Also by Lee Harris

*What's Wrong with the Right Side of History:
Exposing the Roots of Progressive Pathology*

*The Next American Civil War: The Populist
Revolt Against the Liberal Elite*

The Suicide of Reason: Radical Islam's Threat to the West

LINCOLN ROOSEVELT TRUMP

THREE PROFILES IN WORLD-HISTORICAL LEADERSHIP

LEE HARRIS

BOMBARDIER
BOOKS

Published by Bombardier Books
An Imprint of Post Hill Press
ISBN: 979-8-89565-200-8
ISBN (eBook): 979-8-89565-201-5

Lincoln, Roosevelt, Trump:
Three Profiles in World-Historical Leadership
© 2026 by Lee Harris
All Rights Reserved

Cover Design by Cody Corcoran

BOMBARDIER
B O O K S

Post Hill
PRESS

Post Hill Press
New York • Nashville
posthillpress.com

Published in the United States of America
1 2 3 4 5 6 7 8 9 10

For Andy Fuson,
with love and gratitude

CONTENTS

INTRODUCTION
THE TRUMP CONUNDRUM: WORLD-HISTORIC LEADER OR EXISTENTIAL THREAT?

On the afternoon of July 13, 2024, those who checked their smartphones for an update on the news were informed that the sound of gunshots had been heard at the Trump campaign rally being held that day in Butler, Pennsylvania. Later, after some confusion, the news agencies announced that there had been an assassination attempt on the life of the former president. Those who switched on their televisions were able to see replays of the events as they had unfolded.

First, Trump touched his ear, and then he dropped behind his podium, while Secret Service agents piled on top of him. A few moments later, Trump rose back up onto his feet, and, with blood streaming down his face, he lifted his arm in a gesture of defiance as bold as the three words he spoke: "Fight! Fight! Fight!" The photographer who caught this image could not have staged it better.

Unsurprisingly, given the current American obsession with conspiracy theories, there were those on the unhinged left who believed that the whole assassination attempt had been staged by Trump himself, despite the fact that one of his supporters had been killed in the sniper attack. Equally unsurprising, there were those on the unhinged right who claimed that Biden had given the orders for the killing, despite evidence that the would-be assassin, Thomas Matthew Crooks, had apparently considered taking out President Biden himself.

Eventually, even those in the liberal media who despised him came around to accept that Trump had narrowly escaped a genuine attempt on his life. For his many supporters, Trump had been spared by an act of Divine Providence. Liberal critics would later attack Trump's supporters for seeing the hand of God at work in sparing his life. This was part of their broader attack on the allegedly dangerous rise of homegrown fascism under the guise of White Christian Nationalism, by which these liberal critics meant the white, working-class churchgoers who still got goose bumps when they heard the national anthem.

Trump himself, with his skill for turning every adversity into a political opportunity, was delighted that the camera had so perfectly captured him in his spontaneous moment of courageous defiance. Why should he not play it for all it was worth? It was an image as blazingly iconic as Jacques-Louis David's famous canvas of Napoleon crossing the Alps. Yet while David's portrait of the hero on horseback was the product of much labor and David's own considerable artistic imagination—First Consul Bonaparte had brusquely refused even to pose for him—the portrait of the MAGA hero had been as unpremeditated as one of Trump's famous off-the-cuff remarks. Whatever else Trump might be, no one could continue to deny that he was the real thing. In an era of political phonies, Trump's raw authenticity was as winning to his fans as it was confounding to his enemies. Whatever his mission was, Trump was behind it all the way.

But what was that mission?

No sooner had Trump announced his original bid for the presidency on June 16, 2015, than speculation began on what his mission could be. It was entirely reasonable to ask why a man who had never served a day in government should run for the highest office in the land. It was true that Trump possessed a major political asset: By 2016, he had become a household name, thanks to his skill at self-promotion, first as a real estate tycoon, then as a best-selling author, and finally as the celebrity host of the popular reality TV show, *The Apprentice*.

By 2016, Trump was perhaps the most famous billionaire on the planet. Yet though he chose to run as a Republican, he quickly made it apparent that he was as much opposed to the Republican Establishment as he was to the Democratic Establishment. Outsiders had run for the presidency before, but had anyone ever been so outside the Establishment as Trump? Ross Perot had been another billionaire outsider, but in 1992, he had run on a third-party ticket. Trump, in contrast, was determined to win the nomination of one of America's two major political parties.

Had presidential candidates still been chosen in the smoke-filled rooms of old by party big-shots, Trump would have been denied any chance of winning the Republican nomination. But thanks to the progressives of the early twentieth century, the state primary system they introduced had allowed Trump to make an end-run around the Republican Establishment, much to the dismay of party insiders. This was Trump's first coup, demonstrating his uncanny ability to reach out to traditional Republican voters who had grown unhappy with their own party. The Bush dynasty had ended with George W. Bush and was not to be resumed by his brother Jeb, despite the smart money having earlier regarded him as the obvious candidate to lead the Republican Party.

By clinching the Republican nomination, Trump forced those who had previously regarded his candidacy as a joke to take him seriously. By this time, they were dealing not only with Trump the man but also with the political movement that he had ignited under the slogan Make America Great Again (MAGA). This term came into vogue to describe the enthusiastic crowds that attended Trump's signature rallies. Those who cheered and whooped it up at these raucous events were generally working-class men and women lacking a college degree. They went to church, believed in God, and loved their country—and their country music as well. Like Trump himself, many were fans of pro wrestling and McDonald's French fries. In the eyes of their sophisticated critics, however, both conservative and liberal, the MAGA folk were a breed apart: hicks, yokels, and rednecks. Half of them, as Hillary Clinton famously declared, were nothing but "a basket of deplorables."

The fact that so many of Trump's critics openly attacked his supporters was a striking departure from traditional American politics. It had always been permissible to attack a political opponent, indeed to call him or her every name in the book. But their supporters were deemed off limits, and wisely so. No good could ever come from attacking large swaths of the American electorate. Yet this radical departure from the norm showed that the critics of the MAGA movement were struggling to grasp a political phenomenon that they found frankly inexplicable—the resurgence in twenty-first-century America of a style of politics they assumed had long been dead: American populism.

In the post–World War II era, the once powerful tradition of American populism had fallen out of favor as American liberals and progressives began to put their trust in a government run by a highly educated expert elite—a meritocracy, in short. Far better to let such an elite make decisions for the good of the country than to leave those decisions to the ignorant masses. The last significant American populist, Huey Long, had died at the hands of an assassin in 1935 and is mostly remembered dismissively as a power-hungry demagogue. What's forgotten in today's dominant view of populism as a right-wing phenomenon composed of racists and xenophobes, leading to authoritarianism and fascism, is that the populist tradition in this country was historically left wing. Thus Long's program included such radical proposals as a guaranteed minimum personal income and free medical services for all—ideas now embraced by the mainstream American left.

Even more remote from this stereotype was the Democratic Party's own populist hero, William Jennings Bryan, who was by the standards of his time a genuine progressive, advocating labor reforms, government regulation of monopolies, a system of federally insured deposits, and staunch opposition to the rise of American imperialist ambitions. In 1910, Bryan threw his support for the cause of women's suffrage, eight years before the liberal icon Woodrow Wilson.

Today, many are unaware of the critical role the tradition of progressive populism once played in our national politics. They have even come to see populism and progressivism as mutually exclusive. But the progressive wing of the Democratic party would nominate Bryan three times for the presidency, in 1896, 1900, and 1908—a record only matched by FDR and (much later) Donald Trump.

Like all populists in our nation's history, Bryan took the side of ordinary people against the elite of his day. His concern with relieving the debts of poorer citizen led him to embrace a policy of "easy money." In the period between 1776 and 1787, this had taken the form of states that issued their own paper currency. For these early populists, the principle was the more paper money, the better, since inflation would benefit the debtors. Bryan offered another solution: bimetallism. By allowing silver to join gold as the basis of American currency, more bills could be issued, resulting in relief to debtors, but at the expense of their creditors.

The Republican Party under William McKinley had vigorously opposed Bryan's progressive-populist agenda. They especially deplored his bimetallist scheme since by McKinley's day, the once Radical Republicans had become champions of the wealthy and secure. But then, American conservatives have always been stern opponents of populism. Like their perennial hero, Alexander Hamilton, they preferred to see the nation under the management of those they called "natural aristocrats," who, by no very great coincidence, happened to be men like Hamilton himself—men of considerable property, native intelligence, and learning. According to a quite credible legend, Hamilton—a staunch advocate of elite rule, a powerful federal government, and an "energetic" executive—had famously put down the populists of his own era by the remark, "Your people, sir—your people is a great beast."

Suddenly, for many appalled by Trump and the MAGA movement, the great beast was back—only this time, on the right. And it was this fact, in addition to Trump's flamboyant personality, that led many in an elite composed largely of educated liberals to try to assign him and his movement to some historical or conceptual category.

For many, the populist demagogue Adolf Hitler was the obvious antecedent. He too had held great rallies; he too had millions of devoted followers; he too promised to restore his country's greatness, revive its economy, and turn the tables on its adversaries at home and abroad. Efforts were made to plausibly link Trump to Hitler by accusing his father, real estate developer Fred Trump, who had a German background, of being a literal Nazi and a racist who refused to rent apartments to Black tenants.

Those who drew this analogy were not just Democratic Party hacks but also Republican neo-conservatives whose hold on power and influence was threatened by Trump's movement. The Yale historian Timothy Snyder published a bestselling book arguing that America under Trump was on the road to fascism. Snyder's fear of an impending American Reich eventually led him to emigrate to Canada during Trump's second term.

Benito Mussolini, the fascist leader of Italy, offered another historical model. Though widely regarded during the twenties and thirties as a great statesman by figures like Churchill and many American Progressives, he is now mainly remembered as a strutting and posturing egomaniac. And what else was Trump— whose bombastic speech and oversized ego even his warmest supporters found hard to deny?

Yet while Trump did bear some resemblance to these demagogic figures, the analogy ultimately broke down. Thus, as president, he did not shut down the opposition press, throw his opponents in jail, deploy an army of brown- or black-shirted thugs to beat people up in the streets, or ultimately refuse to leave office after initially denying his loss to Joe Biden in 2020. He also lacked a revolutionary program involving a theory of racial or ethnic superiority and an accompanying plan of global domination. (Efforts to paint him as antisemitic fell flat in light of his daughter's marital conversion to Judaism, his recognition of Jerusalem as Israel's capital, and the elevation of his Jewish son-in-law to a prominent peacemaking role in the Middle East.)

But if Trump couldn't be strictly compared to Hitler, he could certainly be labeled a would-be authoritarian dictator fueled by base impulses of greed, hate, and an unquenchable lust for power. To this end, it was useful for a group of psychiatrists to diagnose him as a "malignant narcissist," hence a pathological menace to both the United States and the world.

These public-minded mental health professionals felt that their "duty to warn" overrode the normal ethical constraints against diagnosing a patient they had not personally treated. But this was nothing compared to the liberal journalists who proudly threw professional ethical constraints to the wind by heroically putting their duty to warn, indeed to resist at all costs, above the traditional task of neutrally reporting on events.

For others, it was enough to label Trump a thoroughly bad person: a racist, a xenophobe, a misogynist and rapist, a felon, a crook and a con man. But if Trump were indeed all these things, what did that make his devoted followers? To many critics, it was obvious that his MAGA fan base had erected a "cult of personality" like those that had surrounded Mussolini, Hitler, Stalin, and Mao. Only this explained why Trump's blind followers, many of whom were fundamentalist Christians, were willing to overlook his numerous sins and manifest character flaws. Furthermore, if Trump were guilty of the crimes of nationalism, xenophobia, homophobia, transphobia, nativism, sexism, antisemitism, and racism, then so too were the millions who made up the MAGA movement. This was exactly the kind of man they wanted to see in power, reflecting their own benighted prejudices and hatreds.

The first Trump administration turned into a relentless display of resistance theater: Calls for his impeachment were heard even before he took office; there was obvious collusion among the press, the Democratic Party, and what came to be called the "deep state"; and all of this fueled a growing social, political, and cognitive divide between members of the liberal meritocratic elite and the national populist movement that Trump had ignited. Thus, focused on the deplorable character of their opponents, the liberal elite was slow to catch on to the substantive issues that drove this movement—issues around immigration, the economy, and other social ills—including the perception that the liberal elite and the media were trying to curtail their liberties and foist an alien value system on them.

Of course, Trump being Trump, he did play into his enemies' hands by challenging the results of the 2020 election, which he claimed had been stolen by his political enemies. On January 6, 2021, Trump urged his supporters to protest peacefully as Congress confirmed the election of Joseph Biden. The crowds quickly got out of hand, pouring into the halls of Congress, some intent on trying to disrupt the electoral count, while others seemed to be mere spectators of the ensuing chaos. Conservatives mostly condemned the events of January 6, but they were also inclined to downplay it as an unfortunate incident—a raucous demonstration that devolved into a riot, not a serious attempt to overthrow the government. Democrats and liberal media called it an insurrection, used it as an excuse to impeach Trump a second time, stigmatized his supporters through a campaign of vilification, and launched a massive wave of arrests and prosecutions intended to terrorize Trump's base and drive them out of politics for good. Meanwhile, Trump was slapped with major lawsuits in multiple jurisdictions as part of attempts to convict and jail him on various charges, destroy his businesses by levying massive fines, or at minimum bar him from running for office ever again. Ironically, the obvious politicization of the justice system by Trump's political enemies only served to make him stronger in the eyes of his supporters while calling his opponents' legitimacy into question.

As Trump began to mount his third campaign for the presidency, the attempts to explain him continued. Some historians found parallels to Trump in classical antiquity. Trump was another Julius Caesar, offering an updated version of Caesarism for twenty-first-century America. Other scholars turned to the epoch of European feudalism for an appropriate analogy. Now,

Trump was accused of patrimonialism, a system in which medieval monarchs and emperors treated the state as their own personal property, to do with as they pleased. By supposedly "shredding" the Constitution, Trump was in fact aiming to set up his own dynasty, much like the European kings of old. (Why else had he called his youngest son Barron?) From this, it was a short step to denouncing Trump as aspiring to make himself a king—leading to the "No Kings" protests of June 14, 2025.

What is most striking about all these efforts to reduce Trump to a hateful stereotype is their failure to provide the all-important historical context to the analogies they drew. Hitler, for example, did not produce himself. He was the product of the specific historical circumstances of Germany under the Weimar Republic, which had been created only twelve years before he came to power. By 1932, the German people were struggling with the Great Depression and a 25 percent unemployment rate. In addition, they faced a plague of problems unique to them. There was still bitterness after their shocking defeat in the First World War, even more bitterness over their Draconian treatment at the hands of the victors. They had a hopelessly deadlocked parliament, made up of several parties dedicated to the liquidation of the Weimar Republic, including extreme nationalists whose demands for the restoration of the former German Reich exceeded even Hitler's. Finally, there was the very real threat of a Communist takeover by a party loyal to Stalin. In fact, under the octogenarian President Hindenburg, Article 48 of the Weimar Republic had been invoked over a hundred times in the two years prior to Hitler's election. This permitted the German president to assume dictatorial powers as the only way out of the parliamentary impasses that had rendered Germany's democratic institutions impotent to check the rise of Adolf Hitler. In contrast, by 2016, the American Republic had survived for over two centuries, without Kaisers or Führers—hardly an apt comparison with the floundering Weimar Republic.

The same lack of historical context is an obvious failing of the other charges against Trump. Those who enthusiastically joined in the No Kings protests never quite explained how someone might become a king in twenty-first-century America. The analogy with Caesar also fails the historical test. Trump was not a military leader like Caesar or (later) Napoleon. When Caesar came to power, the Roman Republic had been in its death throes for over a century, while revolutionary France was in disarray and in need of a "republican" monarch to restore order in a society long accustomed to hereditary rule. Neither of these conditions apply to the contemporary USA.

Perhaps the clunkiest analogy is the recent one that accuses Trump of patrimonialism, as if the United States in the twenty-first century had anything whatsoever in common with European feudalism that had passed away centuries earlier and had never taken root in American soil.

The determination to find parallels to Trump in the Roman Empire, the Middle Ages, past European monarchies, and the totalitarian movements of the twentieth century is a bit baffling, considering that most of his positions echo those taken by previous American presidents. Washington warned against foreign entanglements, and Trump wants to reduce those that came about after the end of the Second World War. Like virtually every president of the nineteenth century, from Thomas Jefferson to McKinley, Trump favors tariffs over taxes. Like James Monroe, Trump believes that the American sphere of influence should naturally extend over the Western hemisphere. Like John Quincy Adams and many of his successors, Trump believes in America's manifest destiny. Like Andrew Jackson, Trump led a populist revolt against a dominant elite—deeply entrenched in our capital city—that many voters believed had become complacent, corrupt, and out-of-touch. Like Lincoln, he celebrates the self-made man, although he is not one himself. He shares the expansionist visions of James Polk and Teddy Roosevelt, while seeking new frontiers like JFK. Like FDR, often called a traitor to his class, he is an elite figure who has become the tribune of a populist movement. Like Ronald Reagan, his aim is to keep a meddling government off the backs of the people.

These appeals to ideas and policies from earlier eras of American politics do not necessarily make Trump's adoption of them today correct; however, they do suggest that it is not to European history that we must turn to make sense of Trump, but rather to our own.

To understand the Trump phenomenon, we need to recognize that the populist revival of our era only makes sense within the unique historical context of the American experience. It is here rather than in the faux analogies to European models that we will try to make sense of both Trump and the MAGA movement.

First of all, there is no tradition of sustained authoritarian government in US history. Nor is there any evidence of an appetite for it, then or now. Americans at every stage of history have prized their independence and there is no sign that our heavily armed populace is remotely inclined to hand over dictatorial authority to a "dear leader"–type autocrat such as those we have repeatedly seen arise in Europe, Asia, and Latin America.

Instead, we have had punctuated moments of authoritarian leadership, coming at moments of great crisis, conducted by democratically elected leaders who came to believe that they alone could make the hard decisions needed to save the republican experiment and were willing to break norms, suspend rights, and circumvent a legal constitutional framework that was purposely designed to limit the abuse of executive power.

Moreover, these leaders were not ideologically driven but explicitly pragmatic. These, it so happens, are also the presidents we most deeply admire.

In this book, I will argue the counterintuitive proposition that Abraham Lincoln and Franklin Delano Roosevelt are the presidents who offer the closest analogies to Donald Trump. All three led populist revolts against the rise of a would-be ruling class. All three lived at a time when government by the people was on the verge of becoming a lost cause. All three believed that they were fighting to keep democracy alive not only in their own nation but in the world as well. All three, in short, faced epochal crises.

Epochal crises differ in magnitude and severity from the normal crises that other American presidents faced. First, they were not short-lived, such as (say) the Cuban missile crisis, which was over in a matter of weeks. Rather, they last over many years. Second, these are not out-of-the-blue crises, landing suddenly upon us without warning, as in the case of 9/11. Rather, they gradually emerge over the course of many years and are crises of the political system itself. Third, unlike the crisis brought about by the Second World War, in which virtually all Americans were on the same side, working together for a common goal, the two epochal crises—the Civil War and the Great Depression—led to intensely bitter divisions among Americans, forcing them to take one or the other side of the contest. Finally, an epochal crisis inevitably changes the course of world history. This is what made these figures, in common parlance, "world historical."

In passing judgment on the merits of American presidents, we have to consider what kind of crisis they faced before we can fairly assess them. Calvin Coolidge, for example, is often admired for his minimalist idea of government. This no doubt suited his own political temperament, but such a hands-off approach was only possible because Coolidge did not face a serious crisis during his presidency. We can give high marks to John F. Kennedy for the resolution of the Cuban missile crisis: We avoided a thermonuclear war. In confronting normal crises, we have a set of standards by which we can judge the performance of the presidents who had to deal with them. Did they settle the conflict? Did they exceed the proper limits of presidential power? But by what standards can we grade how a president handles an epochal crisis, since it is the very nature of such crises to call our traditional standards in question? James Buchanan would have gone down in history as fine president had he not been faced with the sundering of the Union.

Even then, James Buchanan was determined to respect the old standards. He could not see a remedy to the crisis within his constitutional authority as president. He was absolutely right; but today many judge him harshly for not abandoning the traditional standards. What many fail to see is that, in an epochal crisis, all traditional standards by which we judge the conduct of a president have been swept away.

This was true in the epochal crisis brought about by the Civil War. Lincoln had only two choices: He could either do nothing, or he would have to assume power that no president had ever claimed before. By assuming these powers, Lincoln violated the traditional standards by which previous American presidents had been judged, which is why—in his own time, and even today— he is often attacked for aspiring to dictatorial power. But these attacks ignore the dismal historical context in which Lincoln made his stand for popular government.

At the outbreak of the Civil War in 1861, the future of the republican form of government seemed bleak indeed. Only thirteen years before, in the Revolutions of 1848, Europeans had established a number of hopeful republics, in the German

Empire, in Hungary, in Rome, in Venice, and most notably in France. Yet this "Springtime of Nations," as it was called, was soon blighted. The French Second Republic lasted less than four years, before being voted out of existence and replaced by the Second Empire under Emperor Louis Napoleon. A similar fate befell the other republics, just as in our own day we have witnessed many false springs across the Arab world.

Thus, when the American Civil War broke out, many astute observers were convinced that, at long last, the American Republic would go the way of all previous ill-advised experiments in popular government. Yet thanks to the populist candidate Abraham Lincoln, a self-made man born into poverty, this did not happen. The republican principle was vindicated, though at an immense cost in American blood, and would continue to inspire other nations around the world.

Again, during the Great Depression of the 1930s, many expected the United States to adopt foreign models of government, such as Mussolini's corporate state or the Soviet model of central economic planning, as a way of dealing with the economic world crisis. But thanks to a populist candidate, Franklin Delano Roosevelt, who was born into privilege, the United States made adjustments but remained fundamentally a government of the people. When other nations were traveling down the road to serfdom during the thirties, FDR refused to follow them. After his death in 1945, American capitalism led and inspired the nations suffering from the devastation of the Second World War to unprecedented levels of prosperity.

Hundreds of volumes have been written on both Lincoln and FDR, but I will offer an interpretation of them that draws on the concept of world-historical leadership developed by the nineteenth-century German philosopher Georg Wilhelm Friedrich Hegel. Though Hegel died in 1831 and obviously did not live to see the presidency of either Lincoln or FDR, both of them clearly fall into the category that Hegel called world-historical.

To call someone a world-historical figure is not to praise them, but merely to indicate their outsized role in shaping the history of their time. One may hate both Lincoln and FDR passionately—and many did hate them in their time: in Lincoln's case, enough to kill him. But no one would deny the immense impact these presidents had on American, and indeed world, history. You are likewise free (as many do) to hate Donald Trump. Indeed, much of the hatred toward him is based on the outsized role he has himself chosen to play on the world stage. I am simply offering a category by which we may best understand him and his sense of personal mission. If you will, take my Hegelian interpretation of Trump as a hypothesis, then test it by what follows. My objective is not to judge but to illuminate.

To many people, the very idea of comparing Trump to Lincoln or FDR will seem outrageous, even blasphemous. This is entirely understandable. Yet we should keep in mind that this response is a reflection of the historical distance that separates us from Lincoln and FDR and the complete lack of such distance from the very much alive Donald Trump. Here, too, we need to provide the proper historical context. When we learn about history as children, it is enough to know simply what happened in the past. History is taught to us as a sequence of events, each of which was the outcome of the decisions made by the various historical actors. How these decisions came to be made is normally passed over in silence. But to get a true sense of history, we must place them in their specific historical context. To simply recount the events of the past in the order of their occurrence is not enough. We must also understand what the actors in any great historical drama *expected* to happen. Moreover, a history that deals only with the outcome of their decisions, while ignoring that confusion and chaos under which they were made, may make both Lincoln and FDR paragons of wisdom in our eyes, but it betrays both the historical record and the world-historical role both men played in dealing with unprecedented crises. The result is bad biography and even worse history.

Much of the difference in the way we see these earlier presidents is due to the image of them that has been hallowed by both popular tradition and by the tendency of later historians to write hagiographies in which they are portrayed as idealistic visionaries, confident of every step they took, without blemish or flaw of character. We quite naturally tend to forget that the historical figures we revere today have been mythologized in our memory of them. Their flaws have been forgotten, their errors forgiven, their crass opportunism erased. Thus, we have a highly sanitized image of them that none of those living among us can hope to compete with.

We also tend to forget that, like Trump in our own day, Lincoln and FDR were despised by their political enemies (and even their allies) during their lifetimes. Like Trump, they were routinely accused of aspiring to be dictators and tyrants. Like Trump, Lincoln and FDR were considered by many to be simply not up to the job, insignificant lightweights who would be crushed by the burden they had assumed—not "presidential" enough, in short. They also were thought to have glaring character defects. Lincoln's critics regarded him as an unlettered bumptious hick; FDR's critics regarded him as a patrician playboy dabbling in politics as others might collect racehorses or show girls. To many, their populist appeal alone was sufficient reason to attack them.

No one can deny that the resurgence of populism has been the most startling fact of our era. Moreover, this resurgence occurred not only in one country but in all the advanced Western nations. This, in turn, made it impossible to blame the political establishment of any one nation without searching for a deeper, more general cause. That cause—as suggested by farsighted works of social criticism, such as Christopher Lasch's *The Revolt of the Elites and the Betrayal of Democracy*—was the rise to power of an international bureaucratic elite produced by the system of merit-based education and professional training that had been instituted throughout the Western world in the postwar era.

If the managerial elites of the various advanced nations had different programs and policies from each other, the various populist revolts against their authority would have little in common. But this is emphatically not the case: All these different national and transnational elites have the exact same programs and policies. Indeed, they are all interlinked. What they all have in common is their belief in what we loosely call globalism. This is an updated version of the old utopian dream of a world government, managed by an elite of enlightened intellectuals, with roots going back to the Abbé de Saint-Pierre and Immanuel Kant in the eighteenth century. Since it was originally the dream of intellectuals, it was little wonder that their scheme should assign the governance of the world to intellectuals like themselves. As a theoretical construct, it was visionary. But today, it has become a potent reality, highly organized and well-funded—a global organization staffed by highly credentialed bureaucrats whose cosmopolitan outlook makes them hostile to the claims of the antiquated nation-states that they hope to transcend and indifferent to those displaced by the march of globalist progress. Its ideology is a strange blend of rich people's socialism and environmentalism. Nonetheless, the earliest opponents of globalism came from the left, whose anti-globalist riots made headlines in 1999, when 40,000–50,000 protestors descended on Seattle, burning dumpsters and smashing windows to protest a WTO ministers' meeting. Parallel protests from the right soon followed, as popular resistance to directives coming from the EU, the UN, and the World Economic Forum (WEF) mounted across Europe.

Unfortunately for the globalist agenda, not everyone was ready for a borderless world without distinct national identities. Political blowback against such high-handed policies was inevitable. Voters naturally expected their leaders to watch out for their interests first; but instead, the meritocratic elites of all advanced nations began to believe that their first duty was to humankind in general. This may sound quite noble, but its implications are deeply disturbing to the common folk whose personal and national interests must be sacrificed in pursuit of the one-world utopia. Hence the periodic protests by French and Dutch farmers who complain that they are being driven out of business by an increasingly restrictive regime of environmental regulations promulgated by unelected bureaucrats in Brussels.

That such populist revolts are underway in all the advanced nations of the West, as well as Japan and Brazil, is evidence that we are dealing with a world-historical event, namely a revolt against those who are determined to achieve a globalist utopia by entrusting the affairs of the world to a transnational meritocratic elite.

When the leadership of a nation believes that it should serve the interests of the global community rather than its own people—who elected them to do precisely that—then the question becomes not why are there many populist revolts in the advanced nations, but rather, why aren't there more. A mother who leaves her own children in order to look after orphans in a distant land might well be a saint, but her own children will still resent the fact that she has abandoned them. This is why we currently see outrage in the UK and Ireland against governments who admitted large numbers of migrants, failed to integrate them or police their behavior, and now seek to suppress and even criminalize popular resentment against them. But what they characterize as merely the expression of reactionary nativist sentiment is better understood as a counterrevolution against the progress of the globalist project.

And this is the ultimate meaning of Trump. Trump, in short, is not the cause of our epochal crisis, but the result. He is the self-appointed tribune of a populist revolt that began not long after the election of Barack Obama. The American Tea Party movement that began in 2007 was the first tremor of this coming revolt against the power of meritocratic elites and preceded Trump's decision to run for president by eight years. During Obama's two terms in office, the United States witnessed the growing rise of populist resentment against what many had come to see as an overbearing meritocratic elite that had become radically out of touch with the political and cultural sensibilities of ordinary voters. Trump did nothing whatsoever to bring on this crisis, though it is one that, like Lincoln and FDR before him, he must tackle if he is to achieve his mission. Properly understood, that mission is not to lead a fascist coup, but rather a democratic counterrevolution against a powerful and increasingly wealthy and privileged elite that holds the common people in contempt unless they think and talk and vote the way their betters think they should. It is this that makes him—potentially, at least—a world-historical figure worthy of comparison to our two greatest presidents.

Lincoln, FDR, and (it must be acknowledged) Trump all possess a charm that approaches the charismatic, as even their opponents grudgingly acknowledge. But without their faults and flaws, it is unlikely that they would succeed in their hazardous missions. It is a sad fact that gentlemen do not make history. Nor, I suspect, would we like the kind of history they made.

A gentleman can deal with normal crises, as Ron DeSantis has amply proved while he has been governor of Florida. He knows exactly what to do in order to deal with them. But it takes an altogether different kind of man to deal with an epochal crisis: What is called for is not the competent administrator, much less the inflexible idealist, but the pragmatic opportunist.

We often hold "opportunists" in contempt and contrast them unfavorably with "idealists." The opportunist is thought to be self-seeking, while the idealist fights for their high moral principles. Naturally, the opportunist has their own personal ambitions: They could never have come to power without them. But unlike the idealist, they are prepared to settle for realistic goals that fall short of their ideals. At times, they may need to set them aside simply to settle a conflict and reach a workable compromise. Aware that they cannot dictate to history, they seek what opportunities they can to influence it. Even so, they know they can only achieve at best an acceptable compromise between their ideals and the stubborn reality they must work with.

Unlike the idealist, whose very ideals will impel them to stay the course with stubborn and even fanatical inflexibility, the pragmatic opportunist is willing to tinker, make mistakes, correct their errors, and reverse their course, even start all over again. This also explains the Machiavellian tendency of these leaders. They have to be willing both to break the rules and to take the abuse heaped upon them in consequence.

The English philosopher Isaiah Berlin offered a helpful distinction between two different types of thinkers, derived from a line of Archilochus of Paros, a Greek poet who lived in the seventh century BC. Archilochus was said to have written such devastating poetic attacks on his enemies that they immediately went off and hanged themselves, but today, he is remembered mostly for his maxim, "The fox has many tricks, the hedgehog just one—but a good one." According to Berlin, thinkers and even men of action could be divided into foxes and hedgehogs. The pragmatic opportunist is naturally a fox. He will possess a whole bag of tricks. The idealist, on the other hand, is too often a hedgehog who knows only one trick—though often, unlike the hedgehog, it is not even a good one.

Seen in this light, Trump may be viewed as the inheritor of a tradition that goes back to the American revolution: American exceptionalism. We began as a people determined never to be subject to a ruling class, as was the case with virtually all other nations of that era. Whenever such a ruling class emerged in our country, subsequent generations would find a populist leader to defend them.

Keeping America exceptional was the challenge that every new generation had to face. But in the case of both Lincoln and FDR, the challenge came in the form of an epochal crisis, when an old order had to be swept away to make room for a new one. Like the American Revolution itself, the outcome of both of these tremendous struggles had implications not only for our own nation but for the world as well, elevating both Lincoln and FDR into the rarefied category of world-historical leaders. How today's version of this struggle is decided will have implications not only for America's future, but the world's. Many populist leaders around the world are closely watching the Trump revolution as it unfolds in America, but none more closely than the global meritocracy itself.

If an age can be defined by the man that everyone is talking about, then we are undoubtedly living in the Age of Trump. Whether you regard this as a blessing or a curse, in the eyes of many, including even his critics, Donald Trump has become the colossus that bestrides our world, with clear ambitions to become a world-historical leader, promising to guide us from an epoch of corrupt and bankrupt liberalism to a Golden Age of American Greatness.

Trump is not the first leader to have such grand, or, as some might say, grandiose, visions. To understand him better, we will now turn to a consideration of those figures from the past who also harbored world-historical ambitions, many of whom discovered that changing the course of history exacted a much higher cost than they had anticipated.

CHAPTER ONE
WHAT IS A WORLD-HISTORICAL LEADER?

1
THE EMPORER AND THE PHILOSOPHER

In 1806, after a decisive win at the Battle of Jena, Napoleon had his Grande Armée occupy the German city from which the battle took its name. Located in Thuringia, Jena was notable for attracting to it the leading German intellectuals of the time. Its inhabitants included Friedrich Schiller, Alexander von Humboldt, Johann Gottlieb Fichte, Novalis, and August Wilhelm Schlegel, all intellectual luminaries of the first magnitude. No star, however, burned so bright as that of the philosopher Georg Wilhelm Friedrich Hegel, who would go on to dominate European thinking of his era and whose influence remains potent even today.

One day, as Napoleon was trotting on his steed through the narrow streets of Jena, the great thinker and the great general crossed paths. Not a word was said between them. Yet, soon afterwards, the thirty-six-year-old Hegel wrote to his friend Friedrich Immanuel Niethammer, "I saw the Emperor—the World Spirit—go out from the city to survey his reign. It is a truly wonderful sensation to see such an individual, who, concentrating on one point while seated on a horse, stretches over the world and dominates it." The phrase "World Spirit astride a horse" would become one of Hegel's most famous utterances.

The term "World Spirit" (*Weltgeist* in German) comes from Hegel's deep meditations on world history—by far the most easily accessible part of his philosophy, and the aspect that has perhaps had the greatest influence on later thinkers.

For Hegel, Napoleon was one of the world-historical figures who presided over the transition from one historical epoch to another. The French Revolution had ended the era of feudalism that had long prevailed in Europe. It had produced radically new ideas, such as the right of the French people to govern themselves. It had championed what became known as The Rights of Man. Yet the Revolution had devoured its own children. It was entirely possible that, like the English Revolution of the seventeenth century, the advance toward greater liberty and equality for the people of France might well be halted and reversed by the swift restoration of the Bourbon monarchy, just as the restoration of the Stuart monarchy had obliterated the Puritan Commonwealth. Yet the emergence of Napoleon had prevented this. Although he had brought the chaos created by the Revolution to an end, he had preserved the cardinal principles that it had embraced. True, he had made himself Emperor, but the *Code Napoléon* that he had initiated would secure for the citizens of France a degree of liberty and equality that they had never known before. Even after his defeat and exile, even after the short-lived Bourbon Restoration, the *Code Napoléon* would live on. Today, it still survives at the basis of French law, though, naturally, it has been updated from time to time.

According to Hegel, the world-historical individual can only emerge under certain quite rare conditions. To understand why this is the case, we need to take a glance at Hegel's overall philosophy of history—fortunately, the most easily accessible as well as the most influential part of his notoriously challenging system of philosophy.

2
HOW EPOCHAL CRISES CHANGE THE COURSE OF HISTORY

Like many other thinkers of his time, Hegel believed that history moved in stages. Each stage had its own ethos and mores, its own distinctive way of doing things and of understanding the world. Each stage had established its own traditions that were held to be sacred and considered its own mode of life as both natural and normative.

The bulk of human history consists of periods in which there are no challenges to the traditional norms and ethos of the culture. There could be wars and other major events, but so long as these did not threaten the fundamental ethos of the culture, no one saw any reason to alter the status quo or reform it, much less to topple and overthrow it. Periods of social and political stability do not get much attention from historians—a fact expressed by Hegel's well-known maxim that "the happy pages of history are blank."

Yet, at certain junctures of history, Hegel argued, a crisis will occur that threatens the status quo. These epochal crises have naturally received the greatest attention from historians. The first book of history was the account given by Herodotus of the crisis brought to the free and independent Greek city-states by the threat of the immense Persian Empire. The fall of the Roman Republic and the rise of Julius Caesar is another crisis that continues to fascinate historians. The American and the French Revolution have hundreds of volumes dedicated to them. So too do the American Civil War and the Great Depression.

In such epochal crises, there will inevitably be a battle between two antagonistic forces. On the one hand, there will be those on the side of the old order, who will fight to preserve the status quo. Against them will be those who recognize that the old order is no longer sustainable. During such crises, the general impulse is to try to save the old order, to patch it up or to bail it out, to put it back on its tottering feet, somehow to keep it on life-support. These desperate remedies are taken not simply out of a sentimental attachment to the status quo, but because no one sees any alternative to it. No one except the one destined to become world-historical.

It may take some time to acknowledge the fact, but the world-historical figure eventually realizes that the old order is too moribund to revive. They then accept its death and realize that there is no point in giving artificial respiration to a corpse. But recognizing this fact, they do not give into despair. They resolutely propose a new path forward, though they themselves can only see the few dim steps in front of them.

This is the critical moment for the world-historical figure. Will other people accept their guidance? Or will they be ignored as a voice crying in the wilderness? Unheeded Cassandras can never hope to have any influence on the course of history. But the world-historical individual always has a rendezvous with Destiny. Many instinctively follow their lead. They see this individual as their champion, because they hear them expressing aloud their own inner convictions and they watch them perform deeds that stir their hearts because these were the deeds they had longed to see done. Others regard this figure as a threat to what they see as a familiar or even God-given order, and resist them, often violently.

The world-historical individual embodies what Hegel called the Spirit of the Times, or the zeitgeist, defined as the sum of all the ideas, beliefs, sentiments, and attitudes of a particular historical era, its intellectual and moral climate. Hegel had borrowed the term from the German thinker, Johann Gottfried Herder, and used it in his own philosophy of history, but zeitgeist has long since passed into the English language, where it is used more or less just as Hegel meant it. There is nothing mystical about the idea. Indeed, today, when we talk about different generations of Americans, such as Baby Boomers, Generation X, Millennials, Generation Z, and Generation Alpha, we are not simply referring to different age cohorts, but rather to the different ideas, beliefs, and attitudes that are broadly characteristic of each of these generations. Indeed, one of the most notable features of our own epoch is how quickly we can switch from one zeitgeist to another.

This, however, is unique to late modernity. In highly traditional societies, in sharp contrast, the zeitgeist may remain virtually the same over the course of centuries. But in addition to the incremental shifts between different generations, which may amount to little more than a change in fashions, there have been those historical periods in which the transition from one zeitgeist to another was both radical and revolutionary.

This indeed is the mark of an epochal crisis: the transition from the zeitgeist of one epoch to that of another. This transition may take generations to complete, or it may occur in the space of a few years, but at the end of the process, people think about the world in very different ways than their predecessors did. Here are a few examples, including periods of transition that occurred after Hegel's own death in 1831.

In 1500, Europeans were all Catholic, aside from the Jews. There had been a number of heretical movements, like the Lollards and the Hussites, but for the most part, the authority of the Pope was unquestioned. Seventeen years later, an obscure but devout Augustinian monk, named Martin Luther, wrote ninety-eight theses (all in Latin) on the Catholic practice of indulgences. Luther accepted the practice, but he thought that it was being abused and he proposed a debate over the question. The issues Luther raised were highly technical and made little sense to those who were not professional theologians. It might well have remained a tempest in a scholastic teacup, but within eight years, Luther was denouncing the Roman pontiff as the Antichrist.

By this time, Luther was no longer standing alone. He had gained many thousands of adherents, who followed him in his break from the Catholic Church. These included princes; former monks, like Luther himself; trained theologians; merchants; artisans; and peasants. Cities were convulsed by religious controversies. The Protestant Reformation had begun, though the followers of Luther would not be called Protestants until 1529.

Seldom, if ever, in history has a culture experienced such a radical and violent change from one zeitgeist to another. Protestant iconoclasts were not merely content to start their own church, but were inspired to deface Catholic churches, to overturn altars, to spit upon crucifixes and to burn statues of the Virgin Mary, to whom as children they had been taught to pray for mercy. This shift in the zeitgeist manifested itself in every aspect of culture. Though Luther's original aim had been to convert all of Europe to his own faith, the Protestant Reformation would permanently fracture Christianity, as various sects multiplied, each equally convinced that they alone possessed the true and original Christian faith. This insistence on believing only what your conscience told you to believe inaugurated the zeitgeist of the modern world, according to Hegel.

In seventeenth-century Europe, monarchs happily ruled by Divine Right, as all agreed. When the radical British Whigs began to dispute this right, they were introducing what would eventually become the zeitgeist of the revolutionary epoch that begin with the Glorious Revolution of 1688 in England, followed by the American Revolution of 1775, followed by the French Revolution of 1789, and innumerable other revolutions in South and Central America as well as in Europe. By the end of this long transition, the Divine Right of kings had been replaced by the demand for government by consent of the people.

Before the American Civil War, most accepted slavery as a fact of life, a blessing to its defenders, a necessary evil to those prepared to keep the Union intact, and an abomination to only a few. But these few ardent abolitionists, though widely despised both in the South and in the North, were the harbingers of the new zeitgeist that would come to prevail in the aftermath of the war, out of which emerged a world committed to the eradication of slavery everywhere. Lincoln did not initiate this movement, but he came to both embody it and to lead to its triumphant conclusion.

The same was true of FDR. Before the Great Depression, most Americans would have agreed with the Republican Calvin Coolidge who, as president, had famously said the business of America was business. By virtue of Americans tending to their own business, both literally and metaphorically, the United States had become the richest nation in the world, with millions enjoying a lifestyle that citizens of other countries envied. They were also the freest. The spectacular success of the period now known as the roaring twenties represented the ultimate and indisputable triumph of America's brand of laissez-faire capitalism, proving that liberty and prosperity went hand in hand. Then came the Great Depression, shattering all previous certitudes. A new zeitgeist emerged in which the American people came to expect their government to look after the national economy, rather than assume that it would naturally take care of itself.

By the time of FDR's election in 1932, the American public was already demanding a leader who could fix their economic woes. FDR did not teach American voters to look to the federal government for help. This is what the American voters themselves now expected the government to do—a lesson resoundingly bought home by FDR's landslide victories in both 1932 and 1936.

Since that shift in zeitgeist, Americans, both right and left, routinely blame a president for any of the economic troubles that occur during his administration, especially inflation and unemployment. There is simply no way of returning to an America where a president could get away with arguing that either sky-rocketing inflation or soaring unemployment was simply not his business.

The populist revolt preceded Trump, but it, too, introduced a new zeitgeist. The government had become too active—in the wrong ways. The meritocratic elite that arose after World War II had failed ordinary Americans badly. Its desire to control what ordinary people both did and thought eventually created a popular reaction against elite domination. This anti-elitism is the rising zeitgeist of our epoch and has gained adherents both in the United States and around the world. It is still spreading today, though how our epoch will end cannot yet be determined. But it is clear which way the wind is blowing.

It is only during these epochal crises that a single individual can play the role of a world-historical leader. This individual instinctively embodies the zeitgeist that is emerging from the womb of time and which, in due course, will replace that of the old order. It is this characteristic that separates this figure from the many other candidates for the list of history's great personages.

3
WHAT'S WRONG WITH THE GREAT MAN THEORY?

The nineteenth-century Scottish sage Thomas Carlyle was the proponent of what became known as the Great Man theory of history. Unlike later theories that emphasized the various impersonal forces, such as class struggle, in shaping human history, Carlyle insisted that "the History of the world is but the Biography of great men." Such men were called Heroes by Carlyle. On his list of great men were two military heroes, Cromwell and Napoleon, but they shared their heroic status with the Prophet Muhammad; Dante and Shakespeare; Martin Luther and John Knox; and Samuel Johnson, Robert Burns, and Jean-Jacques Rousseau.

Carlyle did not invent the idea of the Hero or of the Great Man. The ancient Greek historian and moralist, Plutarch, had written the lives of the eminent men of both the Greeks and the Romans, but his criterion for greatness was both generous and impartial. For example, Plutarch wrote a biography of Julius Caesar, but he also wrote a biography of the man who assassinated him, Marcus Junius Brutus. Obviously both men cannot be heroes. If one is a hero, the other must be a villain, which is indeed how later generations came to look on them. Dante reserved the lowest pit of hell for Brutus, for committing the sin of ingratitude toward a superior from whom he had received benefits. Although Dante himself is typically laconic in *The Inferno*, modern glosses on the text have argued that Dante had it in for Brutus for trying to thwart the Divine plan whereby Julius Caesar, by unifying the Roman Empire, was preparing for the advent of the universal Catholic Church. During the French Revolution, on the other hand, Brutus the assassin became the republican hero, so popular with the revolutionaries that many changed their given names for his.

This will be a problem encountered by any list of the putative heroes of world history. Each of these rare individuals will invariably be the subject of considerable controversy, not only in their own day, but in the judgment of following generations. Even the phrase "great men" implies a favorable evaluation of the individuals in question. Were Hitler and Stalin "great men?" We may decline to count them as such, yet it would be absurd to deny their role as movers and shakers of history.

Yet for Hegel, world-historical figures were not simply those who had an impact on human events. Not all the so-called Great Men who have marched with noisy fanfare across the stage of history have achieved this status. There have been many who moved and shook their own times without leaving anything behind them but the glory or infamy of their names once they departed.

This was certainly the case with Benito Mussolini and Adolf Hitler. Both were convinced that they were men of destiny, whose achievements would be lasting. But the thousand-year Reich of Hitler's dreams lasted a mere twelve years. Both leaders were convinced that they were taking their nations to unprecedented heights of success and power, but left them in ruins, defeated and humiliated. Despite their impact on their own times, neither

Mussolini nor Hitler is counted today among the great men of history, while the catastrophic conclusion of their missions clearly removes them from the category of world-historical leaders, who by definition must achieve something permanent. But Mussolini and Hitler, like many other strutting dictators, marched their people not into a glorious future, but to one of history's dead ends, of which there have been many.

Oliver Cromwell, one of Thomas Carlyle's favorite heroes, is usually counted among history's Great Men. With his immense energy and formidable will, Cromwell brought down the English monarchy, ordered the execution of King Charles I, and established a Puritan Commonwealth. These were truly revolutionary acts. But upon his death, the Commonwealth vanished, the monarchy was restored, and the dead king's son, Charles II, was placed on the throne. Most of the regicides who had ordered the death of Charles I were in their turn hunted down and mercilessly executed. Even the ones who had died before the Restoration were not spared, including Oliver Cromwell himself. Their bodies were exhumed, hanged, taken down, then drawn and quartered, while their skulls were placed on pikes in public squares, as a warning to other would-be revolutionaries. The Commonwealth had lasted a mere eleven years, while today Charles III sits securely upon the same throne as his Stuart namesakes.

If Carlyle had lived into the twentieth century, Vladimir Lenin would certainly fall into his category of Great Man. The USSR that he established in 1917 lasted far longer than the Puritan Commonwealth, but ultimately it too perished. In his own mind, Lenin, who certainly knew his Hegel, was convinced that he was himself another world-historical figure. He would lead backward Russia from the dismal epoch of failing capitalism into the glorious sunshine of a Marxist utopia. But like the Puritan Commonwealth, the Soviet experiment in practical socialism proved to be a dead end, a historical aberration that ended in the neo-Czarism of Vladimir Putin.

4
WHAT MAKES SOMEONE WORLD-HISTORICAL?

These examples provide us with a key requirement of world-historical status. It is not enough merely to shake things up, or to make a big splash. Hitler certainly did all that, but his dream of a Thousand Year Reich dissolved in smoke and ashes. The world-historical figure, on the other hand, must bring about a permanent change. He gives birth to an entirely new epoch after burying the old.

Let us look at Julius Caesar, one of Hegel's world-historical leaders. The Senators who stabbed him to death on the Ides of March in 44 BC were all convinced that, by eliminating Caesar, their beloved Rome could return to the old ideals of the Roman Republic. But this was simply a mirage. The glory days of the Republic had ended nearly a century before. Since that time, there had been a series of bloody civil wars, rule by ruthless dictators like Sulla and Marius, followed by chaos and anarchy. The idea of restoring the old Republic was a fantasy. History has no reverse gear. It can only go forward—though it is always possible to go forward in the wrong direction. The past can never be restored as it really was in all exactitude, though this was the aim of Caesar's assassins and many other movements aimed at restoring a lost Golden Age.

Caesar clearly recognized this fact. The future of Rome lay in one-man rule: that of Julius Caesar himself. By assassinating him, the Senators only proved his point, when at the end of the final bloody civil war, Caesar's nephew, Octavian, became the de facto emperor of Rome. Appearances were kept up. The Senate still had business to do and speeches to make, but it no longer had any real power. From that point on, power was in the hands of Caesar's imperial successors.

Rome would continue in this course, with some interruptions, for the next five centuries, during which time the people of the Mediterranean basin enjoyed security, peace, and the rule of law. The eighteenth-century British historian, Edward Gibbon, in *The Decline and Fall of the Roman Empire*, lamented that the price paid for this increased security was the loss of the old Republican ideal of liberty. There is some truth in this contention, but it overlooks the fact that without the security provided by the rule of law, personal liberty is only available to those strong enough to defend it, allowing precious little liberty for those who lack their strength.

Caesar had not set out to destroy the Republic. He simply recognized that it was already dead, beyond any hope of reviving. The same thing could be said of Napoleon when he proclaimed himself Emperor. He had played no role whatsoever in the French Revolution that had broken out in 1789, nor in the creation of the French Republic that followed the demise of the Bourbon monarchy.

In his first step to supreme power, Napoleon had kept to the venerable Republican tradition, modeled on that of Rome. He made himself the First Consul, using the good old Roman title for its supreme leader. The only difference, though hardly a slight one, was that Rome always insisted on having two co-equal consuls. Eventually Napoleon recognized that the new French Republic was simply not working and replaced it with his empire, to wild popular acclaim. The French had had enough of their own experiment in utopia building.

What role did personal ambition play in the careers of Julius Caesar and Napoleon Bonaparte? Of course, both men were extraordinarily ambitious. They could hardly have accomplished what they did without a personal desire for immense power. Nor were they boy scouts. Both were willing to do whatever it took to reach their goals. They could be ruthless—though Caesar was genuinely magnanimous with his defeated rivals, too much so as it turned out.

But, according to Hegel, such burning personal ambition was a necessary component of all men of destiny. Without it, they would give up too soon and thereby fail in the task of creating a new epoch out of the ashes of the old. But here comes an important qualification. World-historical figures do in fact create a new epoch out of the old, but they are not guided by an ideology that provides them with what they regard as a foolproof blueprint of how this new epoch should be achieved.

As a good Marxist, Vladimir Lenin believed he had an absolutely infallible roadmap to the future. There may need to be minor adjustments along the way, but he had no question what the new epoch he was creating would look like. Unlike many of his ideologically rigid Bolshevik allies, however, Lenin could at times act like a pragmatic opportunist. His decision to seize power in the October revolution, his decision to accept the harsh terms of the German-dictated Treaty of Brest-Litovsk, his decision to abandon the suicidal policy of War Communism and launch the market-friendly New Economic Policy—all of these decisions were strongly opposed by the majority of Bolsheviks. Yet, had Lenin not imposed his formidable will on his party, getting it to reverse its previous positions, the Bolsheviks would have quickly lost the reins of power.

Stalin too could be a pragmatic opportunist, as demonstrated by his willingness to sign the Molotov-Ribbentrop Pact with the Third Reich in 1939. Yet neither Lenin nor Stalin could abandon their commitment to the Marxist-inspired vision of the global triumph of communism. Their own considerable ruthlessness had nothing personal about it. The logic of history, as both Lenin and Stalin understood it, simply required the liquidation of those who were thwarting humankind's path toward the End of History, the final stage of communism. But no genuine world-historical figure can afford to think like this.

True world-historical leaders never think they possess a roadmap to the future, much less a blueprint for utopia. They all must have a mission to accomplish, but how this mission is to be accomplished remains uncertain. If one means does not work to get them to their goal, they will try others. In short, they all must be pragmatic opportunists.

5
THE WORLD-HISTORICAL LEADER BOTH MAKES HISTORY AND IS MADE BY HISTORY

This brings us to the major distinction between the Great Man of Carlyle and Hegel's world-historical leader. Thomas Carlyle believed that his heroes were the active motor of history. His great men made history by their sheer force of will. Furthermore, they even managed to shape the course of events to realize their own objectives. Both Cromwell and Lenin were very much aware of what they wanted to achieve, and they considered themselves as acting in the name of a higher power—in Cromwell's case, God; in Lenin's case, the laws of dialectical materialism as set down by Karl Marx. Both regarded themselves as the heroes chosen by destiny to lead humanity to the promised land of their own making.

Yet for Hegel, this was an illusion. No single individual, no matter how forceful their personality or strong their character, can shape history according to their own designs. The world-historical figure would never have succeeded if they had not been the unwitting agent of vaster historical forces. For all their personal ambition, it would have gotten them nowhere if they had not been unconsciously attuned to the spirit of the times, or zeit-geist. Indeed, the world-historical figure is all too aware of how little influence they can bring to bear on the historical process, if not at the start of their career, then certainly by its end.

The nineteenth-century German statesman Otto von Bismarck succeeded as much as any other Great Man in shaping his own era, yet he displayed a humble awareness of the limited role he played in uniting the various small and independent German states into a single German Reich, the mission to which he had dedicated his life. He once compared his own influence on history to a man lazily floating down a river in a boat, who dangles his hand in the water and waves it about. The effect that the man's hand has on the current of the river is trifling—an apt warning to those who believe that by dipping their hand into politics they can change the course of history by making a big splash.

One of the most unfortunate consequences of the Great Man theory of history, as devised by Carlyle, is that it naturally elevates these rare individuals not just into heroes, but Superheroes, rivaling the irresistible power of the Superheroes of the Marvel franchise, able to bend not just steel, but the course of history, to their inflexible will. This apotheosis of heroes ends in two different distortions of history. First, it leads to the cult of Hero Worship, which has played into the hands of those who were angling for dictatorship. The invincible hero can do no wrong and can make no mistakes. So why not let this hero make all the important decisions? Second, it leads into the kind of fairytale history in which leaders like Lincoln and FDR magically solved the crises they faced by sticking inflexibly to their lofty ideals, never hesitating, never retreating, never compromising. This is a travesty of how such world-historical leaders actually managed to deal with the epochal crises of their day. To point out their flaws and weaknesses, their errors and failures, is not to debunk them, but to return their humanity to them. For it is flawed and erring human beings who make history, and not Superheroes.

Like Otto von Bismarck, the world-historical leader must feel a sense of humility before history. He knows he was made by it and did not make it himself. He is not pursuing a utopia because he knows he cannot obtain one and knows the fate of those who have failed horribly in their aims to achieve theirs. He accepts the world as it is, since it is only by accepting it that he has any chance of improving it. Most importantly, he is not seduced as the idealist so often is, by imagining that we can ever live in a world in which power doesn't count. There will always be a struggle for power, whether among great nations or among members of a small socialist commune. No political reform can ever abolish the desire for power. Every world-historical leader must therefore be prepared for a power struggle when they embark on a mission to replace a dying old order. No Establishment goes down without a fight—often quite vicious.

6
HISTORY HAS A GRAND THEME: THE UNFOLDING OF HUMAN FREEDOM

This brings us to the final characteristic of the world-historical leader. For Hegel, history was more than a mere succession of pointless struggles for power. It had a grand theme, which was the unfolding of human freedom. Certain power struggles were indeed pointless from the perspective of world history. Dynastic squabbles over territories did not matter in the long run. But during an epochal crisis, the struggle for power will inevitably end with the emergence of a new conception of freedom that marks a turning point in world history.

The realm of prehistory did not factor into Hegel's philosophy of history because primitive humans had no genuine conception of freedom. In this respect, Hegel differed from those who, like Locke and Rousseau, believed that human beings were born free. After all, new-born children's freedom lasts only a moment, before they are swaddled both literally and figuratively by the culture into which they are born. More importantly, they have no appreciation of their momentary freedom. For Hegel, freedom required the consciousness of freedom, which no child can possibly have.

This is a point worth examining. Hegel did not believe that humans first had an idea of freedom that they then proceeded to try to actualize in the real world. The European thinkers who celebrated the liberty of the primitive tribes that had been discovered in the New World had it all wrong. The mere fact that the savages of North America could do what they wished did not mean that they were conscious of being free. In fact, a free people would never know they were free until someone threatened them with slavery. The freedom that they had previously taken for granted would only then transform into a consciously held ideal worth fighting for. In short, it was only by struggling to maintain their free way of life that people became conscious that they were free. But in the empires of the ancient Near East, everyone was very conscious that they were slaves, except for the one who sat at the apex of supreme power, who alone was conscious of freedom.

It was in the ancient Near East that there emerged the first states that were based on the principle of hierarchy. There could be no vast empire without an administrative and military hierarchy. But once such a hierarchy emerged, it would easily dominate societies that had not mastered this superior principle of organization. A hierarchical empire would have more personnel, bigger and more disciplined armies with competent generals to lead them. It would easily smash those societies with only a small, undisciplined, and loosely organized band of warriors. It would then reduce these societies into tribute-paying vassal states, which in turn would provide immense wealth to the empire, allowing it to field even larger armies, provided with the best weapons and equipment available at the time.

Such massive empires, however, needed to be governed by a single all-powerful ruler, whose orders had to be obeyed all the way down the chain of command. In the ancient Near East, this was the task of the great king, the prototype of the Oriental despot. Everyone was answerable to him, though he was answerable to nobody. He alone was truly free. He alone took no orders. Everyone was his slave.

In fact, to those living under an Oriental despot, the idea that more than one person could be free made no sense at all. No one could share the freedom that the despot alone was permitted. The only kind of freedom that the subjects of such an empire could imagine was the despot's unlimited freedom to impose his will on everyone else—a freedom, in other words, that was not constrained by any concern with what we today call the rights of others. The others simply had no such rights.

An imperial hierarchy, with its Great King at the head, seemed the secret of worldly success. It is true that in the Near East, these empires would change hands from time to time, but without affecting the pattern of life of those who lived within

19

their wide domains. But for many centuries, mighty empires seemed to be the inevitable wave of the future. Had this been the case, humankind's very idea of freedom would have been stunted at its first growth. The idea that people could share freedom equally could never even have emerged under the conditions of Oriental despotism.

This was why the Persian Wars marked an epoch in the annals of the unfolding idea of human freedom. No Levantine empire had ever been as successful as the Persian Empire that had been founded by Cyrus the Great in 550 BC. Yet when Cyrus's successors, first Darius the Great, followed by his son, Xerxes the Great, decided to incorporate the small city-states of the Greeks into their empire, they were rudely and violently rebuffed. Outraged, the Great King of Persia decided to teach the Greeks a lesson. Indeed, his victory seemed a forgone conclusion, but with astonishing courage and ingenuity the Greeks repelled the invaders, not once but twice.

Much was a matter of luck, as always in human affairs. But the Greeks had developed a new conception of liberty that enabled them to defeat the great hierarchy ruled over by a single man. Freedom was no longer the unique preserve of the despot. Freedom could be shared by many men, indeed, by all the male citizens of the Greek city-states. This obviously could not be the utterly unrestrained liberty of the despot, but a freedom that was careful not to threaten the freedom of other citizens in the same community. The idea of *equal* liberty was a radical innovation, replacing the overwhelmingly unequal liberty of the despot to do whatever he pleased.

It was not merely that more people were now free. Rather, a new idea of freedom had come into the world, one that in time would triumph over the slave empires of the Near East, as Alexander the Great would eventually do by 330 BC. By permitting citizens to cooperate freely, subject to the same law, a highly disciplined military force made up of citizen soldiers could outmaneuver an army of slaves driven by the whips of their imperial master into battles they had no desire to fight. This in turn would become the new secret of worldly success, as the Romans would demonstrate after chasing out their last king and establishing the Roman Republic.

This new idea of freedom was certainly a step forward in human progress, but it left out all those who could not serve as citizen soldiers. After all, it was the courage and military prowess of such men who guarded their communities against the worst of all possible fates: to be conquered by a rival power and left prostrate, despoiled of their property and reduced to abject servitude. From this point of view, it made sense that only these critically important male warriors should be regarded as citizens.

Yet the independent Greek city-states had a tragic flaw. They were too independent. Though they had united in their collective defense to combat the Persians, they quickly fell back into internecine wars and feuds. When Philip of Macedon threatened their sovereignty, the Greeks were unable to rise to the challenge. Yet it was Philip's son, Alexander, who would become Hegel's first world-historical figure by spreading Greek culture into Asia by conquering the Persian Empire. Though of semi-barbarian stock like other Macedonians, Alexander had become intoxicated by Homer's great epic, *The Iliad*, and would become the vehicle for keeping the Greek heritage alive through the creation of a Hellenistic culture that fused East and West together.

In the process, Alexander the Great also performed a deed that symbolized the nature of all world-historical figures. In the city of Gordius on the coast of Asia Minor, there was a great tangle of rope called the Gordian Knot. Legend claimed that anyone hoping to conquer Asia must first unravel it. Instead, according to later tales, Alexander grew impatient and cut the great knot into two with his quick sword. The symbolism of the act is easy to read: The world-historical leader, to achieve his mission, must sometimes not merely bend the rules, but break them.

The genius of the Roman Republic lay in its ability to create a stable empire. Athens had aimed at this feat during the Peloponnesian war but had failed. Rome, in contrast, had successfully come to embrace virtually the entire Mediterranean basin by the time of Julius Caesar's appearance on the world stage. Its territorial empire had become too vast to be managed by its traditional form of government, based on the Senatorial elite. In 44 BC, Julius Caesar was murdered by the members of this elite because he had come to recognize that the Roman Empire had outgrown the stage in which it could be governed by a squabbling elite of patricians. Its vastness required the rule of a single man who would be automatically obeyed throughout the immense expanse of territory that had been acquired under the Republic. Yet this was not a return to Oriental despotism, though there were to be emperors who aspired to become tyrants, like Nero and Caligula.

Despite these hiccups, the Roman Empire retained universal respect due to Roman law, while those who could claim Roman citizenship were scattered from one end of the Mediterranean basin to the other. In the century before the collapse of the Roman Republic, there had been intense debate, often leading to violent conflict, over the question of extending the privilege of Roman citizenship to those who lived outside the walls of the city of Rome. The fate of Rome would have been very different had the decision not eventually been reached to begin the process of granting Roman citizenship to its neighboring allies, especially those who had come to the aid of Rome during its most serious crisis, when Hannibal's army threatened the very gates of Rome.

Later, citizenship was offered even to those peoples whom the Romans had conquered. Finally, in the year 212 AD, the Edict of Caracalla granted Roman citizenship to all free men and women throughout the by then vast Roman Empire. Most importantly, it was thanks to such an expansive and cohesive empire that the Judeo-Christian tradition was able to take root in Europe and to flourish in a culture radically different from that in which it had emerged. Eventually, over the course of centuries, even the ferocious barbarians of the cold north had heard the strange message of the brotherhood of all men.

The period that would later come to be called the European Middle Ages was one in which the same fundamental zeitgeist lasted for many centuries. Virtually all Europeans, with the exception of the Jews and a handful of Christian heretical movements, shared a common and unquestioned Christian faith. This static medieval order, however, was not seen by the people of that era as a dismal lack of progress, as we naturally tend to see it. Rather their social order was understood to be a mirror of the divine order itself, conceived as The Great Chain of Being. God was naturally at the top, and the angels were below Him. Similarly, the structure of Medieval society reflected the natural human order in which kings were at the top, the nobility a notch below, and peasants at the very bottom of the grand celestial hierarchy. Any disruption of this order was by definition a rebellion against both God and the kings whom He had appointed to govern over human affairs. This arrangement was largely unchallenged until the advent of the Protestant Reformation in the early sixteenth century.

The Protestant Reformation found its world-historical figure in Martin Luther. He had translated the Bible into German so that all could read it and could interpret for themselves. He taught that all individuals, in reading the Bible, had the right to interpret it for themselves in the sanctity of their own conscience. This obedience to personal conscience offered another new conception of freedom. And if the people were permitted to freely make up their own minds about the Bible, why not everything else as well? The early Protestant insistence on the liberty of conscience would morph in time into the famous maxim of the eighteenth-century German philosopher, Immanuel Kant: *Sapere aude!* Dare to think for yourself!

The Enlightenment of the eighteenth century owed much to the Protestant Reformation, though it would go on to challenge the religious orthodoxy of all European faiths. It was also during this period that modern science emerged, after breaking the stranglehold imposed by the revival of the physics of Aristotle during the Renaissance. Copernicus offered an alternative to the geocentric system passed down from Aristotle and Ptolemy. Galileo broke with the long-held notion that the celestial realm beyond the moon was immutable and eternally unchanging. He had demonstrated this fact by discovering via his telescope that the moons of Jupiter traveled in circles around their home planet. Kepler would break free of the idea derived from both Plato and Aristotle that all heavenly bodies must move in perfect circles. Finally, Newton was led to abandon the cardinal doctrine of Aristotle that forbade action at a distance, leading him to propose his revolutionary theory of universal gravitation. Action at distance, in the form of gravity, far from being impossible, was what was holding the universe together.

In the middle of the seventeenth century, the Calvinist Roger Williams gained notoriety for proposing that the state had no business dictating people's religious faith. He argued that all religions, including even the Muslim faith, should be tolerated. Eventually the European Enlightenment would catch up with his radical thinking, which was later to be enshrined in the First Amendment of the United States Constitution. The way to modern secularism was thereby opened. By that time, both Europe and North America had witnessed the liberal revolutions that had created the new world order into which Hegel had been born.

By the time of the European Enlightenment, slavery had died out among the European nations, along with the institution of serfdom, with the exception of Czarist Russia, where it began to be introduced just as it was dying out in England. These earlier institutions no longer made any sense to the Europeans of Hegel's own day. Both were regarded as morally wrong and economically inefficient. Yet did the mere fact that there were no longer any serfs or slaves really mean that all men were now truly free and that the last chapter of the pursuit of liberty had finally been written?

True, all men were now formally free, but they were certainly not equally free. The pauper had no master, it is true, but this may have offered them little consolation as they wandered the cities in search of refuse and handouts. True, the most wretched of the earth now had the freedom to think their own thoughts, but even the brightest ideas could not feed a hungry child. Did Hegel really believe that the pursuit of liberty had stopped at this point?

7
HEGEL AND AMERICA—THE LAND OF THE FUTURE

It is often assumed that Hegel believed he had found the End of History in the Prussian state of his own day. Paul Johnson, the popular English historian, criticized Hegel on this very point, using it as proof that Hegel's philosophy was mere "moon-shine"—a harsh, but not uncommon criticism of Hegel popular in many circles. On the other hand, the American scholar, Francis Fukuyama, an admirer of Hegel, claimed to have derived his own ideas about the End of History from Hegel.

The problem with this interpretation is that for Hegel, the End of History would logically entail the end of man's pursuit of freedom. Yet in Hegel's writings on the early American Republic, he made it abundantly clear that he expected Americans to further the progress of human liberty. Indeed, Hegel prophetically suggested that the future belonged to the United States. This meant that the unfolding of the concept of freedom had not been completed in his own time. There was still more to be done. The next chapter in the saga of the pursuit of liberty would take place in North America. There was to be more to the story, and this story would be written in the New World.

Like all thoughtful Europeans of his time, Hegel recognized that what was happening in America was exceptional. It had introduced an entirely new conception of freedom to the world: the freedom of ordinary men and women to chart their own destinies, to make something of themselves. In the virgin land of the New World, ordinary people were offered the chance of social mobility denied them under the top-heavy social hierarchies of the Old World. This was absolutely unprecedented in human history—a society in which even the poor and humble could aspire to rise as far as their talents and abilities allowed, unchecked by a ruling class determined to keep their inferiors in their proper place. For Hegel and many others, the question was not whether America was exceptional, but rather, how long America—a country without traditions of monarchy or aristocracy—could remain so.

Hegel did not normally make prophecies. The proper role of the philosopher was to understand the winding, crooked road that had led from the past to the present, not to try to foresee the future. But his prophecy about America turned out to be correct. America remained exceptional. It did so thanks to the determination of ordinary men and women to resist succumbing to a ruling class. Yet it is doubtful whether this resistance would have overcome an equally determined effort on the part of a government that aimed to establish itself as a despotism, as had occurred in the case of the dozens of other republics that had been inspired by our own revolution.

In the United States, in contrast, it was thanks to a series of remarkable presidents that the spirit of American exceptionalism remained alive. Even in the face of enormous challenges, they fought, in Lincoln's famous words, so "that a government of the people, by the people, and for the people, shall not perish from the earth." As Hegel had surmised, even in its most difficult crisis, the American nation had offered the world "a new birth of freedom." As his words made clear, Lincoln believed that America had a world-historical mission to set a shining example to humanity that would inspire other nations to achieve an even higher stage in the development of human freedom.

This is why America's greatest leaders are world-historical. They kept faith in what they saw as their providential mission. Their words and actions have indeed inspired other nations to resist the domination by corrupt and often brutal ruling classes, from the aristocracies of old, through the totalitarian regimes of the twentieth century, and today against the domination of a meritocratic elite that has lost legitimacy in the eyes of those over whom it aspired to rule.

CHAPTER TWO
A SPECIAL PROVIDENCE: THE MAKING OF AMERICAN EXCEPTIONALISM

1
OLD WORLD BAD, NEW WORLD GOOD

In our own day, the very idea of American exceptionalism has become the subject of controversy. It is sometimes interpreted as a triumphalist vision of a nation that can do no wrong, with the divine right to impose its will on the rest of the world. But let us first note that the word *exceptional* has two different meanings in English. It does not only mean superior or outstanding; it also means statistically rare. The word *exceptional* can apply to both sides of the bell curve: It is possible to be exceptionally ugly or exceptionally beautiful, exceptionally stupid or exceptionally intelligent.

In discussing American exceptionalism, we will begin by simply noting all the various qualities, both of geography and of human capital, that made America radically different from other nations simply as a matter of fact. However, the revolutionary generation produced men and women who were determined to make their new nation exceptional as a matter of principle. They deliberately set out to make it as different as possible from those of the Old World. To many observers, this radicalism was proof that the early American Republic was doomed to be just another experiment in utopia building.

The people of the former British colonies, when they set about creating thirteen independent republics in 1776, were not trying to be different just to be different. If they insisted on developing new institutions, it was to promote and preserve the popular governments that had been created in each of the former colonies, in which the people already enjoyed far more liberty and equality than the rest of the world, and where the humblest were given the chance of social mobility. They self-consciously tried to create a shining example for the world and tirelessly promoted their own unique and sterling virtues, annoying many British visitors (like Charles Dickens) in the process.

This triumphalist reading of American exceptionalism has always offended many highbrow foreigners, both in the past as well as today, but not their poor and oppressed brethren in these same foreign lands who flocked to America in the millions. They were often true believers in the American dream, more so than those who had been born here and who often took for granted what new immigrants were seeking—a land of opportunities where every citizen could start afresh, in a society where social mobility was encouraged rather than rebuked.

Finally, from the very beginning, the view emerged that the Old World was hopelessly and irredeemably corrupt and that America offered an opportunity to start over, redeeming society and humanity itself. It is no accident that the Puritans who established the first British colonies in New England were Separatists. Unlike their Calvinist brethren who stayed behind in England in the hope of purifying the Anglican Church, the Separatists had concluded that the Anglican Establishment could not be purified. The same attitude to the Anglican Church shaped both contemporary and later American ideas about all the institutions of the Old World. There was no point trying to fix them—they were broken beyond repair. Thus, in the New World, the Providence of God had set aside a home for all who wished to start the world afresh. This was exactly why they believed that they were establishing a Novus Ordo Seclorum—a new order of the ages.

This "Old World bad, New World good" dichotomy would be a lasting heritage from the Puritan Separatists. Though Calvinism is no longer the dominant faith in America, even many secular Americans continue to believe they are the Elect of history, a conviction that was still able to inspire Ronald Reagan's Cold War rhetoric, three hundred and forty years after the Puritans landed on Plymouth Rock.

The roots of American exceptionalism can be traced back to the English Puritans who established a new home in the frigid wilds of New England. All of them were staunch Calvinists. This alone made them exceptional. In Europe at the time, the French Huguenots were being persecuted and murdered in their native land. These European Calvinists were already unique, having rejected both of the models of ecclesiastical governance then prevalent in Europe. They did not want to worship in an established church, like the Church of England, nor live under the dominion of the Roman Catholic hierarchy. Rather, the Calvinists were set on worshipping in their own autonomous congregations. They wanted no one to rule over their faith or their way of life. The Puritan rejection of ecclesiastical hierarchy laid the ground for the sweeping rejection of both social and political hierarchies that would make the American revolution so radical.

The Calvinist Puritans who came to North America were also exceptional in believing that they alone had been predestined to be saints. Hence the importance to them of establishing their own commonwealth, separated from the rest of the sinful and fallen world. The final twist in Puritan exceptionalism came from their decision to model their own civil laws on those of the ancient Hebrews, rather than either Roman law or the British constitution.

The impact of the Protestant rediscovery of the Hebrew scriptures that occurred during the Reformation, thanks to translations of the Bible from the original Hebrew and Greek to all the modern languages of Europe, would have a profound and lasting influence on the development of America, far outweighing the European philosophes of the eighteenth century, which modern secularists view as the primary shapers of the American ethos. The popularity among American Protestants of first names taken from the Old Testament is sufficient evidence of the extraordinary impact that reading Hebrew scripture in the vernacular had on the popular mind of that era. Furthermore, just as the ancient Hebrews had devoted themselves to their exceptional faith, radically different from all other world religions, and fought heroically to defend and preserve it, so too would the Puritan Israelites fight to maintain their own separate and exceptional traditions. The American Puritans never doubted that they were Jehovah's new Chosen People. It is hard to be more exceptional than that.

The Puritan Robert Winthrop's 1630 sermon evoking his new colony as "a city upon a hill" would later become, in the words of Ronald Reagan, "a shining city on a hill," although the phrase had come to stand for a multiplicity of meanings that would have struck Winthrop and his Puritan community as bizarre. Having separated from the reprobates predestined to eternal perdition, that is, the rest of humanity, the Puritans certainly would have been shocked to learn that their society would later be hailed as the forerunner of a multi-ethnic democracy that extended religious freedom to all, including atheists. That was the extravagant position of the early American Baptists—so exceptional that their spokesman, Roger Williams, was widely regarded as a lunatic.

2
EXCEPTIONALISM AS A GEOGRAPHICAL FLUKE

The Puritans were exceptional by design, but their long and dangerous voyage to the New World had taken them over two months, which was not unusual. No one had designed America to be so remote from Europe and so difficult to reach. That was a matter of geography, but this natural barrier also contributed to American exceptionalism in two different but important ways. First, only a small minority of Europeans were prepared to leave their native lands and brave the perils of an Atlantic crossing in order to find a new home in the wilderness that was then America. Only the most highly motivated would take on such a risky adventure. This factor assured that, in the age before the steamboat, migrants to America would be tough, energetic, resilient, adaptable, and with a profound belief that their destiny lay in their own hands—a set of characteristics that were exceptional by any standard.

America's geographical isolation provided another feature of American exceptionalism. All the nations of the Old World were incessantly concerned with their relative power vis-à-vis their powerful neighbors. For good reason. The last partition of Poland occurred in 1795, less than a decade after the creation of the American Republic. Bit by bit, Poland had been devoured by its more powerful neighbors, Prussia, Austria, and Russia, until nothing was left. In the dog-eat-dog geopolitics of Europe, national survival could only be guaranteed by a strong state equipped with a formidable military force. Such armed states were expensive, requiring a heavy burden of taxation that fell mostly on those least able to pay them. Those taxes went either directly to supply the military or else to pay off the large debts that the warring states had incurred during hostilities.

The exigencies of war had always demanded a strong leader who could make critical decisions without needing approval from anyone else. Even the early Roman Republic, despite its deeply ingrained abhorrence of one-man rule, conferred supreme authority to a single individual during any serious crisis that endangered their independence, although the appointed dictator, as the Romans called him, could only hold his office for a limited period, just a month or two. In the Europe of the eighteenth century, the same exigencies of war favored authoritarian regimes governed by strong men, like Frederick the Great, or strong women, like Catherine the Great, both of whom had absorbed large chunks of the former Polish Kingdom into their own domains.

America was not surrounded by strong and powerful states like those of Europe. After Americans had won their independence, the European states could still manage to entangle America in their own affairs, as during the War of 1812, but none could ever hope to conquer it. This meant that the early Republic did not need a strong state, a mighty army and navy, or the heavy taxes required to maintain them. Nor did it need a strong leader

33

with dictatorial power simply in order to preserve its independence, as did the European states. This permitted Americans to be concerned mainly with developing the resources of their own country. With the vast territories beyond the Mississippi awaiting their eventual arrival, Americans certainly did not need more territory.

Today, the slogan "America First" is offensive to the globalist meritocracy, but in the eighteenth and nineteenth centuries, it was merely a truism. The American pioneers had more than enough work to do in settling their vast country. They did not need to seek challenges in foreign lands across the seas. Isolationism, far from being a moral crime, as it is often regarded today, had been mandated by geography. The American preoccupation with their own busy and bustling affairs simply left no spare energy to put into righting the wrongs of the Old World, assuming they could ever be righted.

Out of America's geographical isolation emerged another exceptional feature of the American Republic. This was its embrace of the doctrine of quasi-pacifism. Americans shared the British antipathy toward a standing army. One of the causes for the English Civil War was Parliament's fear that the Stuart monarchs, inspired by the Absolute monarchs of Europe, especially Louis XIV, would find ways to fund a standing army that would bypass Parliament. Such an army could then be turned against the English people themselves, the Parliamentarians argued, with good cause. Ironically, however, after the execution of the king and the establishment of the Commonwealth, Oliver Cromwell discovered that he could only rule through the brute force of the New Model Army that he had led to victory in the Civil War. The result was that the English found themselves under military rule and they did not like it.

When the citizens of Boston found themselves living under military occupation, they too bitterly resented it. For Americans, the most abhorrent of all possible systems of government, far worse than monarchy or aristocracy, was a military dictatorship. To fight wars simply for glory of victory, as the French and Prussians did, made no sense to ordinary Americans, while many of the most flourishing Protestant sects either opposed war under any conditions, as the Quakers and Mennonites did, or preached a gospel of peace.

Even the need for a small professional army was a hotly debated issue. Did America really need one? Traditionally, they preferred a citizen militia for purely defensive purposes. Americans disclaimed any interest in foreign wars of conquest. Mere logistics made this virtually impossible. Besides, they had more than enough fighting to do at home.

The Native tribes of North America, many of which, like the Iroquois, were tough and ferocious warriors, posed a formidable challenge. They were a genuine threat to settlers who coveted the land that the Native tribes had always regarded as their own. But divided as they were and lacking military discipline, they did not threaten the existence of the early Republic, although the tiny original English colonies came close to annihilation during their conflicts with the surrounding Native tribes—another factor that limited immigrants only to those who either had immense courage or else equally immense faith in Divine Providence.

There was even something providential about the fact that the Native tribes were so hostile. The Natives of North America had neither a ruling class nor a vast population that had been reduced to the status of peons, as the Aztecs or their predecessors had done in Mesoamerica. Those who arrived in North America were debarred from following the pattern established by the Spanish conquest of Mexico and Peru, by replacing the old ruling elite with themselves, while living off a nation of already subdued peasants. Instead of being settlers who had to work for their own living, they would have become conquerors of a ready-made empire, as the Spanish quickly became in Latin America.

With so much docile labor available to exploit, the British settlers would never have needed to lift a hand, except perhaps to whip a recalcitrant slave to order. Hard work would become the mark of slave labor, to be avoided at all costs by the new ruling class. But the Native tribes of North America could never be reduced to serfs or slaves. They would die first—a quality that many observers both in Europe and America regarded as noble. It recalled to their classically educated minds those heroes of antiquity who, when given the choice between Liberty and Death, always chose death. Patrick Henry had immortalized his own choice in a fiery oration, and in his career, he had expressed both admiration and genuine concern for the fate of the Native Americans who refused to be vanquished. The myth of the "noble savage" was current long before Rousseau, who ironically regarded the "savages" of his own day as degenerates, and it would remain a powerful cultural icon well into our own days.

It was due to the Native tribes' refusal to submit that American settlers had no choice but to do all the hard work themselves. This was true of the small farmers, the artisans, the mechanics, and the merchants of most of the colonies. But the plantation system that developed in the Deep South needed laborers who could work in the torrid heat under conditions unacceptable to those of European descent, many of whom regarded the Deep South as literally uninhabitable. Slaves from Africa had arrived in the British colonies as early as 1619, but the demand for more slaves grew with the booming prosperity of the plantation system. The horrors of both the slave trade and slavery are well-attested and well-known. Those who came to oppose it naturally dwelled on the injustice done to the Black slaves. But in the run-up to the Civil War, what many found so offensive to slavery was its inevitable tendency to stigmatize hard work as servile and degrading. It was a grotesque violation of the famous Protestant work ethic that the German sociologist Max Weber identified with the spirit of capitalism.

3
THE PURITAN SANCTIFICATION OF WORK

As Weber observed, in virtually all other cultures, hard work and exacting labor were looked upon in a negative light. Such work is demeaning and unworthy, fit only for the lower orders. This was the attitude of every ruling class in history. Others, including even Adam Smith, looked on labor as a necessary evil. It was always "toil and trouble." It was justified simply because it was the necessary condition for satisfying our material needs. Labor was merely a means to an end. For Smith, we work in order to enjoy our leisure in tranquility.

The American Puritans, according to Weber, inverted this previously universal attitude to both work and leisure. Work was a good. It was an end in itself. Leisure, on the other hand, was dangerous. Idleness was the devil's playground. The remedy against such worldly temptation was to maximize the amount of work you did. It is true that this work was genuinely productive. It increased the material comfort of the community all around. But this was merely the byproduct of labor, whose true value was to keep people too busy to fall into sinful ways. In colonial America, this attitude to both work and the middle state of life was embraced by all the popular religions, such as the Baptists, Quakers, and Methodists, whose members were made up almost entirely of the working class. The colonial gentry elite naturally retained the code of the gentleman. Their wealth came from land they had inherited. Work was what their slaves did. They could make no sense of the popular religions that condemned their enjoyment of leisure and told them that productive labor was the only path to salvation. For the millions of working-class Americans, in contrast, work became a badge of pride.

This attitude toward labor, derived from religious asceticism, had an unintended consequence. Those who embraced the work ethic became better off, even very rich. The founder of Methodism, John Wesley, who had observed this effect among the working class converts to his faith, loudly bemoaned this outcome, since worldly wealth only led to temptations. On the other hand, Benjamin Franklin, himself raised in the Puritan tradition, was delighted to discover that an ascetic lifestyle was the key to social mobility and worldly success. He endorsed the Protestant work ethic not because it was Protestant, but because it made people rich. Stern frugality and honest work were no longer justified because they were pleasing to the Lord, but rather, because they were the path by which those in a lower station could acquire social mobility and respectable prosperity.

Franklin's maxims, such as "Time is money," offered a fully secular justification for the middling classes to adopt the Protestant ethic not out of a commitment to Calvinist theology, but simply as the best way to get ahead in the world. Franklin's own immense popularity demonstrated that the middling Americans of his era were actually following his worldly advice and by doing so were challenging the fixed social hierarchy that admonished the lower classes to stay in their proper place, well below the gentry elite. It was also thus a revolt against elite dominance of society. Hence it was the American adoption of the Protestant work ethic, especially in its secularized form, that contributed to the anti-elitism of the American working classes.

Thus, it came about that in aristocratic societies, men were ashamed to work, while in America, men were ashamed *not* to work. To be energetic and productive was the prime manly virtue; to be indolent and lazy, a mark of contempt. Benjamin Franklin became a world-wide celebrity during his lifetime, famed as the model and spokesman for the American gospel of entrepreneurial self-improvement. This gospel would produce two of our exceptional traditions. In Europe, men made a lot of money in order to win for themselves and their children the titles and rank of nobility, after which they stopped working. In America, the making of a fortune was an end in itself, and even multi-millionaires were never satisfied unless they continued to increase their riches. At the other end of the economic spectrum, working class Americans were inspired by their opportunity for social mobility and believed that by their hard work, frugality, and temperate habits, they could join the ranks of the rich themselves, along with their children. For the German sociologist Werner Sombart, one of Weber's contemporaries, it was this belief that explained why socialism had never made inroads among the American working class. The class conflict essential to Marx's theory of revolution could gain no traction in a land where virtually everyone believed they could improve their lot by hard work and good behavior. Thus Benjamin Franklin's secularization of the Puritan work ethic became one of the cornerstones of American exceptionalism.

In Europe, however, the diplomatically canny Franklin presented himself to court aristocrats sporting a beaver hat, the emblem of the new breed of man that America was producing: sturdy, hard-working, down-to-earth. Franklin helped to promote the myth that the citizens of the young Republic

39

effortlessly fulfilled Rousseau's ideal of citizenship: industrial, frugal, natural, and simple in their ways. Another source of this myth was the best-selling book, *Letters from an American Farmer*, published in 1782 by J. Hector St. John de Crèvecœur, reenforcing the idyllic visions of America as a utopia of virtue.

4
DID THE ENLIGHTMENT MAKE AMERICA EXCEPTIONAL?

But what about ideas? What role did European thinkers and philosophers play in making America exceptional? This brings us to the widely held view that the American Revolution was the product of the European Enlightenment—a view obviously favored by modern secularists who are reluctant to acknowledge the role that the Judeo-Christian tradition played in shaping America.

The conceit that the European Enlightenment was responsible for the American Revolution ignores the indisputable fact that it was a genuine populist revolt. The British authorities were amazed to discover that the insurrection in their North American colonies was not due to a small cabal of incendiary trouble-makers in Boston, but was supported not only by the urban population but also by outraged farmers from the backwoods who were willing to take up their pitchforks in defense of their liberties, though few had kept up with intellectual debates among the luminaries of the European Enlightenment. It was the explosion of popular resentment against the British that triggered the revolution. Philosophy had nothing to do with it.

The second problem with interpreting the American Revolution as the creation of the Enlightenment is the virtually universal faith that the American people had in the idea of

Divine Providence—the very idea that the foremost thinkers of the European Enlightenment had laughed to scorn. This denial of Divine Providence was the logical consequence of the philosophy of deism so popular among the enlightened thinkers of Europe.

Deism taught that there was a supreme being who had created the universe, but who, after finishing his gigantic task, had resigned his duties and left the universe to its own devices. He had absolutely zero interest in human affairs and certainly could not be expected to violate a law of nature or two merely to help out human beings in their hour of desperate need. Hence there could be no such thing as Divine Providence, a tenet of the Judeo-Christian tradition that Voltaire savagely mocked in his most famous book, *Candide*. But those who had risked all to come to America were not deists. No one could trust luck alone to bring them across the wild Atlantic and confront the formidable Native tribes. Only those supported by their faith in providence would even think of taking up such a daring challenge.

Americans at the time firmly believed that the discovery of the New World had been providential, just as the American revolutionaries saw the hand of God in their victory over the British. This providential reading of American history would become one of the pillars of American exceptionalism. Even Thomas Jefferson deviated from the tenets of enlightened deism, expressing his belief in an "overruling providence." This conviction that God watched over America, still shared by many Americans today, would later morph into the spirit of secular optimism so characteristic of the American people.

But the Americans who waged war on the British Empire were not fighting for an ideology. Unlike the revolutionaries of France, they were not interested in such abstract concepts as The Rights of Man. Their passionate love of liberty had been acquired not from philosophers' treatises, but from the fact that the British colonists of North America had long been permitted more personal liberty than any other people in the world—not as a matter of principle, but simply as a matter of geography. There was no hope of keeping a tight leash on colonies so remote that even a letter would take ten or more weeks to arrive. It was impossible to do much ruling over a people so far out of reach. Hence, for generations before the American Revolution, ordinary Americans had made their own decisions and had been shaping their own lives and destinies. They had acquired and passed down habits of the heart that had made their personal liberty worth fighting for against anyone trying to take it away.

The British critics of the revolution often called the Americans spoiled children. Like all such children, they had been allowed far too much freedom to do exactly as they wished. There was a great deal of truth in this contention, but it was simply the product of the fortuitously benign neglect mandated by the Atlantic Ocean. But if the Americans were spoiled children, they were willing to fight to stay that way.

That is why the revolutionary generation of 1776 fought to create in the New World a government of the people and not a government in the hands of a ruling class, like those of every other nation of the age. The list of the ways in which the early American Republic deliberately deviated from all previous social and political orders is considerable: no monarchy, no hereditary aristocracy, no oligarchy, no state church, no rigid social hierarchy, no arbitrary rule, no laws that did not have the consent of the people.

Nothing like this had ever been attempted on such a scale since antiquity. At the time of the American Revolution, it would have been impossible to find any European observers, whether they supported the American cause or opposed it, who were not aware of how radically exceptional America had become. There was nothing else like it in the world. American exceptionalism was not a controversial issue for those who watched the birth of the American Republic. It was a simple fact.

Alexis de Tocqueville, who visited America during the Age of Jackson is sometimes credited with being the first to recognize American exceptionalism, but his comment is often misinterpreted. He claimed that America was an exception among democracies—which was certainly true enough—but considering just how rare democracies had been in history, this only made America an exception among exceptions. The question, once again, was never whether or not America was exceptional; the question was how long it could remain that way.

From the days of the American revolution, other nations had tried to follow the example we had set. The French, who had both aided and watched our revolution, were inspired to create their own republic in 1792. The countries that had once been part of the Spanish Empire in the Americas would later declare their own independence, with Venezuela the first to claim the title of a republic for itself, on July 5, 1811. During the various national uprisings of 1848, the universal goal of the revolutionaries was to create their own republics with constitutions inspired by ours. Yet most of these hopeful republics failed, often quite quickly, as when the Second French Republic disintegrated after a mere three years of legislative discord and squabbling.

The English firebrand Thomas Paine, the author of *The Rights of Man*, had famously written during the American Revolution that "the cause of America was the cause of mankind." When the French Revolution began, Paine enthusiastically supported it. In 1793, the much-celebrated author was even made an honorary member of the revolutionary French National Assembly. When Paine humanely voted for the life of Louis XVI to be spared, he was thrown in jail by his enemies in the Jacobin club. Fortunately, his American connections saved him from the guillotine, but his experience in France might have caused him to wonder if Edmund Burke might have had a point in the critique of the Revolution that he had published in November 1790, nearly two years before the creation of the French Republic.

Burke had supported the American but opposed the French Revolution. The much-vaunted Rights of Man of both Paine and the French revolutionaries were to Burke merely a lofty but inherently dangerous set of vague abstractions. How many such rights were there and how far did they extend? Who decided what they were? Who was there to defend and protect them? Historically grounded rights could be both enumerated and specified. Everyone knew what they were. There were established routines for defending them. They required only an examination of English laws and tradition, with no need for the dangerous abstract speculation that had swiftly torn the French revolution-aries into mutually hostile camps and unleashed the Reign of Terror that had almost cost Tom Paine his life.

Burke did not accept the doctrine of universal natural rights, a central principle both to Thomas Paine and to all the French revolutionaries on both the right and the left. Instead, like all classical Whigs, Edmund Burke believed that rights and liber-ties were grounded in the peculiar historical experience of the English people. They were inherited rights, the product of their own unique struggles, and had grown organically over the centu-ries. Like a rare plant that could not survive if transplanted to an alien environment, the rights so prized by the English could not be exported to nations lacking its unique history.

At the heart of the debate between Edmund Burke and Thomas Paine was the question whether the American Republic offered a model for all humanity or whether it was so exceptional that it defied imitation—a question that still haunts us today.

In the nineteenth century, America would introduce to the world its own unique brand of philosophy. While much of the world had fallen under the spell of various European ideologies, American thinkers, most notably William James, rejected them all in favor of a philosophy that perfectly expressed the quintessential American spirit, which was dubbed pragmatism.

5
THE TRADITION OF AMERICAN PRAGMATISM

By nature, pragmatism is an anti-ideology. It has no interest in what should work or could work or might work, but only in what actually does work. It is a philosophy that reflected the attitude of ordinary Americans. It offered none of the utopian visions of a perfected humanity that so enthralled European intellectuals of the time. It was not elitist, but down to earth. Instead of the fashionable atheism of European thinkers, pragmatists like James defended the value of religious faith both for individuals and for societies as well. Those who believed Providence watched over them were in fact more successful in their earthly endeavors than those who believed everything happened by chance. When examining an idea, James always wanted to know its "cash value." It wasn't enough for an idea to sound good in theory. It had to prove itself by delivering the goods.

Unlike the European ideologies of his time that aimed at turning European societies upside down, James's pragmatism was an affirmation of the popular traditions in which Americans of every class and background shared. Benjamin Franklin expressed this pragmatic spirit in his own day. Regarded as a sage by the courts of Europe, Franklin did not think it beneath his intellectual eminence to invent such a useful device as the lightning rod. In 1742, he invented the Franklin stove, later improved by David Rittenhouse, an American who was an astronomer, clockmaker, surveyor, mathematician, and inventor.

Less famous than Franklin, Rittenhouse represents one of America's enduring legacies. In most other cultures, a useful invention like the Franklin stove might be good enough. But not in America. Here, what was already good enough could always be made better. The American quest for "the new and improved" had begun with Rittenhouse and would continue until our own time. The founder of Apple, Steven Jobs, perhaps best exemplified this tendency, as each generation of iPhone was indeed an improvement on those already quite marvelous little devices. But he was hardly alone in his quest.

In between Franklin and Jobs came a host of brilliant inventors. Eli Whitney invented the cotton gin; Samuel Morse invented the telegraph, allowing distant nations to communicate at 90 percent of the speed of light. Thomas Edison, who had little formal education, would become perhaps the greatest inventor in the history of the world. In Germany, the brilliant physicist Heinrich Hertz had pioneered theoretical work in the fundamental principles of electromagnetism. But it was Edison who sought to apply his abstract theories to concrete problems of daily life. After hundreds of attempts, Edison would invent the light bulb, and the age of electricity began to sweep across the globe. The Wright brothers would also inaugurate a new era of progress, though they had originally been printers and bicycle makers.

William James, in short, did not invent or discover pragmatism. He was simply providing a philosophical gloss to the activities that ordinary Americans had long been accustomed to doing without reflecting on them: fixing practical problems as they arose, seeing whether these fixes actually worked, abandoning those that didn't (as Edison had abandoned all his failed models for the light bulb), tinkering with and improving what did work, and working tirelessly to keep on improving it. Such indefatigable inventiveness was a national trait, along with the American genius for transforming abstract scientific knowledge into practical know-how.

In addition, it was the same spirit of pragmatism that led Americans of an earlier era to try to reach compromises with their opponents over the political issues that divided them. The art of the deal was already being practiced long before Trump came on the scene. Politicians of both the nineteenth and early twentieth centuries recognized that they had different interests and that it was natural for these different interest groups to advance their own preferred agendas. Trade-offs were to be expected and accepted.

These politicians sought compromise, and not conflict. Innocent of the ideological brand of politics that is the hallmark of our own era, they would have been shocked to discover that compromise had become a crime and that all-out resistance to a sitting president was now considered a virtue. But every political ideology has the inevitable tendency to see the world in terms of black and white, saints versus sinners, the force of darkness against the legions of light. The fact that the Manichaean style of politics has always brought disaster to any nation afflicted by it does not seem to disturb them. If the ravaged twentieth century had any lesson to teach us, it was certainly the danger of ideological fanaticism.

The transition from the politics of pragmatism to the politics of ideology marked a radical shift in the American zeitgeist. This transition came about in the twentieth century, when

American intellectuals, both on the right and on the left, would largely abandon pragmatism as they fell under the spell of one European ideological fad after another, from Marxism and Social Darwinism to existentialism and post-modernism. But this tendency of the intellectual elite to seek ideas in foreign models, often deeply antithetical to the American spirit of pragmatic realism, began shortly after the thirteen former British colonies had declared themselves to be thirteen sovereign and independent republics—indeed, far too independent for many of America's educated elite, who promptly set about plotting how to make them far less independent.

CHAPTER THREE
IF YOU CAN KEEP IT: FROM POPULIST REVOLT TO ELITE REACTION

1
THE REVOLUTION AS A POPULIST REVOLT

The American Revolution was a world-historical event from the first shot fired on April 19, 1775, at the Battles of Lexington and Concord. From this famous shot "heard around the world," as it came to be known, the rebellion in America was closely followed by many European observers. There were those Europeans who cheered it on, like the British Whigs and the French in general, while others looked upon it with contempt as an uprising of a rabble pursuing not liberty but mere license to do whatever they pleased. Among these were both Edward Gibbon and the Tory, Samuel Johnson, who famously quipped: "How is it that we hear the loudest yelps for liberty among the drivers of Negroes?"

Yet all these European observers agreed on one thing: What was unfolding on the North American continent was different from any event that had happened in the world before. What made America exceptional in the eyes of Europeans was its dedication to the principle of equal liberty for its citizens; though property qualifications initially restricted those who could vote, these were gradually lessened until, with the coming of Andrew Jackson, all free males were awarded the franchise.

Yet, even from the very start, it was an audacious attempt to create a social order that rejected the principle of hierarchy that formed the basis of all the major European nations—indeed all nations that had transcended the hunter-gatherer stage. It was difficult even to imagine what a society based on such principles might be like. This is why no one seriously questioned whether America in the wake of 1776 was exceptional.

The most obvious feature of the American revolution was its populist origin—a factor that many members of the political Establishment, both in the British colonies and in Great Britain, found most disturbing, considering how such popular explosions in the past had led to chaos and anarchy. When the British government sought to impose the Stamp Tax on its American colonies, mobs of indignant patriots attacked the homes of those who had been appointed to collect the hated tax. These "Sons of Liberty," as they called themselves, even threatened the lives of anyone who dare to so offend them. Yet though much property was vandalized and destroyed, no blood was shed. The response of the British at this populist explosion was to repeal the Stamp Act that had aroused such fury. This reversal of policy was brought about by the mob, not the learned patriotic pamphlets arguing for the noble principle of "no taxation without representation."

As modern historians have pointed out, the British colonies of North America were the freest and least taxed people in the world when they revolted in 1775. Their grievances against Great Britain, by our contemporary standards, seem both bizarre and quaint. The British had only asked the Americans to pay a nominal tax, in return for the protection that they had offered during the Seven Years War. This was a reasonable request, and yet every effort to tax the Americans was met with violent resistance. When the British once again tried to impose a tax—this time, a minuscule tax on tea—it was met by another populist explosion, known afterwards as The Boston Tea Party. When George III heard of this outrage, he decided to send British troops to Boston to teach his unruly subjects a lesson. Yet when British troops attempted to confiscate the colonial arsenal at Concord, the result was the famous "shot heard around the world." After a brief and desultory skirmish, the British redcoats and their Hessian allies began their retreat back to Boston, but they came under heavy attack as hundreds of ordinary Americans harried them with their muskets and rifles. They had no formal organization. At the time, the American patriots did not even have a general to command them.

Hamilton may have regarded the people as a great beast, but as a soldier fighting in the revolutionary war, he was perfectly aware that without the help of this great beast, American independence would have been a lost cause. The men and women whom the gentry elite called "the inferior or middling sorts" had risked their lives and sacrificed property in the brutal seven-year-long struggle. Without their immense contribution, final victory could not have been possible. Accounts from the British military elite, largely made up of aristocrats, reflect their surprise and dismay when encountering American officers who had formerly been mere farmers, artisans, and petty shopkeepers.

These British officers expected at least to meet with the American gentry elite and not America's riffraff. They weren't expecting aristocrats like themselves. But the American gentry elite constituted a sociological class as clearly defined as the European aristocracy. It was not based on noble bloodlines, as in the old aristocratic families of Europe, but on property, social rank, and breeding. The gentry elite of the British colonies needed to conform to the established code of conduct appropriate to the beau ideal of the English Gentleman. Fairness and civility were essential, as well as good manners and proper demeanor—factors upon which George Washington put great emphasis in his own project of creating himself as the ideal American gentleman. Unlike many of those around him, Washington lacked the college education of which John Adam, Thomas Jefferson, and James Madison could boast. Such a formal education helped to make the grade, but a knowledge of classical antiquity, however acquired, was necessary to understand the political language in which they discussed and debated the issues of the day.

It is no accident that virtually all the names we associated with the heroes of the American Revolution come from the gentry elite. They are the ones we read about, because they were the ones who wrote down their own accounts. Yet although they may have framed the narrative about the American Revolution, it was not the gentry elite, but the ordinary peoples whose names we don't remember, who both made and finished the revolution itself.

Little wonder then that in our retelling of the birth of the American Republic, it often seems as if this gigantic task was accomplished by the learned members of the gentry elite alone, through their erudite debate, philosophical reflection, and elegant prose. We start at the Declaration of Independence in 1776 and then immediately proceed to the framing of the Constitution in 1787. The American Revolution, on this elitist reading, was the work of the well-educated and the enlightened—the Founding

Fathers. In fact, there would have been nothing to found if the ordinary men and women of early America had not been prepared to give their all in the long and bitter struggle for independence.

It was the role played by Hamilton's great beast in achieving our national independence that most surprised those who followed the course of our revolution. In the various populist revolts that occurred in the European past, such as the Peasants' Revolt of 1381 in England and the German Peasants' War from 1524 to 1525, the "people" had indeed acted the part of a great beast. Both of these popular uprisings, and others like them, inevitably ended in violent destruction at the cost of thousands of lives. But the ordinary Americans of 1776 were not peasants; they were independent farmers, artisans, and merchants. Unlike other populist movements in history, American patriots believed that they were only defending the traditional rights and liberties they had long enjoyed as British colonists. Unlike those populist movements that aimed to turn the world upside down, American patriots were fighting to preserve the world they had inherited. This is what has made American populism unique. American populists have always aimed at conserving what they had and were willing to fight against anyone who threatened to take it from them. No one has ever needed an ideology to fight for what is theirs.

It is true that those who remained loyal to Great Britain, known as the American Tories, could suffer rough treatment and humiliation at the hands of the aroused patriot mobs, but no one was strung up from a lantern or led up to the scaffold. This moderation, so characteristic of American populist revolts, would stand in stark contrast to the behavior of the French mobs during the French Revolution that broke out in 1789. Though inspired by our own revolution, the Paris mobs of sans-culottes repeatedly indulged in bloody excesses that pushed the leading revolutionaries of the period into an ever more radical course, ending in the eventual dissolution of the Republic by Napoleon Bonaparte.

Today both France and the United States continue to celebrate their Independence Day. July 4, 1776, is remembered in America for the noble words Jefferson wrote to inspire future generations. July 14, 1789, on the other hand, is a commemoration of the storming of the Bastille and the bloody riotous mayhem that it unleashed. Those guarding the Bastille had surrendered it in the hope of keeping their lives. Instead, they were lynched by the frenzied Parisian mob. Heads mounted on pikes were paraded with raucous fanfare through the winding streets.

The members of the gentry elite back in America who learned of these atrocities wondered if they could be next. This fear of a bloody and violent uprising by the great beast of the people against their betters haunted the dreams of the propertied elite for several generations. In retrospect, we perhaps too easily laugh at their paranoia. No such bloody populist uprising ever occurred on American soil, as we know from history. But the members of the gentry elite of the era did not have the luxury of hindsight. And why should they not fear the idea of handing over power to the ignorant and propertyless masses, who they assumed would quickly despoil them of their position, status, and property?

It is little wonder then that from 1776 on, intelligent observers, both at home and abroad, have wondered how long the American nation could preserve its ideals of a government by that great beast, the people.

The Declaration of Independence had justified the war against Great Britain by invoking "the Right of the People." But who exactly were the People? This would remain a matter of intense controversy throughout the course of American history.

Ordinary people had been indispensable for winning America's independence from Great Britain, but what should they be given once the great patriotic victory had been achieved? That would remain a vexing question, but there was one thing for sure. Aristocrats were to be forever excluded from the ranks of the American People. The nations of the Old World were ruled by hereditary aristocracies, but Americans were determined that no one could claim to rule by virtue of their noble bloodline.

Nothing better displayed the American visceral horror at a titled aristocracy than the indignant stir aroused when, in 1783, some 2,300 officers who had served in the American Revolution decided to found a patriotic organization that they called the Society of the Cincinnati. It derived its name from the Roman patriot who left his farm to defend his Republic, then returned to his fields after victory—the example that George Washington had dutifully followed at a time when many urged him to establish himself as a virtual dictator. Membership in the original Society of the Cincinnati was limited to war veterans, but their sons could also inherit their fathers' title, though this was restricted to the eldest son, just as in England it was the eldest son alone who inherited property and title.

The very idea for such a society was immediately attacked by many prominent Americans, including John Adams, Benjamin Franklin, and Thomas Jefferson. Primogeniture, the curse of the Old World, was back! What came next? Dukes and earls? These American patriots were members of the gentry elite, who had helped to guide the course of the revolution, but they all feared that a society based on primogeniture would sow the seeds of a new hereditary elite, like those that had presumably been left behind in the Old World.

In fact, the Society of the Cincinnati would go on to have a peaceful and obscure life, posing no threat to the American tradition of egalitarianism. The soil of the new Republic was not suitable for the luxuriant growth of an idle aristocracy based on hereditary bloodlines. Instead, the new Republic was to be a revival of the classical republics of the ancient world: Sparta and Rome.

2
RESTORING REPUBLICAN VIRTUE: THE GENTRY ELITE'S UTOPIAN VISION

Unsurprisingly, this mania for restoring ancient republicanism was most prevalent among the few who had mastered the literature that had been handed down from classical antiquity. Many of them had read Livy and Plutarch in the original Latin and Greek. Indeed, to count as educated in the eighteenth century required a decent command of these classical texts, either in their original languages or in translations. This bias toward the study of ancient political systems would have a profound impact on both the American and the French revolutions. It would introduce an element of utopian fantasy into the debate over how these new republics should be constructed.

When learned men read of the patriotic heroes in Livy or in Plutarch, they never doubted the historical veracity of these accounts. Today, we take these stirring stories with a grain of salt, but the educated elites of eighteenth-century America never doubted for a moment that the restoration of ancient republican virtue was entirely possible in their own day. The virtue they all had in mind was the same: the willingness to sacrifice one's fortune, one's life, or even the lives of one's sons—as Brutus the Elder was said to have done—all for the public good.

The American firebrand revolutionary, Samuel Adams, who had attended the Boston Latin School before graduating from Harvard, had frankly stated his desire to create "a Christian Sparta" on American soil. Jeremy Belknap, a learned historian of the era, was so enamored of Sparta that he wanted to revive even its tradition of collective meal-taking. "All men must eat together and their labor be put into common stock—in short, let the individuals be poor and the State rich...." Benjamin Rush had been even more explicit. He believed that it was possible "to convert men into republican machines." But to achieve this goal, the ordinary American must first "be taught that he does not belong to himself, that he is public property." Those who preferred to take the Roman Republic as their model had a no less collectivist version of ancient civic virtue. Private interests were vicious and destructive of civil virtue, which required all personal interests to be set aside in order to pursue the common good. John Adams expressed this ideal when he praised George Washington as "emblematic of republican virtues in sacrificing personal interests to the public good," as opposed to those whom Adams called "the republican riffraff," many of whom were the ones fighting and dying for the American cause.

Though it is often said that the American revolutionaries were followers of the philosophy of the British Whig, John Locke, the members of the gentry elite had no interest in Lockean individualism, an idea antithetical to their cherished ideal of self-sacrificing civic virtue that they regarded as indispensable for an ideal republic. It was rather "the republican riffraff" who upheld Locke's ideas about the right to liberty and to private property, though few of them had ever heard of the English philosopher. They had no need of an abstract theory to defend the liberty to which they had become accustomed. Indeed, as the historian Claire Rydell Arcenas points out in her book *America's Philosopher:*

John Locke in American Intellectual Life, while many Americans often quoted from his *Essay on Human Understanding*, she was shocked to discover that there were no references in the revolutionary literature of the era to Locke's most important work of political philosophy, *The Second Treatise on Government*, despite the later widespread myth that this was the primary intellectual source of the American Revolution—a myth that credited the educated elite alone for the successful outcome of our dangerous break from Great Britain.

Without the enthusiastic support of John Adams's less educated—and indeed often quite ignorant—fellow countrymen, there would have never been a revolution. Yet, by and large, they had no taste for the kind of civic virtue that "the better sort"—the gentry elite with their classical education—had so fervently embraced. The middling sort of Americans couldn't care less about what Livy or Plutarch said. They had no use for the gentry's abstract theories about building an ideal republic on their fanciful notions. They simply wanted to get on with their own lives and to pursue their own personal interests. These ordinary Americans did not first devise a theory of politics and try to implement it in their own communities. Instead, it was the other around. They already had a community that pleased them and they simply wanted to keep it. They championed liberty as a political ideal because they already knew its value and did not want to live without it.

The same attitude would lead the People to oppose the gentry elite's ideal of modeling America on classical Rome or Sparta. They wanted no part of any scheme that would rob them of their ability to make something of themselves. Without having read Adam Smith, whose *Wealth of Nations* had been published in 1776, they were already in the process of creating their own commercial society in which there was no need for a ruling class or even much of a state. Long before the concept of laissez-faire had been promoted as a revolutionary political ideal, ordinary Americans had already been practicing it. And it was out of this practice that the American political system would later enshrine the liberty of personal enterprise as a fundamental right—despite the gentry elite's collectivist visions derived from classical antiquity. The conviction that the best government was the one that interfered the least in their daily affairs was the work not of an intellectual elite, but of ordinary Americans who were simply looking to improve their own lot in life. They were the true champions and defenders of social mobility in the new Republic.

All of this was heresy to many of America's educated elite, who imposed severe limitations on how far the middling and inferior sorts could rise in the world. As Gordon Wood commented, "…some Americans, though they were good republicans, attempted to confine [social] mobility within prescribed channels. Men could rise, but only within the social ranks in which they were born. Their aim in life must be to learn to perform in their inherited position 'with industry, economy, and good conduct.'" But this was certainly not how the People saw the matter. The revolution had promised them the chance to move up as far in the world as their talents and energies allowed. And no would-be ruling elite could take that from them, though the gentry elite would soon give it their best shot.

3
NATURAL ARISTOCRATS VERSUS THE PEOPLE

In the years following the 1783 dispute over the Society of the Cincinnati, the idea of an aristocracy returned, but in an altered form. The tumultuous events leading up to the Constitutional

Convention in Philadelphia in the summer of 1787 had led many of the "better sort" to believe that the time had come to establish a new ruling class of aristocrats—not based on hereditary blood-lines, of course, but rather on merit. The theory supposed that there was a natural aristocracy made up of men of the better sort, men with high social status, whose inherited wealth and property provided them with the leisure required both for a college education and the study of the classical writings of antiquity.

The experiences of James Madison, while serving in the Virginia General Assembly, had opened his eyes to what happened when the middling and inferior sorts gathered together to make laws. None of the intellectual elite had a finer mind than Madison, and none had been more convinced that the revolutionary war was fought in order to restore the classical virtues that he had so admired in his study of the ancients. Yet his abstract faith in "the People" did not last long as he watched and listened to what the representatives of the people actually wanted.

In April 1787, Madison published his "Vices of the Political System of the United States," in which he listed his grievances against popular assemblies. The English reverence for law had been inherited by the Americans, but the state legislatures were making a mockery of it. "The short period of independency has filled as many pages as the century which preceded it," Madison wrote. What was even worse, according to Madison, "We daily see laws repealed or suspended, before any trial of their merits, and even before a knowledge of them can have reached the remoter districts within which they were to operate." How could the Americans have respect for laws made by a legislative mob?

Madison had been born into a wealthy Virginia planter family, had attended college, and held a high social rank. Like his neighbor, friend, and colleague Thomas Jefferson, he had naively assumed that "the People" would select their representatives from the better sort like themselves. True, there was still some respect among the general population for those who occupied a higher station in life, but by and large, the Virginia assembly struck Madison as a collection of riffraff, consisting of men who lack the social graces, the eloquence, the learning, and the prudence that were the natural patrimony of the gentry elite. They could be petty farmers, blacksmiths, carpenters or shop owners, few of whom had much in the way of education. They may have read the Bible and, perhaps, *The Pilgrim's Progress*, but certainly not Plutarch in the original Greek.

Madison was not alone in his dismay at the behavior of these original state legislatures. As the historian Gordon Wood remarks, "Time and again the legislatures interfered with the governor's legitimate powers, rejected judicial decisions, disregarded individual liberties and property right, and in general, as one victim complained, violated 'those fundamental principles which first induced men to come into civil compact.'" What the elite found most disturbing were the economic ideas of the vulgar herd. The thirteen new republics differed, but in most of them, the legislative assemblies were in favor of easy money and availed themselves of the quickest method of procuring it: They printed their own money and made it legal tender. This was obviously designed to help out debtors, since the mandated inflation would naturally be in the favor of those who had to pay back money they had borrowed. Yet, just as naturally, such a monetary policy was anathema to those who were their creditors. Today we may think of the gentry elite of the era as "gentlemen farmers," but they were also gentlemen moneylenders.

The event that finally convinced the gentry elite of the need for a stronger federal government occurred in Western Massachusetts, when a veteran of the Revolutionary War named Daniel Shays left his farm and began the rebellion that bears his name. Like all of his followers, many of whom were also veterans, he believed that the state legislature located in Boston had become corrupted by greed and venality. He believed, with good reason, that the city elite was forcing the farmers in the Western part of the state to pay far more than their fair share of taxes.

Shays's forces organized into formidable battalions. They took over court buildings to stop anyone from trying to sue a debtor who owed them money. The former soldiers also emptied the debtors' prisons that were still in existence then. They even attempted, but failed, to seize the Massachusetts state arsenal, located in Springfield.

The rebellion was not the affair of a day or even a week. It lasted from August 1786 to February 1787. The failure of the state to put down the insurrection within its own borders had to be addressed. The obvious solution to this problem was to create a strong central government, with far more power than the weak Articles of Confederation that, much to Madison's disgust, had refused to provide enough money to pay the soldiers who were fighting for independence. Something obviously had to be done. It was to that end that Madison had devised his cunning strategy. Under the pretext of merely making minor amendments to the Articles of Confederation, Madison and other members of the gentry elite created a constitution clearly designed to put the better sort back in the saddle.

In his own Virginia plan for a federal constitution, James Madison had hoped to establish a permanent and perpetual government in the hands of a natural aristocracy that would be tasked with the job of checking the excesses of democracy in the state governments. He had even hoped to create a method whereby the natural aristocracy in charge of the new federal government could veto laws passed by the popular state assemblies, which were too apt to favor debtors over creditors and to pass a multitude of crazy laws.

Alexander Hamilton had gone much further, arguing that even the governors of the states should be appointed by the federal government. In the Constitutional Convention held behind closed doors in Philadelphia in 1787, Hamilton frankly declared that he would prefer the United States to model its own system on that of the British, which he deemed the best in the world. Fearing the people as a great beast, it was natural that Hamilton wanted to establish a bulwark against further populist agitation, which was his primary reason for wanting to create a powerful federal government, able to subdue the unruly state legislatures. But an America that was merely a transplanted version of the British monarchy, with its president as an elective king and a Senate acting as the House of Lords, would have marked a return to the political and social hierarchies of the Old World, which most of the American revolutionaries had assumed they had rejected in their break from the British Empire. Had Hamilton's advice been followed, the United States might have gone on to achieve success and stability, but it would certainly have had to abandon the claim of American exceptionalism. Even the astute Hamilton, however, recognized that his proposal was a nonstarter. The people would never accept it.

The Constitution that finally emerged from the Philadelphia Convention was a profound disappointment to both Hamilton and Madison. It had not created the immensely powerful central government they had hoped for. Yet it had provided the office of the president with the powers of executive actions that shocked those Americans who had been accustomed to severely limiting the power of their own state governors. As Gordon Wood has pointed out, the revolutionaries of 1776 could not have imagined that in a little more than a decade, they would be asked to ratify a constitution that gave a single individual such immense power, sufficient to provide any ambitious politician with the means of achieving despotism. Fortunately for the supporters of the new constitution, they held a trump card. The new office was destined to be filled by the only man whom everyone trusted not to abuse power: George Washington. Even those who furiously protested the new constitution were careful never to attack Washington.

Against those who warned of the dangers inherent in the newly proposed system of government, both James Madison and Alexander Hamilton, despite their own reservations, immediately rallied to the defense of the Constitution in a series of articles that, in time, became known as *The Federalist Papers*, to which John Jay contributed as well. The controversy was quickly joined by those who became known as the Anti-Federalists. These included such revolutionary luminaries as Patrick Henry and Richard Henry Lee, but it was largely the middling sort who found in the new document a blueprint for constructing precisely the kind of despotic regime that they fought the revolution to overthrow. Many believed that the so-called Constitutional Convention was nothing more than a coup d'etat engineered by America's gentry elite in order to crush the popular radicalism that threatened both their traditional social status and their wealth. Most of the middling sort had absolutely no desire to see any restraint imposed on the liberties they had enjoyed under the weak Articles of the Confederation.

As many modern historians have pointed out, ordinary Americans were prospering quite well without any central government at all. Commerce was lively. There was much social mobility. The middling and even the inferior sort had ambitions to make something of themselves. Many had even ceased to have the traditional reverence for their social superiors, as Madison had discovered. But it would be wrong to dismiss Madison's disillusionment as merely the result of elitist snobbery. All the legislative assemblies of the thirteen independent and sovereign states were behaving like the one in which he had served as a representative. Several, like that of Rhode Island, were much worse. It was not simply that they threatened the economic and social status of the gentry elite. They were also endangering the very existence of the new Republic by their increasing factionalism.

4
JAMES MADISON AND THE DANGERS OF FACTION

Like all the classically educated members of the gentry elite, Madison was well aware that every earlier republic had eventually been destroyed by the struggle between violent factions, each seeking to crush or exile their political enemies, leading to interminable civil feuds that were brought to a halt by the appearance of the necessary strong man to impose order with an iron fist. These factions might represent the rich against the poor, debtors against creditors, but there could be many other sources of dissent representing a variety of other interest groups in conflict with each other. Men could quarrel over religion, social status, and even their artistic tastes.

While sitting in the Virginia legislative assembly, James Madison had seen how quickly factions emerged and had witnessed the calamitous effect they had on the orderly procedures of government. In Federalist No. 10, Madison recognized that factionalism was endemic to any large group of human beings. It could not be eliminated since it was built into human nature. Contrary to those who believed that factions sounded the death knell of any republic, Madison argued that in a nation as large and diverse as America, the threat of factionalism could be controlled and regulated.

Factionalism was most dangerous when there were only two factions in the state, since each would always attempt to seize power from the other. The same could happen with three factions, but, as Madison argued, because of the great size of the new Republic, there would be so many factions that none could seriously hope to seize power alone. They would, in effect, regulate each other.

In making this argument, Madison was also addressing one of the main objections to the creation of a single great nation out of thirteen smaller republics. The earlier eighteenth-century theorists of republicanism, such as Charles Montesquieu and Jean-Jacques Rousseau, had all agreed that a workable republic must be a very small affair. Even tiny Rhode Island was too large to meet their standards. Since a republic could only survive so long as factions did not emerge, only societies in which everyone already shared the same common values, as in a Swiss canton, had a chance of long-term survival. Madison's solution turned this argument on its head by asserting that it was America's multitude of different and various interests that would prevent any single interest from seizing too much power.

Madison undoubtedly came up with this solution after his firsthand experience in trying to realize his and Jefferson's ambition to assure religious tolerance in their native state of Virginia. Away in France, the land of free-thinking philosophers, Jefferson naively believed that all of Virginia's many Protestant denominations would breathe into their sectarian lungs the cosmopolitan spirit of French Enlightenment and see the absurdity of their intolerance of other sects.

Back in Virginia, Madison was quickly disabused of Jefferson's enlightened delusion. The multitude of religious sects and communities had reluctantly accepted the principle of mutual tolerance simply as a permanent truce. All were jealous of the others, and none wanted to be dominated by them. Except for the Baptists, most would have loved to have become the established church of Virginia. Only the Baptists were genuinely horrified at the idea of a state church, which had been customary in the Old World from which they had originally fled. Indeed, the stiff-necked Baptists, rather than Voltaire, were responsible for the American acceptance of religious freedom enshrined in the First Amendment to the Constitution. Drawn largely from the middling sort, the early American Baptists contributed more than their fair share to making America exceptional. They had insisted that, unlike in the Old World, no one could be taxed to support a religion in which they did not believe. Today, we take this idea so much for granted that it is difficult to recognize just how revolutionary it was at the time.

Yet the truce reached among the variously contending religious sects worked, and that was enough for Madison. Indeed, Madison's pragmatic solution to the problem of factionalism in the new Republic might have worked if America had as many political factions as it had religious denominations. But unlike the Protestant tendency to split apart over minor doctrinal nuances, the tendency of political factions is to unite together in their bid for power, setting aside all lesser issues on which they might have differences of opinion.

In addition to his novel theory, Madison also hoped the Constitution had been so deftly constructed as to keep the government from falling into the hands of the fractious many, by reserving positions of authority for America's natural aristocrats, like himself. As originally planned, the Constitution bestowed the unchecked power to choose the president on a group of wise men, known as the electors, not on the people. Another group of wise men, taking the Roman title of Senator, would represent the patrician class of the gentry elite. Finally, a third group of wise men would sit on a Supreme Court as a final safeguard against the dangerous excesses of democracy. The people would be permitted only to vote for their local representatives, but these humble representatives could do little harm considering the various ingenious methods by which the people's dangerously restless will to power could be checked.

With so many wise men, full of the stern old Roman sense of civic duty, guiding the new Republic, there could be little danger of factionalism. James Madison and Alexander Hamilton, after all, had collaborated on *The Federalist Papers*, despite their other political differences. They had set an example that other members of the natural aristocracy were sure to follow.

Yet immediately after the ratification of the Constitution and the birth of the new American Republic, political factions arose among the gentry elite themselves. Madison and Hamilton soon came to quarrel over the question of whether the new federal government should take over and pay the debts of the individual states.

Hamilton had a number of strong arguments for his proposal. As a proponent of a strong central power, he hoped his policy would strengthen the national government and bind the interests of the individual states to that of the federal government. He also saw it as a way of building America's credit in the eyes of the world's investors. A solidified national debt would also become the basis of economic growth by offering predictable interest payment on stable securities. Finally, his program would create sources of federal revenue that did not depend on the states, allowing for the use of national taxes, especially tariffs.

Though there was obviously much to recommend Hamilton's proposal, Madison was growing concerned that it gave too much power to the federal government. A compromise was reached. Hamilton got his way with the state debts, while Jefferson and Madison were able to establish the District of Columbia in what was then a dismal swamp, a spot so uninviting and insalubrious that it was sure to ward off any considerable influx of population. Even in selecting the capital of their nation, Americans were exercising their tradition of exceptionalism. All the old nations of Europe had their capitals in the biggest cities: London, Paris, Madrid, Berlin. Living in the midst of such huge metropolises, there was the unavoidable risk of popular rebellion seizing control of the government, as would happen in Republican France only a few years later.

But the dismal swamp had another claim that appealed to Jefferson and Madison. True, it was a dismal swamp, but it was a dismal swamp located in the South, and not the North. The compromise of 1790 was predicated on the fact that the North and South had both already come to see themselves as different sections with conflicting interests. In time, these two sections would come to violent blows in the Civil War, the end result of a half-century of escalating sectional factionalism.

5
JEFFERSON REINVENTS THE EXECUTIVE

Madison's hope that America's natural aristocracy would be too wise and sensible to feud among themselves had been swiftly dashed. The natural aristocrats, rather than uniting for the good of their Republic, swiftly fell to fighting over other issues than the state debt and the location of the national capital. This quarrel would become violent even during the administration of George Washington, and before long, John Adam's Federalists and Thomas Jefferson's Republicans were at each other's necks— bitter enemies who would stop at nothing to injure the other. Washington was routinely denounced by Jefferson's Republicans as aspiring to set himself up as king. (He's going to be America's George III!—the closest equivalent to Adolf Hitler for eighteenth-century Americans.)

Ironically, Thomas Jefferson, whose study of ancient republics had taught him the dangers of factionalism, would sow the first seeds of a genuine political party, but as a good Whig, he believed that he was only following the radical Whig tradition of resisting too much power in the hands of too few. Fortunately, however, the quarrel between the Federalists and their opponents over the Constitution was resolved by the election of 1800.

During his eight years in office, Jefferson made the presidency a powerful instrument for keeping America exceptional. Unlike Hamilton, Jefferson did not think the people were a great beast. On the contrary, he saw them as the ultimate guardians of the principle of equal liberty. It took a whole people to bring down a despotic government. He saw populist revolts as the people's natural remedy against overbearing social hierarchy.

In a letter written in 1787, while on his embassy to France, Jefferson argued that the Constitutional Convention of the previous summer had overreacted to Shays's rebellion:

> ...what country can preserve its liberties if their rulers are not warned from time to time that their people preserve the spirit of resistance? Let them take arms. The remedy is to set them right as to facts, pardon and pacify them. What signify a few lives lost in a century or two? The

tree of liberty must be refreshed from time to
time with the blood of patriots and tyrants. It is
its natural manure.

On examining the copy of the Constitution that he had just received in Paris, Jefferson found that he especially disliked the novel office of the president, which he compared, with some reason, to the elective monarch of Poland. Since a president could be reelected for as many terms as he could win, what would keep an American president from holding office until his death, like a European king?

When George Washington decided to step down after two terms, he was applauded by the world as the new Cincinnatus. In the process, he also became the one Great Man of History who has been universally admired and acclaimed. But his role in world history is sui generis. No one else was quite like him. Other world-historical figures are defined by what they did, whereas Washington is defined by what he did not do. He did not use the office of the president to seize power. Indeed, it is very possible that the Founding Fathers would have not created such an opportunity for despotism, unless everyone trusted that Washington, as the "indispensable man," was certain to become the first president. Washington's act of relinquishing power was such a political marvel that it also vindicated the principles of the Revolution. Those who had predicted that our upheaval would end either in anarchy or tyranny had been proved wrong. At least so far.

It is often said that Washington established the tradition of two terms per president, but it would not have been much of a tradition if others had chosen not to follow it. The unpopular John Adams served only a single term, but there was no reason to think that a more popular president would follow Washington's example.

In the election of 1800, Aaron Burr and Thomas Jefferson had tied with 73 electoral votes a piece, sending the decision to be made in the House of Representatives, where Burr was narrowly defeated. But what if Burr had become president instead of Jefferson? He was an immensely ambitious man, well-known for his idolatry of Napoleon Bonaparte, the bust of whom he carried around with him wherever he went. Burr also lived until 1836. Would he have honored the two-term precedent, or would he have aspired to become the Emperor of North America? There was nothing in the Constitution at the time that would have kept him from running for nine consecutive terms.

Today, we have come to assume that it was our written Constitution that has spared us from power-hungry men. However, every republic that followed our own model of government also had written constitutions, but these all proved to be made of straw. In each of these cases, the promise of popular government was crushed by ambitious men and their coterie of followers. Burr was just such a man, who would later be accused by Jefferson of a treasonous conspiracy to establish his own independent nation beyond the Mississippi, though the details of his plot remain murky and controversial.

Only a few votes in the House of Representatives kept Burr from the presidency. Jefferson won, and he was determined to set the model to be followed by future presidents. By not running for a third term, which he could have easily won in 1808, Jefferson honorably confirmed the two-term limit tradition set by Washington. As sitting president, Thomas Jefferson also went to great pains to provide the world with the image of the venerable sage, content with only the minimal degree of power sufficient to carry out the duties of his office. Another man with a taste for pomposity and the love of grand display might have filled the office like a European monarch, demanding obsequious obedience from his retainers. But as president, Jefferson went to the other extreme by his rejection of all the traditional trappings of power. You did not have to bow and kiss his feet. You did not even have to take off your hat to him. He was not sheltered by bodyguards, nor did he have courtiers to respond to his every beck and call. No toadies flattered him, no sycophants ate at his table.

Indeed, if you were in the neighborhood of the White House and cared to have a casual chat with the great man, all you had to do was to knock on his front door. Someone would take you up to see him. Rather than sitting in state, invested in the purple robes of royalty, he might be found in his nightgown and slippers, happy to discourse with you on whatever questions you brought to his omnivorous intellect. It might be the teachings of Jean-Jacques Rousseau or the mismanagement of your local post office.

Rather than a Consul of the people, as Washington had been, Jefferson would become their tribune, speaking for and in their interests against those of the patricians. Both of these offices were derived from the Roman Republic. The two Roman Consuls were chosen from the patrician class, the gentry elite of their day. Later, after a protracted period of social conflict between the patricians and the plebs—the middling and inferior sort of their day—these lower orders were granted the office of the tribune, chosen from the plebs by the plebs, in order to defend their interests against those of the elite class. From henceforth, the office of the president could be used either to champion the elite or to champion the people—or to work out a feasible compromise between the two.

Perhaps the most notable case in which Thomas Jefferson acted as the people's tribune arose from his conflict with the Supreme Court. Just as Madison had come to fear legislative despotism, so Jefferson had learned to fear judicial despotism. The Federalists had been voted out, yet they had assumed, by their control of the Supreme Court, the power to thwart the clear will of the people. Of course, this was exactly what the authors of the Constitution had wanted the Supreme Court to do with the powers they had provided to it. But Jefferson saw the potential for despotism in a court over which the people had no control. The justices of the Court could only be removed through the cumbersome process of impeachment and only for treason, bribery, high crimes, and misdemeanors. None of the sitting justices on Chief Justice John Marshall's Supreme Court had committed such offenses. Nevertheless, Jefferson was determined to put the Federalist justices in their place.

On March 12, 1804, the House of Representatives voted to impeach Samuel Chase. The Speaker of the House, John Randolph, one of Jefferson's cousins, had decided to bring charges of impeachment against the most obnoxiously bitter Federalist. Chase never hid his partisanship while on the bench and was loathed by the Jeffersonian Republicans. He made a good first target, though Jefferson hoped that the arch-Federalist, John Marshall, another one of his cousins, would be next on his hit list.

The impeachment in the House of Representatives succeeded, but the Senate voted not to convict. Later historians would regard this as a victory over yet another example of democratic excess. Certainly, American history would have been radically different if the justices of the Supreme Court could be so easily removed by a popular president. As in the case of Burr's defeat in the House of Representatives, the change of only a couple of votes would have set the early American Republic on a far different course than the one actually taken—a healthy reminder that even historically insignificant men can shape the course of history. In the aftermath of the Civil War, it was once again only a few votes that kept President Andrew Johnson in office. Had the Radical Republicans in the Senate succeeded in their mission to remove him, it would have set a dangerous precedent, where a party could unseat a president not for high crimes and misdemeanors, but just because they hated his guts. By such close calls has the destiny of our nation been determined.

Yet Jefferson recognized a troubling fact. Just like any institution, the Supreme Court would always desire to obtain more power for itself. If there was no way of checking its bid for power, then the only recourse was to pass an amendment to the Constitution. Without a more reliable check on its authority, the theoretical balance of power enshrined in the Constitution would be drastically tilted toward the judiciary. This would become a problem that both Lincoln and Franklin Delano Roosevelt had to confront in dealing with their respective crises, while today, we have become aware of how far an activist judiciary can distort and rewrite the Constitution to suit a partisan agenda.

However modestly he may have sat in his office, Jefferson was nevertheless attacked by his enemies for exceeding his authority as president when he made the Louisiana Purchase. Did any president of the United States have the constitutional right to add roughly 828,000 square miles to the nation and to double its size by the stroke of a pen? Yet Jefferson's bold stroke showed what a president could do with his power if he was adamantly determined on a point. He had thereby shown the flexibility of presidential power. It was there when you needed it, but that didn't mean you had to use it all the time, just in cases of emergency.

By agreeing to the Louisiana Purchase, Jefferson had in effect evoked another Roman office: that of the Roman dictator. Despite its fear of too much power in the hands of a single man, the Roman Republic recognized that there were certain emergency situations that demanded immediate executive action. A war that imperiled Rome called for a single man to be put in charge. Cincinnatus himself, the model of civic virtue, had twice been appointed dictator, to deal with enemies at the gate. The position, however, was only temporary. Once the crisis was over, the dictator relinquished his power and returned to normal life.

When debating the Louisiana Purchase within his cabinet, Jefferson had at first argued that as president, he lacked the constitutional authority to accept Napoleon's offer of the vast western lands. Already, in New England, there were many who were vehemently opposed to the expansion of the United States, fearing that it would inevitably diminish their own power to influence the course of government. The Federalists spoke strongly against the purchase, as did many of Jefferson's own party.

With so many opposing him, at first, Jefferson felt that he could only proceed if the Constitution could be amended to give the president such powers as he required. But such an undertaking would be time-consuming, creating controversies in every state debating it, and without any assurance that such an amendment to the Constitution would ultimately be ratified. Eventually, Jefferson was able to persuade himself that the purchase was indeed constitutional, but only with a good bit of dubious rationalization. But in effect, what Jefferson decided to do was to be dictator for a day, arguing that future generations of Americans would in time come to thank him for his high-handed action.

Today, we consider the idea of "manifest destiny" as a fundamental principle of American exceptionalism. Yet the heated debate over the Louisiana Purchase indicates that this destiny was by no means manifest to those who bitterly opposed adding vast new territories to a nation that they believed was already big enough. Furthermore, those who see manifest destiny as merely a pretext for imperialistic aggression by American jingoists should consider the fact that it was the genteel John Quincy Adams who most fervently championed the future expansion of the United States to the distant Pacific Ocean—a quarter of a century before the phrase manifest destiny was coined by the journalist John L. O'Sullivan in 1845.

The judicious and erudite Adams was familiar with the ways of European powers from his earlier career as a diplomat. He foresaw a threat to the future of the Republic if these vast territories were to be absorbed within one or more of the European empires. Czarist Russia had already taken Alaska and was in the process of expanding into California. The British, already in possession of Canada, potentially posed an even more formidable threat. In short, Adams perceived that if the United States did not expand into these vast domains, sooner or later they would fall into the hands of a rival power.

Eventually, most Americans accepted manifest destiny. Indeed, it quickly became one of the key themes of American exceptionalism. The fact that so many had originally opposed the Louisiana Purchase demonstrates that the principle of American exceptionalism was not fixed at any specific point in our history but was capable of evolving and growing over time. Equally important is the fact that this expansion, opposed by the Eastern elites, was enthusiastically supported by the middling and inferior sorts who longed for the opportunities offered them by the newly expanded frontier. And Jefferson proved to be right. Later generations would indeed bless his name for his decision to violate his constitutional authority.

In summary, the office of the president under Jefferson had become unlike any other political office in the world. The president could play the role of Consul, Tribune, and Dictator, depending on the needs of the hour. The president could even be the Revolutionary-in-Chief, as Jefferson had demonstrated. His own vision of presidential authority exceeded those of the Founders as well as some of the presidents who followed him, but without question, Jefferson had prepared an office that would be equipped with all the powers necessary to face the epochal crises that confronted later presidents. All these powers would be needed and exercised by both Lincoln and Franklin Delano Roosevelt. When confronted with the crises of the Civil War and the Great Depression, they also had to assume dictatorial powers far beyond the strict letter of the Constitution. Like Jefferson, both assumed that future generations would forgive them for exceeding their Constitutional authority in order to meet unprecedented challenges that otherwise threatened to destroy the Republic. In fact, future generations have not only forgiven but applauded them. The scruples that would have kept America from fulfilling its manifest destiny were never those of the people. You can find many today who are still indignant over James Polk's "Wicked War" to win California for America. But no one wants to give it back. The sins of the father can also be blessings to the son.

CHAPTER FOUR
POPULISM IN THE AGE OF JACKSON

1
END OF FACTIONALISM OR RISE OF A NEW RULING CLASS?

No one in the early American Republic was more patrician than Thomas Jefferson. He was a paragon of gentlemanly erudition and virtue. The three presidents who would follow him in office, James Madison, James Monroe, and John Quincey Adams, were cut from the same cloth, though of a slightly rougher fabric. They were all born into inherited wealth, were highly educated and possessed the highest social rank available in the American Republic. By any standard, they were the best and the brightest, the elite of the elite.

By 1824, ordinary people began to notice that the government of the United States had fallen into the hands of a ruling elite, which was even assuming the form of an aristocracy of sorts. With the exception of John Adam's one term, every president before 1824 had been a scion of old wealthy planter families. Washington, Jefferson, Madison, and Monroe all belonged to what became known as the Virginia dynasty. John Quincy Adams, elected in 1824, shared their aristocratic attitude. He was himself part of an American intellectual, if not political, dynasty that had started with his father and would be passed on to his son, Charles Francis Adams, and to the latter's son, the brilliant historian Henry Adams. As scions of the social and economic elite known as the Boston Brahmins, they dominated American intellectual and cultural life for much of the nineteenth century.

It is true that perhaps no other nation had ever been blessed with such a brilliant and able ruling elite, yet an elite it had become. Shades of the hated European system of hierarchy seemed to menace the egalitarian ethos on which the nation had been proudly founded.

The election of Thomas Jefferson to the presidency in 1800 would transform what had been a political faction, the Republicans, into the dominant party. By 1814, the Federalist Party had completely collapsed, after having deeply injured its prestige by flirting with the idea of New England's secession from the Union. As in the case of Jefferson's factionalism, there is considerable irony that the party that had most wanted to make a strong and powerful Union was the party that first considered leaving a much weaker one.

2
JACKSON AND BACKWOODS ANTI-ELITISM

Later historians would describe the following period, during which James Monroe was president, as "the era of good feelings."

There was a great sense of national purpose that left little room for political factions to emerge. The partisan rancor of the past appeared to be at an end. Indeed, beginning with President Madison, efforts were undertaken to eliminate the very idea of political parties. By eradicating party rancor from the hearts of its citizens, it was hoped that they would have good feelings toward each other, even toward those with whom they might differ on a few minor points.

There was something else that made political parties seem unnecessary. They had no role to play in selecting the next president. This was handled by a tradition borrowed from the Golden Age of the Antonines, where each of the good emperors chose as his successor the man whom he believed to be the most competent to govern wisely the vast Roman Empire. Adopted for American purposes, it meant that a sitting president could in effect appoint his own successor. It thus transpired that the man chosen to be secretary of state was virtually assured of becoming the next president. Jefferson picked Madison who picked Monroe who picked John Quincy Adams.

However well this tradition may have worked for the Antonines, to revive it in America was yet another attempt to return to the models of government offered by the Old World. It may well have been the means of creating the best and wisest of all possible ruling classes, but it remained a ruling class all the same and a violation of the basic principle of American anti-elitism.

This predictable line of succession might have gone on forever, except for Andrew Jackson. Andrew Jackson was the first self-made man to be elected president. Furthermore, he did this at a time when many of the gentry elite were not willing to allow men of humble and obscure origins to ascend more than a few notches above the station into which they were born. Family, wealth, and social position still mattered to the elite. But Andrew Jackson had lacked all of these. The child of Scotch-Irish parents living in the backwoods of South Carolina, his father died only a few months before Jackson came into the world. His schooling had been rudimentary. His teenage years were spent amid the British campaign to exterminate the American rebels in the Southern Atlantic states. One of his two brothers had been killed by the British, another left by them to die. His mother, to whom he was strongly attached, died while nursing a wounded relative in Charleston. From that point on, Andrew Jackson was on his own.

But Jackson had the itch to leave his mark on the world. In an age of generally colorless figures, like John Quincy Adams, Jackson burst forth in living color. He managed to get a law degree and then set himself up as a frontier lawyer, where he gained both wealth and notoriety. Known for his quicksilver temper, Jackson fought duels, in one of which he killed a man who had insulted him. He would later become judge. He married the woman to whom he was devoted, while she was still married to another man.

A natural leader of men, Andrew Jackson quickly earned the steadfast loyalty of the ragtag soldiers he led in battle against the Cherokees of Georgia. Later, while undertaking an "unauthorized" invasion of what was then Spanish Florida, Jackson had ordered two citizens of Great Britain to be hanged, bringing down on him the wrath of both the British and the Spanish Empire.

By far Jackson's greatest and most unexpected triumph was his victory over the British in the Battle of New Orleans fought on January 8, 1815—a victory that revenged the humiliation that the Red Coats had inflicted on the young Republic in 1812 when they burnt down the White House. Yet even saving New Orleans from the British was not enough to convert his detractors who disliked that Jackson had imposed martial law on the city and complained that their rights were being taken away.

Even his admirers had to admit that Andrew Jackson was not much for following other people's rules. His taste for autocracy may have simply been due to the tendency of every man in a hurry to get to his goal as expeditiously as possible. But his open and glowing admiration for Napoleon Bonaparte unnerved many, who warned that if elected president, Jackson would immediately set about imitating his idol by declaring himself the Emperor of North America. After all, Napoleon had demonstrated to the world just how far a self-made man could rise.

Eventually, after serving in both Houses of Congress, Jackson set his sights on becoming the president of the United States. He had much popular support, but not quite enough. In a five-man race for the presidency, Jackson had indeed received the most popular votes, but not enough votes in the electoral college to secure a victory. By the rules set down in the Constitution, the election was thrown into the House of Representatives, which chose John Quincy Adams, despite his poorer showing in the popular vote than Jackson. The will of the people had been denied—at least as Jackson's many supporters saw the matter.

Jackson later claimed that there had been a "corrupt bargain" between Henry Clay, a congressional firebrand who ruled the House, and John Quincy Adams. Adams, it was said, had promised to make Clay secretary of state—the hitherto automatic launch pad to the presidency for which Clay desperately longed all his life. In return, Clay would muscle the House he controlled into selecting Adams over Jackson.

Whether or not such a corrupt bargain had actually occurred, Adams was elected and Clay became his secretary of state. Perhaps just a coincidence? No, howled Jackson and his supporters. The ruling clique had denied the will of the people, they thundered. Four years later, Jackson ran again and won in a land-slide on the basis of his promise to clean out the whole corrupted Washington establishment. Far more Americans voted than ever before, and the majority of them—nearly 60 percent—voted for Jackson. Upon taking office, Jackson sacked most of the various government officials who had been appointed by the previous administrations.

Most of these men were highly competent, some even experts in their fields. Nevertheless, they had been appointed through the patronage system, which effectively made them loyal clients of the president who appointed them. They owed their job, their status, and their position in society to him. Indeed, the patronage system had come straight out of the Old World, where it had been used to amass political power for the monarch. For those who had begun calling themselves democrats, the patronage system smacked of the corrupt politics that inevitably led to despotism. It was un-American, and Jackson campaigned on ridding the government of this new threat to the will of the people.

Once elected, Jackson put new men into the jobs vacated by those loyal to the old order. Naturally, he chose men who were personally loyal to him. His critics objected that the new men were less fit for their posts than those who had previously held them. In many cases, they were undoubtedly right. Jackson's critics, however, assumed—or at least pretended to assume—that the appointees being replaced did not already have their own loyalties, namely to the old order that was being replaced. However competent such an official might be, it mattered little to the new president if the official was not loyal to him. Indeed, out of loyalty to the old order, the official might even use his superior administrative competency to undermine the new order. It is little wonder then that in taking on the Establishment, the leader

of a populist revolt will always prefer loyalty before efficiency. It
would be suicidal not to.

3
JACKSON TAKES ON THE PLUTOCRATS

Jackson, however, had another even greater target on his radar
than the small federal administration of his day. This was the
Second National Bank of America. Like Jefferson and many
other Americans of the time, Jackson was deeply suspicious
of banks. This had been one of their chief complaints against
Hamilton, who had urged the establishment of America's first
National Bank, as a part of his grand design to make America
a manufacturing power that would rival and hopefully eclipse
Great Britain. Whatever merits they saw in the proposal, both
Jackson and his supporters feared it would become the power
base of a new elite. (Hamilton, on the other hand, did not see
this as a drawback to his program, but one of its chief benefits.)
But for those of the populist persuasion, real wealth was always
something tangible, like land and coins minted out of silver or
gold. The idea of credit spooked them. A bank made money by
charging interest on the paper notes that it issued. This by itself
constituted usury, long considered a serious offense against both
God and humanity.

Worse, the notes that the bank floated were not "hard currency," but merely promises that the bank could exchange these
magical pieces of paper for gold and silver on request. Since the
banks printed more magic money than they had hard currency,
it was always possible for a bank to fail if it had issued far more
bank notes than could be reclaimed from its stock of gold and

silver. This occurred whenever a bank was operated by reckless or imprudent people.

At the head of the Second National Bank, however, sat Nicholas Biddle, a Philadelphia grandee—imperious, aristocratic, and not given to recklessness or imprudence. He and Jackson loathed each other. In his first effort to crash Biddle's bank, Jackson had argued that it was unconstitutional. When this failed, Jackson resorted to other devious methods, including withdrawing government funds, until he eventually succeeded ending both the bank and Biddle's reign over it.

Biddle was naturally unpopular with Jackson's followers. He represented a new elite of men who mysteriously made money out of money. They did not farm, or collect rents, or make barrels, or sail on ships. In fact, most people had no idea what they did to amass their immense fortunes. Ordinary Americans had the same suspicious attitude to bank notes that most people today have toward what is to them the equally baffling crypto-currency of our day. Eliminating the central banking system that was an obvious imitation of the Bank of England made sense to those who did not want America to adopt foreign ways. But at what cost?

America would eventually see the rise of a plutocratic elite in the decades after the Civil War, but it is highly likely that the rise of this new elite would have occurred much sooner had Jackson not brought down the Second National Bank. Money men like Biddle did not automatically step into positions of power and influence earlier held by the gentry elite. Jackson had managed to both bring down the reign of the gentry elite and prevent the rise of a plutocratic elite in their place.

No elite goes down without a struggle. In the election of 1828, the gentry elite attacked Jackson with scurrilous savagery. Jackson's gentlemen opponents accused his long dead mother of being a prostitute and libeled his beloved wife, Rachel, with a thousand insults, hounding her to her death shortly after Jackson's victory in 1828. On the other hand, the rising elite of money men, like Nicholas Biddle, could be equally vicious. In his efforts to preserve the charter of his bank, he severely tightened credit, thereby contributing to the Panic of 1837.

Prying power out of the hands of both a declining and a rising elite will inevitably have serious consequences. It cannot be otherwise. If the elite does not deliberately sabotage the efforts to reduce their power, as Biddle did, the displacement of the elite will by itself create confusion and uncertainty. The elite had made the rules by which the game was played. Changing these rules will naturally be disconcerting to those who have become accustomed to them.

Jackson's victory was a turning point in American history. After him, there was no longer any hope, or even much desire, to revive the idealized party-free republic of the framers of the Constitution. From this point on, politics in America would become party politics. Yet, somehow, the framers' worst fears never materialized. In the America of Andrew Jackson, political parties did not degenerate into the violent factionalism that had terminated the careers of so many other virtuous republics. Class conflict between the rich and poor had brought down many hopeful republics of the past, but in America, the poor had been given the opportunity denied them in the Old World.

4
THE PROMISE OF THE AMERICAN FRONTIER

Thanks to Jefferson's constitutionally doubtful purchase of the Louisiana Territory, the middling and inferior sorts had been offered America's vast new frontier in which they could start afresh. Vehemently opposed by the moneyed and educated Northern elites, Jefferson had scored a major victory for ordinary Americans. He had pulled off a populist coup, which readjusted the balance between the people and the elite just when it appeared that the latter were winning. And the elite would have won, if it had been able to cut off the westward movement of ordinary men and women into new territories, as they had hoped to do. Or if Jefferson had not set aside the Constitution.

The frontier truly made America an exception among nations. Hegel lived just long enough to see the first three years of Andrew Jackson's presidency, but he already recognized the critical importance of America's vast frontier in preserving the country's exceptional political system. Hegel believed that America in the Age of Jackson had not yet become what he called a State. This may sound odd, but the paradox is just a matter of terminology. Hegel used the term State for what we would call a strong central government—precisely the kind that the Jeffersonian tradition feared and opposed. A State was what all European nations had, with their professional standing armies and unelected bureaucratic administration. Such a strong State, Hegel argued, was a necessity whenever a society had divided into distinct economic classes, since those with property needed a powerful bulwark to defend their interests against those who had no property. But such a condition, Hegel argued, had not yet emerged in the early American Republic. The reason for this was its vast and still mostly unexplored frontier. This was why America still remained a land of natural libertarians, people who bitterly resent any attempt to infringe on their own personal liberty. Since America always had a frontier untouched by the fussy constraints of civilized life back in the city, those unhappy with their lot, or who simply wanted to move up in the world, could always move further west.

The most famous American novelist of the Jackson Era, James Fenimore Cooper, had dramatically portrayed this westward quest for personal liberty in his *Leatherstocking Tales*. The five novels recount the life of his most famous character, Natty Bumppo. As a young man, he lived in upper state New York. But as the rising tide of civilized life began to threaten his own personal liberty, he moves to the frontier, but one that is constantly shifting further and further west. As an old man, he finds himself on the lonely prairies of the American Midwest. Yet, even here, Cooper's rugged hero discovers that his splendid isolation is under attack (quite literally) from the new settlers. Hegel had no doubt that the energetic new country of natural libertarians would eventually dominate the North American continent—his version of manifest destiny. But this inevitably meant that at some point, Americans would run out of frontiers. Hegel probably did not expect this to happen as quickly as it did. No one else did. But he recognized the profound transformation that this would have on the American concept of liberty. The lifestyle that was sacred to Cooper's hero was doomed to pass away. The ethos of the natural libertarians would have to give way to the demands of civilized life.

With the end of the frontier, Hegel predicted, America would face a crisis. The conflict between rich and poor—which the frontier had kept to a minimum, acting as something of a sociological safety valve—would begin to grow, and with it the need for a state apparatus strong enough to hold off the revolt of the common people. What would happen when the frontier closed? This was the same question that the American historian Frederick Turner made famous when he declared the end of the frontier in 1893. Did this mean the end of American exception-alism, as Hegel anticipated?

This would be the challenge facing future American presidents, but in the 1830s, the democracy that Jackson created in the New World attracted the attention of many other European thinkers besides Hegel. Alexis de Tocqueville came to the United States to study it, producing perhaps the most famous account of that creative period of our national history. Jackson's administration was therefore an event in world history. Yet Andrew Jackson does not qualify as a world-historical figure. True, he was an innovator whose influence would spur on the hopes of other democratic movements around the world. But Jackson faced no great epochal crisis. The forces arrayed against him moaned and complained about him, but there was no counter-revolution that threatened to topple him. The transition to the new democracy was astonishingly painless and entirely without bloodshed.

Furthermore, for many observers, like de Tocqueville, Jacksonian democracy no longer seemed like a historical fluke, but rather, the shape of things to come. In 1830, the restored Bourbon monarchy under Charles X had been forced into exile after a mob 14,000 strong had driven the king and his family to flee to England. The rise of democracies around the world was now widely seen to be inevitable, just as nineteenth-century socialists came to believe in the inevitable triumph of socialism. This was the same spirit that inspired those European optimists to establish their various republics in the Revolutions of 1848.

But as we observed earlier, the abysmal failure of all these republics by 1860 made the future of democracy look dark indeed. Jackson certainly had the right stuff for a world-historical leader, but history did not provide him with the opportunity. But Jackson had created the Democratic Party that would go on to become one of the most successful political parties in world history, whose populistic appeal would become the secret of its coalition-building, managing to unite both farmers and working men and women to its side. Furthermore, both the Whig Party and, later, the Republican Party would adopt Jackson's populist style of campaigning. The zeitgeist had changed dramatically. From now on, it was essential to represent any candidate for the president as "a man of the people."

In 1860, the new Republican Party nominated their own "man of the people." It would be Abraham Lincoln's fate to face an epochal crisis in his great battle to save the Republic, along with the egalitarian spirit it embodied. Fortunately for Lincoln and the world, he had inherited an office that both Jefferson and Jackson had made powerful enough to deal with the greatest challenge any president had ever faced. An American president now had the power to change the course of world history.

CHAPTER FIVE
LINCOLN AND THE SECOND GREAT AMERICAN REVOLT

1
HISTORY'S MOST IMPROBABLE WORLD-HISTORICAL LEADER

Few would question Abraham Lincoln's greatness. Yet there can be no better example of the difference between Carlyle's Heroes, who bend history to their will, and the world-historical leader, who must carry out his mission in the face of adverse historical circumstances over which he has little or no control. Had events not put Lincoln in office in 1861, he could easily have become merely another obscure politician of the antebellum era, forgotten by all but antiquarians. Yet the mysterious currents of history would fatefully bring him to prominence during the great controversy over the future of slavery.

After his nomination in 1860, Lincoln was asked to provide his biography. He quoted from Thomas Gray's "Elegy Written in a Country Churchyard." His early life had been summed up by the line, "The short and simple annals of the poor." He might have added that, unlike Gray's poor English villagers, he had been raised on the American frontier, far wilder and more unruly than any English village, full of drunken men engaging in fist fights and other brawls. Lincoln spoke of his mother with decent respect but avoided any mention of his father. From boyhood, in order to feed his family, Lincoln had been a day laborer, and he learned to respect those who worked with their hands. He was consequently unable to acquire much formal education—perhaps only eighteen months at most. But he had early on become an avid reader of any book he could get his hands on. Entirely self-taught, Lincoln entered the legal profession. At the time, this was one of the favored paths by which the sons of the poor could achieve social mobility by diligent study and native intelligence.

During his early years, Illinois was still considered the frontier. It was where the West began. Like many others, Lincoln was impressed by the growing commercial vitality of his region. The city of Chicago had demonstrated that the East had no monopoly on the economic interests of America. From an insignificant village, it had rapidly transformed into the center of a Western economic boom.

What the West needed most, according to Lincoln, was help in developing "internal improvements" in the region, or what we today would call infrastructure, which in the antebellum period meant the expansion of turnpikes, railroads, and canals. Like his political idol Henry Clay, Lincoln believed that the federal government should provide the funds for these projects, though this became a bone of contention with the South and even New England, which believed that the federal government should not favor one section of the nation over others.

As an attorney, Lincoln naturally championed the railroad interests. This suited his own political visions for the West, though it also made him a rich man. The railroads paid well. Later, when he entered Illinois state politics, he became an advocate of dredging and expanding local waterways.

Later in his life, Lincoln would recall the time when, as a young man, he traveled down the Mississippi to the thriving city of New Orleans, where he had encountered the city's slave market. He had heard about slavery before, as everyone in America had—it was an issue that was just starting to divide Americans. But witnessing firsthand the selling of human beings shocked him and left a lasting distaste for the peculiar institution of the South.

Despite his deep distaste for slavery, Lincoln had never been an abolitionist, like the more radical members of the newly created Republican Party, formed in 1856. The patrician Bostonian, Charles Sumner, graduate of both Harvard College and Harvard Law School, had been urging the immediate and complete abolition of slavery for decades when Lincoln ran for president in 1860. In fact, Lincoln had been nominated by his party precisely because of his moderate views on the slavery issue.

Unlike the radical abolitionists, like William Lloyd Garrison, who attacked both the Constitution and the Union for their acceptance of slavery as a matter of fact, Lincoln never wavered in his insistence that the Union must be preserved at all costs. This explains both why he was willing to reluctantly tolerate slavery before the Civil War and why he persisted in his efforts to restore the Union even after five years of bloody carnage. The Union always came first. It had to come first, because Lincoln was deeply convinced that the American Republic represented what he called "the last best hope of earth" in his Second Annual Message to Congress, delivered in 1862. The following year,

Lincoln, in his Gettysburg Address, put the question even more impressively when he told his audience that "we here highly resolve…that government of the people, by the people, for the people, shall not perish from the earth."

Ultimately, what was at stake for Lincoln was whether the cause of freedom would prevail not only in the fractured United States but in the world at large, and at a point in history where it was Lincoln's stubborn persistence alone that kept the cause of liberty alive. This is the factor that has bequeathed to him his indisputable standing as a world-historical agent, the guardian of America's exceptionalist ethos in a world in which republicanism was on the verge of being a lost cause. Yet his emphatic insistence that the vast Western territories of the United States must be kept free from slaves would eventually lead him into fighting the bloodiest war Americans ever fought.

Today, we call it the American Civil War, but it might just as easily be called the Second American Populist Revolt. Unlike most other politicians, north and south, Lincoln was deeply committed to helping the middling and inferior sorts, like himself, to have a fair chance in the world. Both the aristocrats of the South and the elite of the North suffered from the most inveterate sin of snobbery: They looked down on those who labored with their hands. Lincoln did not; he had labored with his own.

Only Lincoln, with his humble background, could have led the North to victory. The war only became a popular cause in the North because of the arrogance of the Southern aristocrats who despised the egalitarianism of the vulgar Yankee rabble. The average man and woman of the Northern states, regardless of their views on slavery, were fed up with a Union in which the Southern states had come to play a dominant role, despite their inferiority in numbers. They blocked every measure to help the common man of the North. Eventually, with the humiliating

Fall of Fort Sumter, these middling and inferior sorts had had enough. They would teach the arrogant rebels a lesson they would never forget. And they did.

The common myth that the North was solely motivated by the cause of abolitionism obscures the populist origins of the conflict. Charles Sumner, for all his patrician eloquence, could never have moved the Northern masses to take up arms in the cause of abolition. It took Lincoln, born in a Kentucky log cabin, who had risen by his own efforts to political prominence in Illinois, to lead the populist revolt that would eventually bring an end to the old order and begin a new one.

A man of the West, Lincoln was as distrustful of the Northern Establishment as he was hostile to the aristocracy of the South. Both elites were equally opposed to his own vision of an American future that offered the promise of free land to ordinary people. He wanted to boost and build a nation based not on elite values but on those of the common people, unconstrained by either money power or slave power. The New England elite had opposed the Louisiana Purchase in the hope of cutting Americans off from moving into the vast new frontiers it offered them. The same selfish motives had made the frontier virtually off limits to the poor. There was no better way of keeping labor cheap than by denying the laborer the right to pick up and start a new life along the frontier. Lincoln's championing of the poor came naturally to a man of his background, but it brought down on his head the wrath of the elite, both South and North.

Lincoln's enemies to the South openly regarded him as "white trash"—the only category of humanity that they regarded as below that of their black slaves. His Northern critics, including members of his own cabinet, were no more polite. He was an uneducated bumpkin whom they believed to be utterly unfit to lead the Union through its greatest crisis. His polished and urbane secretary of state, William Seward, even made a bid to assume the role of acting president in the Fort Sumter crisis. Fortunately for the world, Lincoln had the gritty determination, the stubborn gumption born of his own hardscrabble struggle, that gave him the backbone to resist the counsel of his better-educated and far more sophisticated colleagues. It was these qualities that would transform Lincoln into becoming the least likely of world-historical leaders. The great irony is that Lincoln desperately hoped to keep the old order intact. He did everything he possibly could to preserve the Union. Yet his decisions and actions as president led to its collapse and the unforeseen emergence of a new one.

2
LINCOLN'S CHECKERED RISE TO POLITICAL EMINENCE

Lincoln's political career had been less than stellar prior to his nomination as the Republican candidate for the presidency in the Chicago Convention held in 1860. Although Andrew Jackson campaigned as an outsider, he had held a vast array of positions in both his state and national government. Against this venerable record, Lincoln had spent eight years in the Illinois state legislature followed by a single term in the US House of Representatives. He was still a member of the Whig Party in those days, and when the Democratic president, James Polk, declared war on the Mexican Republic, the Whigs opposed him. Although Polk simply wanted to expand American territory to the Pacific, fulfilling his nation's manifest destiny as a continental power, he had offered a somewhat lame pretext for the war, arguing that the Mexicans had fired on the Americans first, down in a "spot" in Texas. Lincoln repeatedly insisted on knowing exactly where this spot was—was it in Mexico or in Texas? If in Texas, the war was just; if in Mexico, it was wicked. Hence the unflattering nickname "Spotty Lincoln."

The Whigs' united opposition to Polk's "wicked war" did not, however, keep them from nominating the general whose glory had shone brightest in the conflict: Zachary Taylor. Lincoln, of course, supported him—as did his Whig colleague, Alexander Stephens. But in 1856, a new political party suddenly emerged on the scene—the party that would forever after call itself the Party of Lincoln.

It was within the ranks of the Republican Party that Lincoln first came to notice as a national figure. There was something about him that many found strongly appealing. Lincoln had one big and undeniable thing going for him. He was, as everyone had to admit, a self-made man. He had pulled himself up by his bootstraps. He had educated himself on his own. He had become a successful attorney and attained considerable prosperity. He had even married Mary Todd, a local belle whom Stephen Douglas had also courted earlier in his life. Her family belonged to the aristocracy of Lexington, Kentucky. She had received a fine private education and was at home in social circles many notches above Lincoln's lowly origins. She had always wanted to become the First Lady. She had almost married the man who almost became president, Stephen Douglas, before deciding to marry the man who eventually did.

After his brief and inglorious career in the House, Lincoln decided to challenge the formidable Douglas, who had held the position of Illinois Senator since 1846. Douglas was not only the incumbent, but he was also considered the greatest orator of his age, nicknamed the Little Giant, due to his diminutive stature and magnificent eloquence. Lincoln's bid for his seat might have gone down as a footnote to a footnote in history but for the fact that the confidently magnanimous Douglas had granted Lincoln's request for a series of public debates, which were closely followed by political observers around the nation. Surprisingly, the towering Lincoln held his own against the Little Giant. Even more surprisingly, their debates, unlike the televised debates of our own day, had genuine substance. They concerned nothing less than the preservation of the Union, and the issue that was currently endangering it: the question of slavery.

In the celebrated debates, Lincoln had made it clear that, unlike the Radical Republicans, Charles Sumner among them, he was not an abolitionist. He even angered the abolitionist wing of his party when he declared during the debate that he supported the Fugitive Slave Act of 1850. This was among the most controversial of the many compromises that the North had made with the South in order to save the Union. But it was bitterly resented. Many in the northern states were outraged whenever fugitive slaves were apprehended in one of their own free states, just on the point of obtaining their liberty. The Southerners in Congress had demanded that the fugitive slave law be strictly enforced everywhere in the Union, a foolish policy that aroused the North's indignant fury, while returning only a handful of slaves. Out of approximately 10,000 who had escaped to freedom, only 400 were dragged back to their house of bondage. Once again, the South's shrill insistence on its abstract rights alienated the North and was instrumental in bringing about its own final defeat.

There was, however, one point on which Lincoln stood absolutely firm. There must be no expansion of slavery into the federal territories. Like many of his fellow Republicans, he had been deeply disturbed by the infamous Dred Scott decision that the Supreme Court under Chief Justice Roger Taney had issued on March 6, 1857. Lincoln even suggested that there had been a backroom conspiracy between then-President Buchanan, a Democrat, and the Chief Justice, for the purpose of settling the slave question in America once and for all. By declaring that the American Blacks were not, in fact, citizens of the United States, the Court had in effect granted to slaveholders their right to move their human chattel into the federal territories just as much as they had the right to bring along with them their horse and buggy. In coming to this decision, the Court also hoped to scotch the ambition of the recently created Republican Party to halt the spread of slavery into the federal territories.

Instead of providing a permanent fix to the question, the decision had only inflamed it. The South now had the Supreme Court and the Constitution on its side. Most Democrats supported the decision, although many were uneasy about the reasoning behind it. But even those who regarded the decision as unjust felt that they could not go against the decision of the highest court in the land.

The platform of the Republican Party in 1860 unequivocally rejected the decision. They stood firm on the principle that slavery must not be extended into federal territory. The South could keep its peculiar institution of slavery, so long as they did not seek to expand it into the free soil of the West. This moderate position angered many of the Republican Radicals who urged immediate abolition, but it angered the South even more. During the Georgia Secession Convention, held in the town of Milledgeville from January 16 to March 23, 1861, Alexander Stephens, who would soon become vice president of the Confederacy, had argued forcefully against secession. But even the moderate and sensible Stephens, a friend of Lincoln during the days when both were Whigs, told the Convention that he himself would pick up a musket and fight against the

Yankees if the new Republican administration tried "to exclude us, by an Act of Congress, from the [federal] Territories, with our slave property." This was, in fact, the most burning grievance in the South during the Secession Crisis.

By refusing to accept the Dred Scott decision, the Republicans were in effect challenging the Constitution of the United States. But on what grounds? Some Republicans claimed that there was a higher law than the Constitution, but where was it to be found and who could tell us what it was? For Lincoln, this higher law had been invoked in the Declaration of Independence, the spirit of which should guide any interpretation of the Constitution. For Lincoln, as for Tom Paine, the cause of America was also the cause of humankind, and nowhere has this cause been more elegantly and forcefully stated than in the Declaration of Independence. The doctrine of natural rights evoked by Thomas Jefferson was not limited to any specific race or breed of men. It applied to Black slaves as well as to the oppressed in every country or clime. It was a universal clarion call for a future in which all enjoyed the liberty that was their natural birthright. Yet only the Supreme Court had the authority to interpret the words of the Constitution, as Lincoln well knew. The fact that the Republicans could never square their position on slavery with the Constitution left them vulnerable to the charge of being too radical to govern.

Yet if we look back on the origin of the Constitution, it should come as no surprise that Taney's court was opposed to the radically egalitarian ideas introduced by the Republicans. The Constitution had been designed to guard against populist agitation and democratic excess. The Taney Court looked upon the Republicans as dangerous revolutionaries, ready to sunder the Union in pursuit of their hopeless cause of abolitionism. In the eyes of the justices of the Court, they had used the Constitution exactly as the Founding Fathers intended it to be used.

Lincoln was thereby presented with a serious dilemma. What could justify resistance to the decision of the Supreme Court? He found his way out by appealing to the radical Whig tradition. In his famous "House Divided" speech at the Republican State Convention held in Springfield, Illinois, on June 16, 1858, Lincoln charged that the Dred Scott decision would inevitably transform the nation into a "dreary region of despotism." Since all free men had the right to resist despotism, according to Whig doctrine, the Republican resistance to the Dred Scott decision was fully warranted. The rights of slaveholders to take their slaves into federal territory should be determined not by the justices on the Supreme Court but by the people. Anything else was despotism.

Yet implicit in this resistance was the recognition that the Constitution alone could not prevent the rise of despotism—it had not stopped Taney and the other justices from issuing their decision, had it? This had a further disturbing implication. If the Constitution could permit the rise of despotism in any of its branches—the executive, the legislative, and the judiciary—then, as the Whigs had argued of old, it would be up to the people themselves to defend their liberties from tyranny by resisting it by whatever means necessary.

In writing the Declaration, Thomas Jefferson had been perfectly aware that England had its own constitution, not written down in a single document, but adhering to a vast assortment of precedents and traditions. He also knew that the English constitution had long been the envy of the world. But it had not prevented the British assault on the liberty of America, and hence the need for America to declare its independence. Just as the English constitution had not defended the rights of the British

Colonists, so now the American Constitution was not enough to defend the right of the American people to govern themselves.

Lincoln, who had started his political life as an American Whig, opposed the expansion of slavery on grounds that any eighteenth-century British Whig would recognize. Every person had the right to the fruits of their own labor. If you denied them that, how could they ever be expected to achieve what Lincoln and so many other white Americans had achieved? With his characteristically earthy wit, Lincoln had once summarized the contrasting Southern theory of labor as "You work; I eat." If every person should be allowed the chance to make something of themselves, as Lincoln had, on what grounds should the Black slaves of the South be denied the same opportunity?

Historians have argued that the real origin of the Civil War lay in the westward expansion of the American Republic. During the administration of James Polk, vast new territories had been acquired, from Texas to California. Just as in the debates over the Louisiana Purchase, the other sections of the country were concerned about how the admission of new states would affect the balance of power in both Congress and in the election of presidents. The free states insisted that the new territories should be free as well, while the slave states insisted that they had the right to bring their own slaves into these virgin lands. Attempts to achieve compromise between these two extremes would pre-occupy the best political minds of the nation, and there were many instances where the fate of the Union hung in the balance but was saved by a last-minute settlement by political geniuses such as Henry Clay and Stephen Douglas.

Lincoln observed these sequences of compromises with growing concern. Above all, he feared that once the peculiar institution of the South had spread into the federal territories, slavery would endanger the cause of free white labor that he championed. Not only would slavery introduce unfair competition, but it would have the same effect in these western territories as it did elsewhere—it would degrade all forms of manual labor, stigmatizing them as servile, no matter how productive and useful they were to the society as a whole.

3
THE REPUBLICAN PARTY GOES POPULIST

Lincoln, despite the caliber of his debate performances, failed to beat Douglas. Yet it may well have been fortunate that, despite his dazzling performance in the debates, Lincoln was defeated in the election for the Senate. If he had won, he might well have lost what the Chicago Convention regarded as his greatest asset, his status as an outsider who was undeniably a man of the people. If anything, in the campaign of 1860, the Republicans went a bit overboard on the populist theme. They could not say enough about Lincoln's humble origins, the extreme poverty of his youth, his conspicuous lack of polish and urbanity. They even hailed the fact that Lincoln, by his own admission, had received at most only one year of formal education. And those damn rails! They were everywhere.

There is some evidence that in his obscure early years, Lincoln might actually have split a rail or two, but the rails at the convention certainly had not been split by Lincoln, as no doubt all the attendees knew in their hearts. But it was all great fun, and it showed that Lincoln was a man of the people. It reminded many observers of the "Log Cabin and Hard Cider" campaign of the Whig candidate for president, William Henry Harrison, which took place twenty years earlier.

Though indisputably born in a log cabin, Lincoln had no relish for hard cider. He was a teetotaler. The temperance movement had grown strong in the intervening years, and Lincoln, who had witnessed much disorderly drunkenness in his frontier youth, himself promoted it. Naturally, there were many at the convention who were not practicing temperance, and it showed. Still, the nomination of the absent Lincoln was greeted with thunderous ovations.

On May 19, 1860, a delegation was rapidly dispatched to Lincoln's home in Springfield, Illinois, to make a formal offer of the nomination to the standard-bearer they had chosen. Those who had never set eyes on him were a bit taken aback by his physical appearance. No one had ever called Lincoln a handsome man. He was six feet four, but rawboned and ungainly. Some would even call him a bit uncouth, but everyone knew of his well-earned reputation for integrity. He was, after all, Honest Abe.

When the Democratic press tried to puncture his image for scrupulous honesty, the worst they could come up with was the claim that back in the late 1840s, while serving his one term in the House of Representatives, he had billed the government for three pairs of boots. In fact, Lincoln had paid for them with his own money, but the triviality of the accusation was perhaps the best evidence that he was just as honest as his many supporters claimed him to be.

This aspect of his character was a major factor in his success. The reason for this is simple. Just as in the Age of Jackson, the conviction that members of the federal government had become corrupt led to seeking an outsider to drain the swamp, so, by 1860, the same conviction, even better grounded than in 1828, led the Republicans to seek an outsider whose reputation for integrity stood in sharp contrast to the general run of politicians of that era. Even Lincoln's great rival for the nomination, William Seward, though an honest man himself, was tainted by the corrupt practices of many of his colleagues in his home state of New York, where he had been first the governor and then Senator. By the time of the Chicago Convention, Seward had been an important figure in government for twenty-one years. Yet the Convention chose Lincoln in the hope that he might appear more moderate to voters on the question that was agitating the nation—the intractable slavery question.

The Republican Party had been created in 1856 by men who, like Lincoln, were agitated by the slave question. They were all united in their loathing of slavery, though no one was quite sure what to do about it. The most conspicuous feature of the new party, however, was that it was the first major American political party that consisted only of men from the free states, with the exception of the fervent Kentucky abolitionist Henry Clay. There had been various small political parties that had opposed slavery, like the Free Soil Party, but they were all perfectly aware that they had no chance of winning a national election. Many of these fringe parties had united with the Republicans, who made no secret of their ambition to win the control of the government in Washington, including the election of a Republican president. In 1860, there were some abolitionists who were members of the party, but it is hard to calculate how many, though, at best, they constituted a small minority. But like many other small political minorities, they naturally alarmed many moderate voters. Later, the moderate Lincoln himself would have to contend with the extremists in his own party, the powerful political clique known as the Radical Republicans.

This in itself was a major break with the unwritten tradition that to be genuinely American, a political party must appeal to both sections of the nation, as previous parties had done. Despite their differences, the major parties, such as the Federalists, the Jeffersonian Republicans, the Jacksonian Democrats, the Whigs, and even the American Party, a.k.a. the Know-Nothings, had supporters on both sides of the Mason-Dixon line. Lincoln himself had earlier been a Whig, along with his friend, the brilliant Alexander Stephens, who shortly after Lincoln's election in 1860 would become the vice president of the Confederacy.

4
WRITING OFF THE SOUTH

To many sober Americans of that era, the very emergence of a purely sectional party endangered the Union. In the 1856 presidential campaign, the platform of the Republican Party had attacked "the twin relics of barbarism," namely Slavery and Polygamy. The denunciation of polygamy was sure to lose votes among the Mormons, but they were only a scattered minority, far too small to affect the outcome. But the inflammatory condemnation of slavery was political dynamite. It meant that the newly created party could not expect to win a single slaveholding state, of which there were then fifteen, close to half of the thirty-three that made up the Union.

The creation of a purely sectional party by the Republicans did not violate the Constitution, yet it was a flagrant violation of the traditional rules by which American politics had hitherto been played—the rule that no American party should appeal exclusively to one section of the nation, without consideration of the whole. To cast this sacrosanct tradition to the wind was to embark into the wholly unknown.

During the Secession Crisis, many Southerners would have agreed with the sentiment of Thomas R. R. Cobb of Georgia when he said that while the election of Lincoln may be according to the letter of the law, "I am compelled to decide that the election of Lincoln is in violation of the spirit of the Constitution of the United States." He had a good point. A political party that had put their president in office without a single vote from the South would have horrified the Founding Fathers.

Yet to blame the Republicans alone for this radical departure from the old order would be unfair. The party was created as a response to the profound changes in American popular feelings among the many Northerners who had come to abhor slavery and to resent the power of the slaveholding states. The spirit of the times had made further compromise impossible. The Republican Party was not the cause of this change but merely its symptom.

The movement that had begun in England among the Evangelical Christians, like William Wilberforce, had held African slavery up as an abomination unworthy of modern civilization. The abolitionists had won many converts to their cause, beginning in England (which abolished the slave trade as early as 1807), and the movement quickly spread to other nations, including America. The charge that slavery was an offense to God was powerful in a world in which the Judeo-Christian faith was still strong. But the ideal of moral progress introduced by the Enlightenment also played its role in turning people's minds against slavery.

People were no longer willing to put up with moral outrages simply because that was the way of the world, as in earlier times. Improving the world had now become the duty of Western civilization—indeed, its mission. The Republican platform of 1856 invoked this trope when it declared slavery (along with polygamy) to be "relicts of barbarism." By this time, the world had won the moral argument against African slavery in the American South.

Proof of this deeper change in popular sentiment over slavery quickly became evident in the Democratic Party as well. Stephen Douglas, despite his indefatigable efforts to keep his own party together, failed in the end to stem the tide of sectionalism.

At the 1860 Democratic convention in Charleston, the split between Northern and Southern Democrats had become glaringly obvious. A second convention in Baltimore made the split final, resulting in an election in which the Republican candidate Lincoln faced three candidates who all claimed to represent the fatally splintered Democratic Party.

The popular forces of sectionalism had wrecked the old order with its tradition of exclusively national parties. Where a political magician like Stephen Douglas had failed, who could have succeeded? The tradition that had once been able to keep the Union together was now gone with the wind.

Acute observers of the American scene were fully aware of the dangers of a Republican presidency, of seeing the White House occupied by a man who had not received a single electoral vote from the South. Many had tried to warn of the danger this radical innovation posed. Yet Lincoln won the election. Though he had clinched the electoral college, he had received only 39.7 percent of the popular vote, lower than any presidential candidate before him. Even more alarming, though quite expected, not a single individual vote had been cast for him in any of the states of the Deep South. But then he wasn't even on the ballot, so no wonder.

The news of Lincoln's victory was flashed across the telegraph wires that now stretched all over the United States. The telegraph, invented by Samuel Morse back in the 1840s, would be the first in the series of technological breakthroughs in communication that would increasingly influence the political thinking of Americans. Unlike the floridly verbose newspapers of the day, the telegraph was by nature laconic. It just blurted out the bare facts.

Lincoln won—that was all the telegraph reported when it reached Charleston, South Carolina, but that was more than enough. No editorial was needed to explain what it meant. It meant secession. On hearing the grim news, the men in the Federal Court House of Charleston, assembled to try a case before it, looked at each other in dismay, and promptly went home. They had nothing more to do with the government in Washington, now that it had fallen into the hands of the wicked Republicans. The South had given fair warning. In this grave eventuality, they had pledged to secede from the Union, and this time, they really meant it.

Lincoln, however, was not convinced. He had heard such talk many times before, and as president-elect, he repeatedly stated his conviction that it would all blow over. The South was only engaged in its customary posturing. But tension throughout the nation was increasing, with the secession movement advancing rapidly in the states of the Deep South, while in the North, there were nightly parades of Lincoln supporters, young men known as Wide Awakes, who held aloft rails upon which torches had been mounted. They had something of a paramilitary aspect and could be threatening. They were certainly not abolitionists; they were simply furious over the secession of the South states. It was the first stirrings of the populist revolt against the Confederacy that would be the real spark that set off the Civil War. Unlike many Democrats and even many in Lincoln's administration, the Wide Awakes were prepared and even anxious to go to war to teach the South a lesson. Like many others in the North, they had watched as the politicians in Washington endlessly offered the South compromise after compromise, including the politicians they themselves had chosen. It was time, many believed, that the affairs of the nation be taken out of the hands of compromising politicians and put back in the hands of the now wide-awake young men of the North, hundreds of thousands of whom could not wait until they had the chance to kill a rebel traitor.

Barred by tradition from campaigning for himself, Lincoln could only sit back and watch the hoopla, uneasy with all the noise and commotion. But the secession crisis did not blow over, and by the time he took the oath of office, all the states of the Deep South had left the Union. At this point, anger in the North had reached the boiling point. War was virtually inevitable, no matter what the politicians in Washington did. Lincoln, like world-historical leaders before, ultimately had to yield before the inevitable, but this took both time and the confluence of events.

There were many who, after the secession of hot-headed South Carolina, had taken Lincoln's overly optimistic view of the situation. Yet there was one man in America who immediately recognized the chasm of danger that yawned before the nation. Stephen Douglas was so convinced that the two sections were heading toward catastrophe that he threw tradition to the wind and scandalized many observers by stumping across the country and brazenly campaigning for himself, convinced that he alone could head off the impending crisis.

Even after he had been defeated by Lincoln, Douglas did not let up, but immediately headed to the Southern states, where he used his spectacular skill as a public speaker to try to talk sense to the rebel hot heads. He told them plainly that there would be a long and horrible war, and that no matter how valiantly the Confederates fought, it was a war that they were doomed to lose.

Douglas represents the finest example of the man who hero-ically strives to preserve the old order, even as it is about to go under. Yet all his energetic efforts were in vain. But when at last war broke out, he instantly rallied to Lincoln's side and threw his heart into championing the Union cause, until his premature death due to typhoid fever on June 3, 1861, before the first American soldier had drawn blood in battle.

Though Lincoln had been elected, President Buchanan was left to deal with the secession crisis that the Republican victory had triggered. With mounting anxiety, he watched as the states of the Deep South left one by one. Buchanan has generally been criticized for doing nothing, but this is profoundly unfair.

Unlike the Southern firebrands, Buchanan did not believe that the states had their much-vaunted right of secession. Yet he knew of no Constitutional remedies. Indeed, the Constitution provided none. The document had wisely omitted any mention of secession. It was too dangerous a topic to bring up just as the Founding Fathers were trying to create an admittedly imperfect Union. It would have been reckless to provide any of the states in the newly formed nation with an easy way of getting out of it.

The authors of the Constitution realized that it would be a serious enough challenge to get all the thirteen fiercely independent states to ratify their controversial new document as it was, but to inform them that once in the new Union, they would be unable to leave it, let alone that they would be compelled by arms to return to its bosom—that was out of the question.

By dodging the question of secession, the Constitution also left unanswered what the government in Washington should or could do in case such an event ever came to pass. Since no state had ever seceded before, despite frequent threats to do so—mostly from the South, but from New England as well—Lincoln had no precedent to which he could appeal. To attack Buchanan is to imply that there was some obvious remedy that he was too feeble-minded to hit upon. But this is to cheat Lincoln. Because there was no obvious solution, and no one was more aware of this than Honest Abe himself. The Constitution, which both sides cited in their defense, could provide no help whatsoever in resolving the great crisis. This meant that in the end, like Jefferson and Jackson before him, Lincoln would be forced to take measures that exceeded the Constitutional authority of the president. Indeed, according to Roger Taney and his Supreme Court, they were serious violations of the Constitution that he had sworn to obey.

CHAPTER SIX
DECISION AT FORT SUMTER: LINCOLN'S WORLD-HISTORIC CHOICE

1
LINCOLN'S TOUGHEST MORNING

On an April morning in 1861, not long after the states of the Deep South had all seceded, Lincoln's Secretary of the Navy, Gideon Welles, walked into the office where the recently inaugurated president was working. Before Welles had time to set down the heavy stack of papers and documents he was carrying, or even to say good morning, a despondent Lincoln looked up at him over his shoulder, noticed Welles's discontented countenance, and asked, "What have I done wrong?"

This is not the image of Lincoln to which we have long been accustomed. It is certainly not the Lincoln rendered in gleaming marble in the immense memorial dedicated to him in Washington, DC. There he sits with sublime confidence, the calm and steady captain of his nation's destiny during the greatest crisis it had ever faced. In his martyr's death, Lincoln had become majestic and awe-inspiring, even God-like. Unshakable in his resolve, unwavering in his aims, he was now the Great Emancipator, the savior of his country, indisputably one of the Great Men of history.

This was not the Lincoln that Welles found on that April morning. This was a Lincoln who did not know what to do next, a Lincoln troubled by his mistakes and profoundly uncertain of the future, a Lincoln surrounded by critics and naysayers, many carping, even insulting. He was fully aware of the names they had begun to call him both in casual conversations and in the press just as soon as he had been elected president, and especially after the war had begun: Backwoods Bumpkin, Weakling, Yahoo, Gorilla, Ignoramus Abe, Despot, Old Scoundrel, Filthy Storyteller.

It was true that Lincoln loved to tell stories, anecdotes, and jokes, many of which were a bit off-color by the standards of his time. Most were so corny that, while they might have raised a guffaw among yokels, they were greeted with unamused silence by the more sophisticated members of his cabinet.

Yet sometimes his tale would hit both the mark and the funny bone. When he was asked about the feud brewing between his Democratic rival, Stephen Douglas, and the head of the Democratic Party in Illinois, Lincoln said he felt like the old woman who found her husband in the backyard tangling with a bear and shouted, "Go husband, go bear!"

On that first morning in April, however, Lincoln was not in the mood for jokes. The Deep South had already created the Confederate States of America on February 4, 1861, and at its head was the gentlemanly and dignified Jefferson Davis: a man who, unlike Lincoln, really looked like the president of a great

Republic. Now there was nothing to guide Lincoln about what to do next.

2
CAN SUMTER BE SAVED?

Everyone knew that the situation of the garrison on the tiny island in the mouth of Charleston harbor was grim and rapidly becoming hopeless. After Major Robert Anderson had relocated the federal forces to Fort Sumter, the shore batteries surrounding the harbor had been controlled by roused Confederates, with cannons now trained on the Union bastion. Lincoln had two questions before him. Could the garrison at Fort Sumter be resupplied and, more importantly, should they attempt to resupply it?

Everyone knew that President James Buchanan had tried to pull off this feat but had failed. The previous January, the steamship *The Star of the West*, owned by Cornelius Vanderbilt, had been sent by Buchanan with both provisions and fresh men, in the hope that it would be permitted to land the much-needed aid. When the ship sailed toward the harbor, it was promptly attacked by Confederate forces. Though the steamship sustained no major damage, its captain John McGowan decided not to risk further combat and departed for safer waters.

The incident set off indignant roars of protestation in both the North and the South. The Yankees had dared to try to hold onto *our* fort. For that was the very question in dispute. The states of the Deep South had contributed more than their fair share— so they believed—toward the system of federal forts and garrisons that had dotted the old Union. The Yankees were welcome to retain those set up in their own territory, but the Confederates insisted that they had no right to those in the seceded states, such as Fort Sumter. The Confederates approached the matter like one of the partners in a sensible modern divorce: Let us divide up our common property fairly. You get your half. I get my half.

Unfortunately for the South, the other partner in the marriage refused to recognize the divorce. The North did not see the Union as a partnership, from which any partner was free to leave whenever they wanted. The Union was indivisible. You could not leave it; you could only turn against it, which is exactly what the Confederates had done by attacking *The Star of the West*. The rebels had dared to fire on *our* flag—that became the focus of Yankee indignation. Yet in both the North and the Deep South, though emotions were heated, there were no calls for war.

During the Secession Crisis, the Republican stalwart Horace Greeley wrote an editorial in his paper entitled, "Let our erring sisters go in peace." There were few men at the time who had opposed slavery more vigorously than Greeley, yet he placed his hopes on the idea that there could be "a peaceable secession." He spoke for many in the North. Yet Greeley could only influence opinion. Whether or not to heed his counsel was a decision for the Lincoln administration. William Seward, the suave New Yorker whom Lincoln had appointed as his Secretary of State, agreed with Greeley, though he had a different reason for wishing to avoid hostility. Seward had been a far more prominent national figure than Lincoln before the Chicago Convention, but he had acquired the reputation of a red-hot radical abolitionist and was passed over in favor of the moderate Lincoln. Yet, ironically, it was Seward who argued most forcefully that Fort Sumter should be handed over to the Confederacy, just as he had promised its commissioner only the previous week. Seward believed that there was no need to start a firestorm over Fort Sumter. He was convinced that within months, our Southern sisters would see the error of their ways and return voluntarily to the Union fold. Seward was certain that throughout the South there remained legions of Southerners who were still stout Unionists, prudent people of property and education, like Seward himself, who were simply biding their time until they could wrestle power from the firebrand insurrectionists.

Even Lincoln himself long gave credence to this notion, though he abandoned it after sending a few discreet observers down to Charleston, who were genuinely shocked and dismayed to find that it contained nothing but firebrand insurrectionists. There was nary a Unionist in the whole city.

The great army of southern Unionists in which Seward had placed all his hopes was a phantom. It did not exist. A few Unionists remained in the South, but, like Andrew Johnson from Tennessee, no one was listening to them. Despite Johnson's successful career in Tennessee politics, secession fever in his home state drove him to depart for Washington immediately after Tennessee had formally left the Union.

William Seward had unwittingly based his entire policy during the Fort Sumter crisis on an illusion. He could not imagine that the Union had already been shattered beyond any hope of repair. Like all those intelligent and sensible men who are unable to discern the spirit of their times, Seward had failed to recognize that the road leading back to the past had been washed away in the flood of violent emotions from both North and South. He could see no other way of going forward than by retreating to the now vanquished status quo of the Old Order.

Lincoln became a world-historical figure from the moment he realized that it was mere illusion to fantasize, as Seward did, that the Southern states would ever come to recognize the error of their ways. During the Fort Sumter crisis, Lincoln knew that there were only two choices: to continue to fume impotently over the South or to declare war against it.

Buchanan had been right. There was nothing in the Constitution that gave the president the power or authority to force the states that had seceded back into the Union. We only dispute that question today in order to protect Lincoln's spotless reputation, but by doing so, we are also ignoring one of the qualities that made him a world-historical figure: his willingness to set aside the Constitution in order to preserve the Union. He did not want to choose between the two. No president ever had been given this choice before. But like Alexander the Great, Lincoln cut the Gordian Knot.

Those who point out Lincoln's assumption of dictatorial powers normally do so to debunk him, but they are in effect stating the best case for regarding him as a world-historical leader. Lincoln could either preserve the Constitution or save the Republic, but he could not do both. His was an example of the tragic choice that every world-historical figure is forced to make, according to Hegel. The choice that the world-historical individual has to make is not between good and evil, but between two different goods.

The Republic that had existed prior to the Civil War was unquestionably something very good, and Lincoln was prepared to do whatever he could to preserve it. But the Fort Sumter crisis spelled the death of the old Union, no matter what choice Lincoln made. If he did nothing, the Union would be irretrievably sundered. If he acted to resupply Fort Sumter, it would be taken as an act of war by the Confederacy, making a Civil War unavoidable. It was akin to being forced to decide which of your two beloved children you can save. Lincon chose war in order to save the Republic, and few today regret his choice.

Cutting the Gordian Knot is a moment of high drama, but it may take decades before its historical consequences fully unravel. The ultimate judge of whether or not it is wise to cut the Gordian Knot is the future world produced by its cutting—though, of course, we can never know what the world would be like if the knot had not been cut.

By electing to resupply Fort Sumter, Lincoln knew he was risking war, but even a million speeches on the order of the Gettysburg Address could not have made men march off to war unless they had already decided to do so. Indeed, millions would soon be ready to march. Back then, public opinion could not be manufactured wholesale. The Yankee sense of outrage may have been fueled by an incendiary press, but the spark that ignited it was once again the brutal terseness of the telegraph: Rebels seize Fort Sumter.

In his cabinet, Lincoln found support only from his allies in the powerful Blair family from Maryland, led by Montgomery Blair, the man Lincoln had appointed as his Postmaster General. Blair, along with Lincoln, had decided to ignore Seward's counsel on Fort Sumter as well as that of General Winfield Scott, the highest-ranking military man in the Union, both of whom felt that any attempt to resupply the garrison was both hopeless and a dangerous step toward war. Instead, Lincoln had been seduced by the assurances of Gustavus Fox, a naval officer who convinced Lincoln that if the president entrusted the command to him, he would be able to land the much-needed supplies and extra troops at the embattled garrison at Fort Sumter.

As it turned out, Fox was suffering from delusions of competency. His mission failed abysmally, as had Buchanan's. Contrary to the sanguine expectation of Lincoln, there was absolutely no way that Fort Sumter could be saved. The rescue mission had all been for naught. A blunder of such magnitude might well have run Lincoln out of office, indicted for his impetuosity, his poor judgment, his lack of political skills, and his amateurishness. Maybe a president really did need more experience than having split rails as a lad.

3
JEFFERSON DAVIS SAVES THE PRESIDENCY FOR LINCOLN

Lincoln's political career was saved by Jefferson Davis, the august president of the new Southern Republic, another of the many bizarre ironies that shaped both the outbreak and the course of the war. When Jefferson Davis learned that the Union was intent on holding the fort, he believed that Seward had lied to him about abandoning it as part of the plot that the nefarious Lincoln was weaving to ensnare the South. He immediately issued orders to the batteries on both sides of the island.

The bombardment began in the early hours of April 12, 1861. Robert Anderson's weary and hungry men held on for two days before surrendering to the rebels. They were chivalrously allowed to lower their own flag. Miraculously, the only loss of life through the whole ordeal came at its very end, when a canon, instead of offering a salute to the Union flag, exploded, killing one man. Writing in her diary in Charleston, Mary Boykin Chesnut expressed her joy and jubilation that no Yankees had been killed by the Confederate forces, assuming that this unexpected twist of fate would naturally lead all the combatants to seek a compromise peace. She could not have been more wrong, though her belief that the terrible Yankees would return to their senses was no more fanciful than Seward's belief that red-hot rebels would return to theirs.

There was no more critical moment in Lincoln's life than the fall and surrender of Fort Sumter. The North had been humiliatingly defeated in its first battle. What could be more natural than for a Northern tide of indignation to put the blame on Lincoln for the fiasco? Yet the tide of indignation that flooded the North was not aimed at Lincoln, but at those who had dared to fire on the Union flag.

The rebels had fired first. To the already bitter resentment over secession, which had been given months to boil over, was added a new sense of righteous indignation that quickly turned into wrath. Leaving the Union was bad enough, but now the Confederates had dared to attack it. In the North, there was a swift sea change in popular sentiment: Overnight, the rebels became traitors. War was now inevitable. The people of the North demanded it.

This was America's second great populist revolt. Like all such movements, the people knew exactly what they were against without being very clear of what they were for. A minority in the North had long loathed the peculiar institution of slavery on which Southern economic power was based. But those who had accepted slavery as a fact of life were now also up in arms, many of whom were no friends of the abolitionists and, indeed, hated them for their relentless obsession with the plight of the African slave. It is too often forgotten today that in the North, there were people who wanted to see Black slaves liberated, but most would have been just as happy to see them disappear. Many who hated the slaveholders despised the slaves they held no less. But all differences of opinion over the slavery question vanished in the collective outpouring of populist wrath against the traitors to the Union. A mere two days after the fall of Fort Sumter, Lincoln called for 75,000 militia volunteers to serve for three months.

He found no shortage of Northern boys and men eager to wreak vengeance on the rebels.

On April 4, 1861, the Virginia Secession Convention had voted not to secede. But now, as popular passions swept the South, Virginia joined the Confederacy, severing its connection with the Union only two days after Lincoln's call for volunteers. Virginia, along with everyone else, knew that Lincoln's call to arms signaled imminent war against the South. But what Constitutional justification did Lincoln have to declare war on the Confederacy?

Lincoln faced a dilemma. If he had accepted the contention of the Confederacy that it had established a new and independent nation, then he could have simply declared war on it, just as he might upon Mexico or France. Of course, he would have needed the approval of Congress, but with all the rebels gone, that would not have been much of a challenge.

But from the start of the secession movement, as we have seen, Lincoln had maintained its illegality. In his First Inaugural Address, delivered on March 4, 1861, he argued "that no State, upon its own mere motion, can lawfully get out of the Union...I, therefore, consider that, in view of the Constitution and the laws, the Union is unbroken." In other words, the State could not secede, and therefore, none had. They were still in the Union, whether they saw it that way or not. But while the Constitution provided a procedure for declaring war on a foreign and independent nation, it gave no authority for the president to declare war on one of the states within the Union.

On July 4, 1861, Lincoln delivered an address to Congress in which he defended both his decision to call up the militia and the decision to suspend habeas corpus. Earlier, on May 28, 1861, the Chief Justice of the Supreme Court, Roger Taney, had declared that Lincoln had exceeded his Constitutional authority by suspending habeas corpus, but Lincoln ignored Taney's ruling, just as he had ignored the 1857 Dred Scott decision of which Taney had been the author.

Since the Habeas Corpus Act had been passed by the English parliament in 1679, it had been enshrined as one of the chief guardians of personal liberty. Without it, Taney and others agreed, there would be the threat of a presidential dictatorship. Lincoln's response to Taney became famous: "Are all the laws but one to go unexecuted, and the Government itself go to pieces lest that one be violated?"

This was a good point, but clearly Lincoln was treading a slippery slope. If one law—and a sacrosanct law to boot—could be violated to keep the government from going to pieces, how many more laws might be violated in the name of preserving the Union?

In his address of July 4, Lincoln also used the state of emergency to justify his call for volunteer militia. On July 13, 1861, Congress held that there was an "insurrection" in the South, and on August 16, 1861, Lincoln made the same formal declaration. The Constitutional basis for this decision was Article I, Section 8, Clause 15, which gave Congress the power "to provide for calling forth the Militia to execute the Laws of the Union, suppress Insurrections and repel Invasions..."

As noted earlier, the framers of the Constitution had given the federal government the power to "suppress Insurrections" after they had been deeply disturbed by Shays's Rebellion. This was later supplemented by the Insurrection Act of 1807. But what was an uprising of disgruntled farmers in Western Massachusetts compared to a united Confederacy made up of eleven states formerly belonging to the Union? Could the original intent of the framers be twisted to apply to a situation that they had never even imagined?

4
BOTH SIDES QUOTE THE DECLARATION OF INDEPENDENCE

Naturally, the Confederate states were deeply insulted to be called insurrectionists. In their defense, the Southerners cited the opening words of the preamble to the Declaration of Independence that gave "one people" the right "to dissolve the political bands which have connected them with another, and to assume, among the powers of the earth, the separate and equal station to which the Laws of Nature and of Nature's God entitle them...." What could be clearer, the Confederate apologists on both sides of the Atlantic argued. Their new Republic clearly represented "one people." Virtually all white Southerners supported it with tremendous enthusiasm, as was later to be proved by the defiant energy with which they held off their Yankee invaders during four years of bloody struggle. If the mere fact that Southerners owned slaves somehow abolished their natural right to seek their own independence, then the Declaration of Independence was a lie. At the time it was written in 1776, slavery was legal in all thirteen colonies of Great Britain. If the presence of slavery in their midst disqualified Southerners from seeking to establish their own Republic, then America's justification for breaking with England was equally null and void.

Lord Acton, a representative of the English Whig tradition, took the side of the Confederacy. He was appalled by "The War of Yankee Aggression," as Southerners were apt to call it, both during hostilities and in their later apologetics. His hero was not Lincoln, but Robert E. Lee, with whom Acton corresponded after the war was over. His fervent support of the Confederacy has often baffled and embarrassed later libertarians, but it is really not so hard to understand. The United States emerged from the bitter war with a far stronger and more powerful central government than it had possessed before. For Acton, this immense accession of centralized authority was an obvious threat to the liberties of the people that the Whig tradition had always championed.

On the other side of the political spectrum, Karl Marx took the side of the North. If wage slavery was bad, chattel slavery was obviously much worse. In articles Marx sent from England to Horace Greeley's *New York Tribune*, he championed the Northern cause and defended Lincoln at every turn. Like Hegel, Marx saw history on a grand scale. To him, the Northern cause represented a step forward in the progress of human freedom, while slavery was a relic of barbarism, just as the Republican platform had insisted in 1856. Unlike Acton, Marx was not afraid of the concentration of power, provided that it lay in the hands of those guiding history toward its ultimate goal. Indeed, until the end of his life, Marx regarded the United States as the promised land of socialism. It was the most progressive nation in the world. In his old age, he even toyed with the idea that socialism could be peacefully achieved in America without the need for a violent and bloody revolution. Even Karl Marx believed in American exceptionalism.

Paradoxically, both the North and the South ultimately rested their case upon the radical Whig right of resistance. Northerners believed that they were threatened by the despotism of the Southern slavocracy, while Southerners were equally convinced that they were threatened by the plutocratic despotism of the North. Both sides had somehow to square their cause with the Constitution—and neither had any trouble managing this feat. Lincoln had finessed this matter by calling the Confederacy an insurrection. But the army of the South would quickly demonstrate that the Yankees were not dealing with a small body of farmers up in arms, as in Shays's Rebellion. The South was solidly behind their new Republic. They had shown that they were prepared both to fight and to die for it. They were no rabble, as the North would discover quite early in the war.

CHAPTER SEVEN
TO FREE OR NOT TO FREE: THE SLAVERY QUESTION AND THE WAR

1
THE CROOKED ROAD TO ABOLITION

Today, we look back on Lincoln as the Great Emancipator, the man who freed the slaves. We naturally regard this as his mission—indeed, his world-historical mission. But as we noted earlier in this book, this was not his original mission. As with other world-historical figures, Lincoln, in his battle against the entrenched status quo of the Southern slave states, was forced to alter his course many times. Even the Emancipation Proclamation was an ad hoc solution, brought about by the exigencies of war.

The initial mission of Lincoln, his administration, and virtually the entire North was to restore the Union, even if they had to kill every last Confederate soldier and burn every field, home, and barn across the South. Their position was a bit like a man who is determined to recapture his runaway wife, to bring her back to the happy home where she belongs, even if he has to drag her back as a corpse. But the populist revolt in the North was literally blind with rage. There was no possibility of talking sense to them, even if Lincoln had wanted to.

Yet a Union restored at the barrel of a canon—what would such a Union be worth to the victors, not to mention the vanquished? Little wonder that observers around the world believed that the Civil War would leave the United States united in name only, while nothing remained in the South except bitter hatred and resentment at the perfidy of the now eternal Yankee foe. Yes, most agreed: The North would triumph, but only after any hope of restoring the Union had been crushed by the armies of the Yankee invader, who naturally looked on every last Southerner as the enemy, just as rebels came to hate every last Yankee.

Seldom have two peoples gone to war more certain of the righteousness of their cause. Only the Yankees, with their visceral sense of their own righteousness, could have continued to wage so long a war of bitter attrition. But only the Confederates, with their heroic defiance, could have prolonged the war to the point where the Yankee objective became not just the restoration of the Union, but the abolition of slavery. Needless to say, this was an unintended consequence of the protracted Confederate resistance. Herein lies one of those historical ironies that make predicting the future so risky a venture. Had the South not fought so courageously, it is difficult to imagine that Lincoln would ever have taken the desperate step of issuing the Emancipation Proclamation. To see why this is so, let's consider what would have happened if the South had been defeated in the first great battle of the Civil War.

The Yankees called it the First Bull Run. The Confederates called it the First Manassas. As the morning of July 21, 1861, broke, the Yankees were supremely confident that the cowardly rebels would turn tail and flee before their own army of righteousness. They were so confident of a victory that they thought it would be a picnic.

In the same picnic spirit, the ladies and gentlemen of nearby Washington, DC, rented lavish carriages to take them to relish their first great victory over the South. Many even assumed that it would also be the end of the Confederacy.

The new Confederate capital of Richmond, Virginia, was also close to the site of the battle. Many a Yankee had high hopes that their soldiers would soon be marching into Richmond, crushing the head of the viper of treason, hanging Jeff Davis from that sour apple tree.

The sensible southerners, knowing that they were licked, would rush back into the arms of the Union. Since Lincoln refused to acknowledge that they had ever left the Union in the first place, the episode would have gone down as the insurrection of rebel firebrands, just as Seward had predicted. The Union would not need to be restored, because it had never been broken. But in this case, what would be the fate of the slaves?

To demand, after their quick defeat, that the Southerners should now free their slaves—that was certainly out of the question. Such a step would only plunge the Union right back into an even more desperate and bitter struggle. It was easy to imagine the South abandoning its claimed right of secession, but to ask them to abolish their peculiar institution was nothing more or less than to demand the unconditional surrender of their entire way of life.

Furthermore, aside from the radical abolitionists, there were few in the North who were ready to take such a drastic step in 1861. After all, if the slaves were freed, what would happen to them then? It could only lead to major disruptions in the established social order, and no one wanted that. If combat had ceased after the first great battle, the status quo would be quickly resumed.

Fortunately for the cause of human liberty, the South won the first battle and would go on to win many more. Had the Confederates not fought so hard and for so long and with such stubbornness, their slaves would never have been emancipated by the North.

2
A TERRIBLE WAY TO END SLAVERY

Today, the Emancipation Proclamation is hailed as a turning point in the history of freedom. But that was far from the view of it taken by both the South and by many European observers as well, who saw it as a sinister scheme to achieve what John Brown had failed to do: to incite an insurrection of slaves in the Confederate States.

Those who held this view could marshal arguments for it by appealing to the document itself. It was tellingly billed as a wartime emergency act, and Lincoln justified it because it would shorten the war. But how could a piece of paper shorten the war? Only if it incited slave rebellions in the states of the Confederacy could the Emancipation Proclamation have possibly brought a quicker victory for the North.

Even more telling was the fact that only the slaves in the rebellious states had been emancipated, not those in the states that were loyal to the North. The slaves in the South were declared to be free though they remained in chains. The slaves of the states allied to the North remained in chains as well. The only real difference between them was that if the South's slaves rebelled, the Yankees would cheer them on, whereas if the slaves in the North's allied states rebelled, the Yankees would hunt them down. If Lincoln had really been animated by humanitarianism, he would have begun by freeing the slaves he could free, rather than pretending to free those he couldn't.

From these facts, it was easy for the skeptics to conclude that the Emancipation Proclamation was a Machiavellian scheme designed to incite a vast slave insurrection in the Confederate camp. The soldiers who had been fighting against the Yankees would be forced to leave the fields of battle and rush back to their home states in order to defend their families against the roaming and raging hordes. Yet both the Machiavellian scheme and the fear that it would succeed were chimeras.

There were no slave revolts in the South after the Emancipation Proclamation was issued by Lincoln on January 1, 1863. Though there were nearly 180,000 former slaves in the Yankee army, they bravely fought as soldiers and not as marauding maniacs. Indeed, compared to the behavior of the whites of the North and South, both slave and freedman displayed a remarkable degree of sanity and humanity.

Southerners had often bragged about their land of happy and contented slaves. This was a self-deception that assuaged the conscience of many slaveholders, but the abolitionists went to the other extreme by assuming that all slaves would be happy to cut their masters' throats if they just had a chance. After the war, tales abounded in the South of how former slaves had helped their now impoverished former masters to get through the worst days that followed the cessation of hostilities. These tales were mostly true.

The loyalty of these former slaves is embarrassing to those today who confuse such loyalty with mere subservience. But loyalty can be the expression of a noble heart. That former slaves could be moved to pity at the sight of their vanquished masters is nothing for them to be ashamed of. It is a sign that the message of Christianity had been better understood by the former slaves than the white folks who had taught it to them. Of all the parties to the Civil War, the slaves alone managed to do nothing that they would be ashamed of when the war was done.

The only military benefit that the Emancipation Proclamation brought to the North was that it inspired many slaves to gain their freedom by crossing Yankee lines to fight for the Union cause. Yet their contribution did not lead to a swift Union victory. There was only more war, two years and four months of it, in fact. But, as we have seen, it was only by virtue of their stubborn and long defiance of the North that slavery was finally abolished in the South. A premature peace would have simply given slavery a new and perhaps even a permanent lease on life. Had the Confederacy become an independent nation, plans were already afoot to implement its own vision of manifest destiny, which was to spread their slavocracy even farther, into Cuba, Mexico, and the tiny central American nations.

By the time of Lee's surrender at Appomattox, the die had been cast. As Stephen Douglas had presciently warned, the South had at long last been defeated. The first question that the victorious Yankees faced was what to do with the vanquished rebels; the second, what to do with the slaves. The period known as Reconstruction only angered the defeated whites, while it ultimately failed to provide the freed Blacks with the means of making a fresh start in life by offering them the forty acres and a mule they had been promised. They had been liberated from their chains only to become hopeless peons.

The Civil War was a terrible way to end slavery in the United States, but the brutal truth is that there was no other way. It is true that the British had earlier emancipated the slaves held in

Jamaica and other outposts in the Western Hemisphere without a blood bath. The English people even paid the slave-owners for the cost of their slaves—a sensible remedy that America's abolitionists found abhorrent to their lofty principles. But only a few Englishmen were directly affected by the liberation of their slaves. In the American South, on the other hand, emancipation meant the destruction of an entire way of life—and that will always be something people will fight and die for. There was simply no other option than that which Lincoln had taken.

The American Civil War was an epochal crisis that had long been brewing and that had reached a point of no return when Lincoln became president. Once Lincoln had realized that there was no way to restore the old order, he steeled himself to launch a war the outcome of which no one, and certainly not Lincoln himself, could predict at the time. Eventually, this war freed the slaves, though it had not begun with that objective, but rather to teach the Southerners a lesson they would never forget—and which, in fact, many still have not forgotten.

It is difficult not to sympathize with the defeated South. They had not created the social order into which they were born. The generation that fought in the Civil War had not brought the slaves across the Atlantic Ocean to work in their fields. The Yankees had done this for them. By 1860, almost every slave had been born in America, with no memories of the Africa from which their ancestors had been stolen.

Like all human beings, the white Southerners had to make do with the social order in which they found themselves. When their social order was attacked, they fought with astonishing courage and stubbornness to defend their traditional way of life, as people have done from time immemorial. No one wants their world turned upside down, especially at the hands of a bitter enemy. And never had a world been turned upside down with such violent suddenness as happened to the vanquished rebels in 1865. It is a world that still haunts us, as the perennial success of Margaret Mitchell's *Gone with the Wind* demonstrates.

Karl Marx had simply said good riddance to the Old South, as progressives do today. But Hegel would have been sympathetic to the Old South, despite his own hatred of slavery. The Confederates represented a set of genuinely noble, even aristocratic, ideals: chivalry, a deep sense of community, dedication to a higher cause, ferocious independence, dauntless courage, and the capacity for tenacious resistance. These are all admirable qualities, and any culture that had produced them deserves our respect. Yet, tragically, these good qualities conflicted with the greater good of preserving the principle of popular government upon which the American Republic had been based. This is why the Old South had to go.

Looking back at Lincoln from our own day, we can see clearly what neither Acton nor Marx could have anticipated. Had the American Union been shattered by the Civil War, the cause of free government and of democracy would have been damaged perhaps irretrievably around the world. In the great ideological struggles of the twentieth century, against both fascism and Soviet communism, there would have been no great power to fight for the right of ordinary men and women to decide what to believe and how to live. But then, it is characteristic of world-historical figures that it is often only after many generations that the scope and scale of their accomplishment can be grasped. This is also one of the main reasons why their contemporary critics always seem in hindsight to appear so obtuse and even perverse to later generations. But this is unfair to the critics, who could see no farther into the future than is allotted to ordinary mortals.

Our hindsight also permits us to see in Lincoln a forerunner of the populist progressive tradition that would later be taken up by William Jennings Bryan. Studies of Lincoln take note of the importance he gave to the self-made man, who alone and against all odds managed to lift himself up by his own bootstraps, as the adage goes. But what if the man (or boy) is so poor that he doesn't even have a pair of boots? In that case, the answer was obvious: Give him the boots, and let the national government provide them.

Lincoln's opposition to the South was not just based on slavery but also on the fact that the South had been united against the Free Soil, Free Labor, Free Men movement that sought to give the white working class of the North access to the federal territories. Lincoln had enthusiastically supported the principles of the Free Soil Party that had been created in 1848, only to merge with the Republican Party in 1856. By Free Soil, the Party had originally meant soil free of slavery, but Lincoln took this idea more literally.

3
THE RISE OF THE PLUTOCRATIC ELITE

In the Homestead Act of May 1862, which Lincoln supported and signed, Americans were provided with up to 160 acres of virgin land free of charge once they had paid a nominal registration fee. Many in the North had long supported the idea but it had been blocked at every step by the recalcitrant South, who were opposed to the very idea of slave-free soil. The act could only be passed once the South pulled all of its members out of Congress.

The Homestead Act was revolutionary in its intent. Previously, Americans had been permitted to make a fresh start, but how they went about this was left entirely up to their own resources and devices. Yet it is extremely difficult to make a fresh start if you literally have nothing to start with. By offering free land on which even the very poor could begin a new chapter in their lives, the Homestead Act had introduced the germ of a new and radical idea into American politics, one that would have a tremendous future. It was the duty of the federal government to guarantee its citizens the means and materials by which they could actually make a fresh start.

The Homestead Act no doubt expressed a noble ideal. The law made every household eligible for the free land, including those headed only by women, and it was not restricted to whites. No piece of legislation passed by Congress had ever been so progressive economically. The vision was that of happy self-made men and women, their fresh start having been provided by the government. They would naturally transform the virgin soil they had been freely offered into prosperous farms. This, in turn, would push back the wild frontier and lure immigrants from Europe with the promise of the fresh start that was every American's birthright.

Unfortunately, this attempt to aid the landless men and women for whom it was intended was wrecked by speculators who, as usual, quickly figured out various ways to game the system. They hired agents to fill out claims on the free land, though neither the speculators nor their agents had the slightest interest in setting foot on it, much less trying to cultivate and improve it.

These land speculators were the harbingers of a new threat to the core principle of American exceptionalism that wanted every American to be given the same chances and opportunities and, thereby, a level playing field. But the land speculators had demonstrated that the clever and quick could swiftly outwit both the people and their government.

In the decades following the Homestead Act, a new elite rose to power, as the inevitable result of America's unprecedented economic growth after the Civil War. The populist revolt under Andrew Jackson had granted unlimited social mobility to all American citizens, which many had taken full advantage of. As a result of this radical political innovation, and with both luck and initiative, a few Americans had become fabulously wealthy, while others remained poor. As so often happens, the solution of one era became the problem to be fixed in the subsequent one. Social mobility, intended to give all a fresh start, had resulted in the plutocratic rule of a very few.

Those who had amassed great fortunes began to use their wealth in order to manipulate the politicians in Washington to do their bidding. The extent to which the federal government had fallen under their thumbs soon became an open national scandal. This time it was not the wealthy planters of the Old South who threatened to establish an aristocracy, but the captains of industry who naturally wanted their workers to be obedient, to know their place in the pecking order, and to not rock the yacht.

Their ideal society of efficient robots laboring to create even vaster empires of riches for their owners was as antithetical to American exceptionalism as was the slavocracy of the Confederates. Wage slaves might be freer than chattel slaves, but they were no more in a position to make a fresh start in life than those who had been held in real chains. The natural libertarians, like Cooper's fictional Natty Bumppo, were not made to be good worker bees. They were too independent, too ornery, to sacrifice their liberty in order to be cogs in the well-oiled machine of capitalism, while self-made individuals were only respected as long as they had become very rich self-made individuals. Otherwise, such energetic persons were frowned upon as potential competitors. Neither the natural libertarian nor the self-made individual was fit material for the work required on an assembly line. Those who were fit were only fit because they had no other choice. This was a far cry from the Jeffersonian vision of an America populated by sturdy and independent yeomen.

Capitalism is a fine economic system, which has proven itself by producing high standards of living for those who live in free-market societies. Yet when capitalists gain political control over any society, as happened in the United States between the time of the American Civil War and the Great Depression, they will naturally set themselves up as a ruling class. Like all ruling classes before them, they will be primarily interested in preserving the social order that put them on top.

By 1900, anxiety over the growing economic inequality between the rich and the poor was shared by all the progressives, including the Republican president, Theodore Roosevelt, who was concerned with the long-term effects this inequality would have on American society. The progressives of that era attacked the great corporate trusts, which they saw as a grave threat to the small and independent businesses that provided a livelihood for many middle-class Americans. Judge Louis Brandeis summed up the attitude of these early progressives in his book, *The Curse of Bigness*. Unlike the progressives of today, Brandeis and those of like mind wanted to wind back the clock, to return to the simpler way of life before the advent of gigantic corporations, like Rockefeller's Standard Oil. They liked small towns and small businesses. They hated heavy industry and assembly lines.

So, too, did William Jennings Bryan, whose populist movement would take up the cause of those that the American system of capitalism had left behind. The "forgotten man" whom FDR would seek to represent during the Great Depression worked on these assembly lines, if they were lucky, but were otherwise condemned to menial labor, with no chance of bettering themselves. Up until FDR became president, this had come to seem like the natural order of things, just as chattel slavery had been looked upon in the Old South. Both the British and American Whigs had long assumed that the despotism they so deeply feared could arise only from the executive branch of government. James Madison, through his personal experience in the Virginia Assembly, had come to recognize that there could be legislative despotism as well. Thomas Jefferson had come to fear the rise of judicial despotism, and for good reason, as we have learned from the judicial activists of our time. But plutocracy was a new kind of threat. You could not vote it out of office or impeach it. You could not wage war against it. Instead, it invariably managed to win over to its side senators, congressmen, judges, and even presidents. It was a despotic power that seemed beyond the control of the people. How to keep the plutocrats from becoming a ruthless and corrupt ruling class would become the greatest challenge that the American tradition of egalitarianism had ever faced. It would eventually have to be met—and by another world-historical president, only slightly less improbable than Abraham Lincoln.

Franklin Delano Roosevelt would also take a page from Lincoln's playbook. The Homestead Act had failed to achieve its noble goals, but it had been a valiant effort to use the power of the newly strengthened federal government to offer ordinary Americans a fresh start in life. FDR would use the federal government to try to achieve the same purpose for the forgotten man of his own day. In doing so, he initiated a new epoch in American history, just as Lincoln had done before him.

CHAPTER EIGHT
CHAMELEON ON PLAID: FDR'S MACHIAVELLIAN MOMENT

1
LOVING FDR, HATING FDR

When Franklin Delano Roosevelt was elected in 1932, no one expected that he would die in office thirteen years later. No president had been elected for three terms, let alone the four terms that the nation granted him. What FDR might have done had he completed his fourth term in office is mere speculation. But on the day that he died in the polio haven of Warm Springs, Georgia, on April 12, 1945, millions upon millions in America and around the world mourned this death.

In the eyes of many at the time, FDR had both saved the nation, during the Great Depression, and defeated fascism in the Second World War, which was then drawing to a close. Today, this is widely regarded as his legacy. But, as in the case of Lincoln, FDR was not one of Carlyle's Heroes, able to shape and control events through the majesty of his imperial will and supreme intellect. Like all the world-historical figures of the past, he was the product of events beyond his control. He erred and backtracked; he fumbled and failed; yet in the end, the world FDR left behind him was radically different from the world into which he had been born. One epoch had passed and a new epoch had emerged, and no one played a greater role in this radical transformation than Roosevelt himself.

With the exception of Lincoln, no president had ever been so intensely loved or so intensely hated, so admired or so vilified. Until the advent of Donald Trump, FDR held the record for the number of former allies who would later turn against him, including his first vice president, John Nance Garner; the chief of his Brain Trust, Raymond Moley; Postmaster General James Farley; and his ambassador to England, Joseph Kennedy.

Among the intellectuals who had at first supported him but who later became his foes, the most prominent were Walter Lippmann and the progressive historian Charles Beard. William Randolph Hearst had originally backed him in 1932, but two years later, he ordered his formidable chain of syndicated news-papers to attack him. Even Al Smith, the Democratic candidate for president in 1928, a party loyalist if there ever was one, was so upset by FDR's policies that he became the head of the Liberty League, an assortment of businessmen convinced that FDR was leading America down the path to socialism. On the other hand, the genuine socialists, both within his administration and out-side of it, were irked by FDR's stubborn refusal to follow their directives.

Many were angry at FDR, but often for contradictory reasons. He was moving too fast; he was moving too slow. He was too far to the right; he was too far to the left. Some urged him to join the British in their darkest hour and declare war on Nazi Germany; others, like Charles Beard, savaged him for abandoning the principle of non-intervention. He was criticized for trusting Stalin too much; he was criticized for not trusting him enough.

With a list of such die-hard enemies, it is a wonder that he was elected for a second term in 1936. Yet in no previous election had any candidate won by such an enormous landslide. Nearly 61 percent of the voters cast their ballots for Roosevelt. He received 523 electoral votes; his hapless opponent, Alf Landon, won 8.

Had FDR been re-elected because his various New Deal initiatives had successfully put Americans back to work? No. In fact, 1936 saw the hopes of renewed prosperity dashed. Even more Americans were out of work. Yet FDR had persuaded the vast majority of voters to give him another chance. How can we explain this feat?

Two of FDR's predecessors in office, Woodrow Wilson and Herbert Hoover, had entered politics late in their life. Indeed, their political careers came about almost by accident. But FDR was a born politician. He could charm the birds out of the trees, if he wished, but he was just as capable of Machiavellian cunning. It became notorious among those who spoke privately with FDR that everyone came away convinced that the president was eager to take their advice, but he seldom did. Roosevelt's favorite device for achieving this result was the phrase "fine, fine, fine." His populist rival on the left, Huey Long, complained that FDR would hail his ideas as "fine, fine, fine," but he'd later discover that FDR used the same phrase when talking to reactionary politicians on the right. To many observers, this was proof of shallow character—a man who changed his mind depending on the last person he was talking to. This was exactly how Herbert Hoover sized up Roosevelt, calling him "a chameleon on plaid."

It is a tribute to FDR's political genius that he could so easily convince others of his wishy-washiness while he himself was pursuing a Machiavellian policy. By appearing to approve of everyone else's ideas, he was able eventually to maneuver them into accepting the idea he had all along. There had never been an American politician whose right hand was more aware of what his left hand was doing, though both friends and foes were never quite sure which hand FDR was extending them.

As a pragmatic politician, FDR had no interest in political ideologies. He knew elections were won by the old-fashioned methods of building coalitions, of rewarding with patronage those who had stood by him and ignoring, when not punishing, those who had strayed from the fold. He could also be astonishingly vindictive.

When Millard E. Tydings, Senator from Maryland, did not go along with a New Deal program at Roosevelt's urging, the president personally campaigned to defeat him in his 1938 Senate race. It was part of his wider campaign to "purge" conservative Democrats from the party, though FDR's definition of *conservative* was anyone who bucked his will. Tydings won by a handy margin. But FDR's futile and childish attempt to get revenge on a Senator of his own party was an indication that FDR's buoyant self-confidence was on the verge of becoming hubris.

In addition to his stick, FDR also knew how to provide carrots—lots of them—to those who stayed on his side. The British Whigs of the eighteenth century decried the power of patronage as a threat to liberty. Handing out government jobs to party followers allowed the monarch to reward loyalists. But no British king or queen had ever had access to the largesse of the American federal government, as FDR had. The New Deal spawned a host of programs designed to provide jobs to the unemployed. These, too, were filled with functionaries dedicated to Roosevelt.

No president before FDR had ever had the opportunity to create his own administrative state within the state. This was due to several factors. In 1932, roughly 1,800,000 Americans worked for the federal government. In 1945, that number reached 3,300,000, though much of this increase had been due to the Second World War. While this growth extended the reach of FDR's power, by far the most important factor was Roosevelt's unprecedented thirteen years in office. During this period, many left the government, and their positions were naturally filled by loyalists. During the three full terms FDR served, the administration of the federal government had been filled to the brim with liberal Democrats. The first deep state was the result of FDR's carrot policy. It worked marvelously for Roosevelt but sowed the seeds of an administrative bureaucracy far more liberal than the ordinary Americans it was administering, with portentous consequences for the future.

What can we make of such a man?

2
ROOSEVELT CONFRONTS THE CRISIS OF HIS TIME

The first thing to note is that FDR, like Lincoln, faced an epochal crisis—not a civil war, but the Great Depression. Unlike normal crises, there was no rule book for how to fix the collapse of the world's economy. The finest economists of his time had not a clue. Yet in 1933, it would have been fatal for the newly elected president of the United States to announce to the world that he himself had no idea how to get out of the global depression. So he had to put on a brave front.

As the victim of adult polio, FDR was accustomed to putting on a brave front. His famous words, "We have nothing to fear but fear itself," delivered in his first inaugural address, have become trite, but they electrified Americans when they were spoken, though credit for writing the address is usually given to Raymond Moley. They tapped into the spirit of American exceptionalism, which held that no matter what might befall our nation, we its people could handle it. Neither despair nor scapegoating tempted us. We had faced overwhelming odds since the time of the American Revolution. Now, Roosevelt called upon Americans to face another epochal crisis with courage and grit. And, miraculously, they did.

Today FDR's reputation has become so absorbed into the legends of the Democratic Party that it has become difficult to see the man through the mist of adoring propagandists. On the other hand, the counter-legend offered by his modern detractors is equally off the mark. FDR was not a socialist; he was not even a progressive. He began his presidency with a deep belief that the American economy could still right itself, embracing laissez-faire capitalism and a balanced budget. Little by little, as the Depression dragged on, FDR would recognize, just as Lincoln had, that there was no going back to the past.

Yet he stoutly refused to adopt any of the radical remedies proposed for the American economy. He rejected Soviet-style Five-Year Plans, with their state-managed economy, and had only contempt for the fascist solution of an open dictatorship, though many Americans—including some of his closest advisors—had urged him to take one or the other of these courses. In the end, though he failed to cure America of its economic malaise, FDR succeeded in preserving the basic principles of American exceptionalism during a crisis in which there were widespread calls to remake America along the lines of the European fascist corporate states or the centrally planned economy of the USSR. Today, America is still standing strong, while both European fascism and Soviet communism have been relegated to the trash bin of history.

Clearly, FDR chose the right course, but it was one that only the most consummate of pragmatic opportunists could have navigated. Here, and not in any ideology, right or left, we will find the real FDR. No one was more aware of what power could do, and FDR knew how to use it. He often asked for more power than was granted him, and few today regret that he was not given it. But no one had ever been more astute at using the power he had than FDR, though his greatest source of power came from his innate gift of persuasive and overpowering charm.

Like Abraham Lincoln, FDR did not become a world-historical figure by design. He certainly never imagined that he would become one when he took his oath of office in 1932. Roosevelt was certainly ambitious all his life, but world-historical greatness was thrust upon him, just as it had been in the case of Lincoln. Indeed, there was nothing in FDR's background that would have suggested that destiny had chosen him for the role he came to play in shaping American and world history.

This was certainly not due to his obscure and humble origins, as in the case of Lincoln. FDR was no self-made man. He had split no rails in his youth, nor book-learned himself like Lincoln. He was as close to a genuine aristocrat as it was possible to be and still be an American. The Roosevelts were descended from those sturdy Dutch settlers who had arrived in New York in 1624 when the Dutch West India Company set up a trading post on Manhattan Island. FDR's own family had inherited both landed estates and the wealth that went with them. Even as a child, FDR knew that he would never have to work a day in his life, though his doting and often smothering mother had observed in her young son a budding talent for political leadership. She would later recall how she had told her son not to boss his little friends around in the games they played, to which the young FDR replied, "If I didn't give the orders, nothing would happen"—an attitude that FDR would not relinquish until the end of his eventful, bossy life.

Another childhood experience that shaped the young Roosevelt came from the time he spent in Wilhelmine Germany before the Great War. He developed an intense antipathy to the German passion for military parades as well as for crude German chauvinism. He would later come to detest the Third Reich, not for its antisemitism, but because he saw in it the recrudescence of Prussian militarism. This aversion to militaristic societies was characteristic of all Americans, but it was especially intense in FDR and would come to dominate his attitude to both Germany and Japan leading up to the Second World War. The ideologies invoked to justify militarism were of little interest to FDR. He was familiar enough with history to know that military empires, with their innate tendencies to territorial expansion, were a threat to liberty.

Needless to say, such a child of privilege received the best private education, and there had never been any doubt that he would attend the most prestigious college in the United States, though his academic career at Harvard had been less than stellar. But neither then nor later would the elite opinion makers have much regard for the quality of FDR's intellect. Most would have agreed with Justice Oliver Wendell Holmes's famous assessment of Roosevelt as having "a second-rate intellect, but a first-class temperament."

Like his distant cousin, Teddy Roosevelt, whom he greatly admired and hoped to follow into politics, Franklin chose a career of public service. But unlike his cousin, FDR came from a family of Democrats. This was an anomalous situation for a family as old and wealthy as the Roosevelts. In the presidential election of 1908, the Democratic Party had nominated the populist candidate, William Jennings Bryan, for the third time. The Eastern Establishment hated and feared him. He was for easy money in the form of bimetallism, which made him the friend of debtors and the enemy of their creditors. But in 1912, the Democratic Party finally abandoned the people's peerless leader and selected Woodrow Wilson, a former college professor who had served a tumultuous term as the president of Princeton University, where he exhibited the penchant for self-righteous idealism that would characterize his two terms as president. But Wilson was the beau ideal of the new progressivist movement under the management not of folk heroes like Bryan but of highly trained experts in government. The influence of the Prussian academic system ran high in those days. They had the finest and most demanding universities in the world, which had produced outstanding men in virtually every scientific field. Wilson wanted to model the American educational system, and especially its colleges, on the Prussian model.

The Constitution had claimed to embody the will of the People, but Wilson believed that it had outlived its usefulness. Again, the Prussian model of an efficient and incorruptible state bureaucracy, manned by suitable experts, beckoned Wilson and other members of the new progressive elite. Under their direction, the American government would become the engine of moral and social improvements. The masses would benefit from experts' sure guidance, though they would have virtually no say in the matter. Yet as a concession to those in the party still loyal to their veteran standard-bearer, Wilson made Bryan his Secretary of State.

After three defeats in his run for president, it is no surprise that Bryan's agrarian brand of progressive populism had become unfashionable. In addition, the urban Eastern progressives of the time, under the leadership of Wilson, were starting to separate themselves from the agrarian populism favored by both the South and the Midwest—a split that would eventually wind up with the two political movements occupying opposite ends of the political spectrum, as today.

Nowadays, Bryan is mainly remembered for the role he played in the so-called Scopes Trial, in which a Tennessee high school teacher named John Scopes was charged with violating state law by teaching Darwin's theory of evolution. Bryan, who led the prosecution, is routinely condemned by modern liberals for his simple-minded adherence to Biblical literalism and his refusal to accept Darwin's theory of evolution. But what this retrospective dismissal overlooks is that the brand of Darwinism championed by progressives in the twenties was Social Darwinism.

This was not a theory of biology, but a political ideology that was deployed to justify an economic order in which those at the top were predestined by natural selection to be on top, while those at the bottom were equally predestined to be on the bottom. Bryan's defense of the Bible against the Social Darwinists was a plea for the brotherhood of man against an ideology tailor-made to justify the rule of the new plutocratic elite that had come into being after the Civil War.

Indeed, the then-fashionable notion of "the survival of the fittest" gave the Social Darwinists of that era a presumed scientific basis to justify subjugating not only Black Americans but all those who had been left behind in the evolutionary struggle for supremacy at the top of the social totem pole. Biology had condemned these losers to their lowly position in the natural order. And who would be such a fool as to defy the laws of biology?

The rich were charmed by such a convenient theory, and they never doubted its status as science. It was not their fault that nature had put them on top, just as nature had fortunately provided them with a multitude of workers willing to work for a pittance. Both rich and poor were simply obeying the laws of evolution, each in their own way.

The fact that many of the new progressives, like Woodrow Wilson, had adopted Social Darwinism as their pet cause put them at odds with Bryan's agrarian populism. Perhaps here we might find the origin of the culture wars that have come to divide America. Bryan was on the side of the common people, many of whom the new progressives might have deemed unfit to reproduce. Like Moses, Bryan chose life. The Eastern progressives chose sterilization. But what kind of people would have the arrogance to decide who should be allowed to have descendants and who should not?

Woodrow Wilson, for one. As the governor of New Jersey, he had signed into law an act requiring the involuntary sterilization of those deemed unfit to reproduce. Though hailed as a progressive by later liberal historians, upon becoming president he immediately imposed the Jim Crow laws of the South on the federal government. While Bryan had supported women's suffrage, Wilson had endlessly waffled on the issue. So why is William Jennings Bryan derided and forgotten, while Wilson remains a hero to liberal historians? The answer is both simple and obvious. Wilson was approved by the establishment of his day. Bryan wasn't.

3
ROOSEVELT'S RISE AND THE END OF THE ROARING TWENTIES

It was under Woodrow Wilson that Roosevelt was appointed Assistant Secretary of the Navy. He had earlier attended Columbia Law School, though he dropped out before earning his degree. Later, after passing the bar, he would join the prestigious law firm of Carter Ledyard & Milburn, perhaps attracted by its specialization in admiralty law—the sea always being close to FDR's heart. Yet closer still was politics—his true passion and hobby. Given the prominence in New York of both sides of his family, the Delanos and the Roosevelts, and his own considerable charm, he was urged to run for the position of New York State Senator, which he duly won. At the end of his one term, he was tapped by Woodrow Wilson to become the Assistant to Josephus Daniels, the Secretary of the Navy, and another Southerner like Wilson himself.

We are so accustomed to picturing FDR crippled by polio and condemned to his wheelchair that it may be hard to imagine what the young, handsome, and perfectly fit Roosevelt was like when serving under Daniels, who would later say that he fell in love with the slender and dashing young FDR from the moment he set eyes upon him. (Back then, men could say such things without a blush.) Daniels had been appointed Secretary of the Navy despite being a declared pacifist. Woodrow Wilson, though a resident of New Jersey when elected in 1912, had also grown up in the South during the Civil War and the Reconstruction that followed and shared Daniels's aversion to war, no doubt influenced by their firsthand experience of its ravages.

When the European War broke out in August 1914, Teddy Roosevelt, who had been defeated two years earlier in his second run for the presidency, immediately urged Wilson to enter the war on the side of the Allies: Great Britain, France, and Czarist Russia. Wilson, backed by his Secretary of State William Jennings Bryan and Josephus Daniels, declared that Americans must remain neutral both in heart and mind. In their view, the Great War was a strictly European affair. It was simply another European struggle for power and, as such, it did not concern the United States. The peculiarly American brand of pacifism rejected military aggression against other nations carried out merely for selfish national interests. Wars waged in national defense were another matter, and all the American pacifists agreed on that point. But so too were wars carried out in the name of a lofty principle, such as freeing the slaves.

By 1917, however, the mood of the country had changed radically. Most Americans did not just want to enter the war; they demanded it. Wilson had genuinely sought to avoid sending American troops off to a European war, but on April 6, 1917, before a solemn assembly of Congress, he announced that a state of war existed between the United States and Germany.

The idealist in Wilson required him to justify his decision to go to war on loftier grounds than the ones on which the European nations had broken the peace. The pedantic professor in him tried to make this difference clear when he proclaimed that the United States was an associate, and not an ally, of England and France. They might have started the war for their own narrow and selfish purposes, but Wilson was determined to transform it into something noble, awe-inspiring, and, of course, idealistic. Under his guidance, it had become, in that famous phrase, "the war to end all wars."

By 1920, those Americans who had been so eager to fight the war to end all wars had been bitterly disillusioned by its outcome, especially after the European victors had imposed conditions on the defeated Germans that virtually assured another European war within a generation. French Marshall Ferdinand Foch declared that the Treaty of Versailles was only "an armistice for twenty years," thinking it was too lenient on the Germans, while John Maynard Keynes, who attacked the treaty as crushingly harsh, prophetically warned that its consequences would be instability and extremism in Germany, paving the way for the next war. Many Americans were equally appalled by the terms of the treaty.

To make matters worse, the millions of dollars that had been loaned to the Allies could not be repaid, deeply affronting thrifty Americans who believed in repaying their debts. The general sentiment of the time was the desire to return to normalcy, as Republican Warren G. Harding put it in his campaign for the presidency in 1920. This was the implicit rejection of both Wilson's high-minded idealism as well as the activist and meddling government championed by Teddy Roosevelt and the other progressives of his era.

In 1920, the still vigorous FDR was chosen by the drawn-out Democratic Convention to be their vice-presidential candidate in a race that the Democrats were foredoomed to lose. Their platform had been a virtual paean to Wilson. It even demanded that Wilson's treaty for the League of Nations be passed without the slightest amendment—a lost cause if there ever was one. This perverse insistence on affirming Wilson's legacy inevitably ruled out nominating William Jennings Bryan for a fourth time, despite his continuing popularity. His style of progressive populism, so warmly championed in the Midwest, was now considered a hopelessly lost cause by party insiders. So, on the forty-fourth ballot, the party chose James Cox, who had been the Governor of Ohio and a staunch defender of Wilson and his policies.

The Democrats had hoped that by adding Roosevelt to the ticket, his famous name alone would be an asset. Although relatively young for the job of vice president at thirty-eight, FDR was recognized by veteran politicians as possessing the valuable political gifts of immense personal charm and a supreme sense of self-confidence. Yet the American people had had enough of ambitious presidents. The unassuming Harding won over 60 percent of the popular vote, while crushing the Democrats in the Electoral College 404 to 127. It was the worst defeat ever suffered by a presidential candidate up to that date.

It is against this background that the subsequent political career of FDR must be understood. Although FDR had faithfully supported Wilson as a good party man, their temperaments could not have been more different. FDR would go on to become one of the most gifted pragmatic opportunists of all time, famously willing to tinker and experiment. Unlike Wilson, FDR was no intellectual, and in his political career, he was fully prepared to renounce any principle, however lofty, that prevented him from doing what he thought best at the time.

Yet thanks to his consummate political skills, FDR was able to appeal to the Wilsonian Democrats as well as to those voters who had been the most devoted followers of William Jennings Bryan, though as president, FDR initially resisted the various progressive programs that Bryan had long advocated. Politics for FDR was never about championing an ideological cause, but about building coalitions. Though many progressive Democrats urged him to take a stand on civil rights for African Americans, FDR steered clear of championing a highly controversial cause that would inevitably endanger the Democrats' hold on the solid South. For the young FDR, the goal of the politician was to win elections and not to reform the world. This was FDR's creed. It was not an ideology, but an instinct.

Yet the glowing political career that awaited FDR appeared to be at an end when he was struck down by polio at the age of thirty-nine. His doting and overprotective mother advised him to give up politics altogether, but FDR refused to be beaten. With the encouragement of his wife, Eleanor, and his closest advisers, FDR continued to play a role in New York State politics. He backed Al Smith both for governor and for president in 1928, although FDR disliked Smith's progressive politics, while Smith—born to poverty—never trusted the patrician Roosevelt. The fact was that FDR realized that neither Bryan's brand of populism nor Smith's brand of progressivism had much appeal for the American voters in the 1920s. They had wanted normalcy, and they had gotten it.

Calvin Coolidge, who became president on the death of Harding, had caught the mood of America perfectly. No more wars to save the world. No more entanglements with Europe. Congress passed a multitude of laws that were designed to make American neutrality permanent. No president could ever again inveigle the American voters to send their sons off to foreign lands to fight foreign wars.

In addition, although Coolidge was a staunch Republican, he subscribed to the Jeffersonian tradition of minimalist government. He had no use for populism, of either the easy-money kind or the new elite progressivism that aimed to improve and uplift American life through innovative policies and programs. Coolidge, and the millions who voted for him, did not think their nation was in need of much improving—and certainly not at the hands of progressive eggheads. After all, just look at the economy. It was roaring. It could take care of itself, just as it had in 1921, when a post-war recession hit America.

In response to this crisis, President Warren G. Harding did absolutely nothing. The economy was allowed to adjust itself according to market principles. Wages fell, but that was the natural cure for recession. In time, wages would rise again, and all would be well. The government had virtually no role to play. And, indeed, the recession of 1921 was soon over, and the Roaring Twenties were in full swing. Everyone was getting rich.

Americans were still getting rich when they went to the polls in the election of 1928, which Republican Herbert Hoover won in a landslide against Democrat Al Smith. Hoover, left an orphan at an early age, was the quintessential self-made man, the rugged individual whose talents matched his aspirations. First, he had made a fortune in mining. Resourceful and energetic, he became known as the man who could fix everything. When in the aftermath of the Great War, millions of desperate Europeans faced starvation, Hoover was put in charge of the relief efforts aimed at providing food for Europe's starving masses, a truly Herculean task that he handily accomplished to the surprise and satisfaction of a grateful world. He had richly earned his nickname The Great Engineer.

A third career awaited Hoover when President Harding appointed him Secretary of Commerce, a position he retained after Harding's death in 1923. When in 1927, the winding Mississippi once again flooded its banks, President Calvin Coolidge sent the redoubtable Hoover to provide relief for its victims. Both he and Hoover, however, were in agreement that this relief should only come from the governments of the states affected by the flood, along with donations from charitable individuals and organizations, and not from the federal government. The campaign Hoover launched to marshal such funds was successful, another feather in his already much be-feathered cap.

Yet the very fact that Coolidge had sent his Secretary of Commerce to deal with what had once been regarded as a strictly local problem represented a not inconsiderable shift in the traditional approach to such crises by the federal government. It showed that the government cared—at least a little. Yet Coolidge continued to believe that the federal government should not care too much. Unlike presidents of our own day, Coolidge declined to visit the devastated area. That was not what presidents were for.

The stock market crash had occurred just seven months after Hoover was sworn in as president. The prudent Hoover could not be held responsible for the speculative frenzy that had seized investors all across America and in every station of life. As the Secretary of Commerce under Coolidge, Hoover had repeatedly warned that the unbridled speculation in the stock market by all and sundry was creating a potentially explosive bubble and should be curbed. It had gone too far. The stock market was running wild. Moreover, the recession that followed the crash did not heal itself as it had done in 1921. It only got worse. And Herbert Hoover was just the man to fix it.

Unlike Harding and Coolidge, Hoover was congenitally incapable of doing nothing. His style of leadership was as different from that of the pragmatic opportunist as it was from the high-minded idealism of a Woodrow Wilson. To begin with, Hoover approached problems with the attitude of the engineer—the very attitude that had been so immensely successful when it came to inventing new technology and better, faster machines. This kind of engineering know-how had made America the world leader in using scientific breakthroughs to provide ordinary Americans with more and more conveniences. Yet the fatal error of the engineering mindset is to believe that human beings can be fixed just like machines. They can't.

Hoover's first concern was to make sure that wages did not fall. He jawboned captains of industry into keeping wages high, higher than the dismal market would have set them if left to itself. This departure from the previously sacred principle of laissez-faire marked an epochal transition in American politics. From now on, the public would naturally come to expect the government to do something when hard times hit.

President Hoover continued to maintain that "prosperity was right around the corner." But that corner seemed to grow ever more distant—and with it, the golden reputation of the man once known as The Great Engineer. His name was now cursed by the millions who had voted for him out of the sincere conviction that whatever might break in the USA, Hoover was just the man to fix it. Hoover's optimism was seconded by most of the leading American economists of the time. By 1932, however, the American economy had still not turned around Hoover's hopeful corner, and the crisis was deepening day by day. Later economists of various schools would offer their own explanations for what made this economic crisis different from previous ones, both in severity and length. But the majority of American voters in 1932 came to the same conclusion: It was all Herbert Hoover's fault. Though Hoover refused to see it coming, he was defeated in a crushing landslide by Franklin Delano Roosevelt, whom he had dismissed as an opportunist lightweight—an assessment with which many other observers concurred.

The American economy was not like a broken machine. It all came down to how people felt. What it needed was not a brilliant engineer like Hoover but a brilliant politician like FDR. Hoover never realized that, despite his genuine engineer's itch to fix America's economic woes, he had become a folk villain. The shantytowns springing up across the United States were dubbed Hoovervilles. The newspapers under which the unemployed

159

slept in the winter became Hoover blankets. Never before had so many Americans been so happy to see their president—one they had voted in by a landslide—turned out of office.

By the time Roosevelt took the oath of office, the world economy was in a tailspin. The landslide majority that had elected FDR now expected him to achieve what Hoover had failed to do: Fix their economy. Gone forever were the days when an American president could wash his hands of an economic crisis. He was now expected to tackle it with bare fists.

But was FDR the man to succeed where the redoubtable Herbert Hoover had so signally failed? In fact, FDR's instinctive ideas about the American economy were not much different from those of Calvin Coolidge. On the campaign trail, FDR had attacked Hoover's bold venture into deficit spending as "a veritable cancer in the body politic and economic." He had a homespun notion of economics and believed that if going into debt was dangerous to a household, it must be even more dangerous for the national economy. It would be several years before John Maynard Keynes would revolutionize economics by championing deficit spending as a means of dealing with a weakening economy. Yet on the very day that FDR took his oath of office, the world economy had been brought to the brink of collapse by the escalating banking crisis that had originated in Austria and was spreading throughout the rest of the globe. Something had to be done immediately, and the American people were ready to give their new president as much power as he needed. Indeed, after the election of 1932, there was a great deal of talk about a coming dictatorship. This was because a new zeitgeist had set in among Europeans after the Great War. Parliamentary governments had failed—to many, that was the harsh lesson of the worst war in history. This was certainly the lesson that Lenin, Mussolini, Stalin, and Hitler had all learned. Rather than trusting to rowdy debating clubs, a.k.a. parliaments, better to have a single wise leader you can put your trust in. Just as by 1860, Lincoln had faced a world in which popular government teetered on the verge of extinction, so too by 1932, FDR faced a world where democracies were being rejected around the globe in favor of authoritarian governments. Both presidents seemed like they were up against the forces of historical inevitability. Indeed, even many Americans, rather than fearing the advent of a dictatorship, were praying for one. Only the coming of such a dictator could save them from their present desperate crisis.

As Adam Cohen has written in his superb account of FDR's first hundred days, *Nothing to Fear*, "The nation expected Roosevelt to claim the powers of a dictator, or close to it." The desire to see FDR assume such power was shared not only by many liberals, but by Republicans as well, such as Senator David Reed of Pennsylvania, who said, "I do not often envy other countries their governments, but I say that if this country ever needed a Mussolini, it needs one now." Walter Lippmann, the weightiest commentator on the public events of his time, agreed that given the severity of the crisis, a resort to "'dictatorial powers,' if that is the name for it—is essential."

The call for a dictator made a certain sense. The crisis brought about by the Great Depression, many argued, was not a normal crisis, and they were certainly right. The Constitutional means put at the disposal of a sitting president were simply not adequate to deal with such a catastrophe. The body of laws that had traditionally prescribed the limits of presidential power did not permit him to take the kind of dramatic measures that were needed to halt the nation's rapidly increasing descent into economic ruin. These traditional constraints, the heritage of the Whig fear of a too-powerful executive, were designed precisely in order to keep the American head of state from aspiring to autocracy.

Even worse, the Constitution gave the president precious little control over the American economy, and certainly not enough to deal with the Great Depression. This lack of authority had long been seen not as a handicap, but as the counsel of prudence and wisdom. No one wanted a president who meddled at will with the economy. The economy should take care of itself.

FDR himself had run on a platform based on the traditional Democratic preference for a limited government that dutifully balanced its budget. But by the time he took the oath of office on March 4, 1933, events had rendered those pious platitudes null and void. Banks were now failing at such an alarming rate that something had to be done to stop the hemorrhaging of faith in America's financial institutions. There was only one possible solution: to declare a federal bank holiday. But like holidays in general, everyone knew that this one, too, had to come to an end. It was easy to close the doors of a bank suffering from a run on its accounts. But what would happen when these doors were thrown open again?

CHAPTER NINE
CHARM AND CUNNING: FDR PULLS A RABBIT OUT OF HIS HAT

1
THE BANKING CRISIS OF 1933

By the time FDR declared a federal bank holiday, all forty-eight states had already done so. This feat had been accomplished by the banking wizards of the lame-duck Hoover administration.

The idea had first been introduced by those states most at risk of a financial meltdown. Later, other states joined voluntarily. But in the days and nights before FDR's inauguration, Hoover's banking wizards, fiscal conservatives by both temperament and ideology, had used every means at their disposal to convince the remaining holdouts among the states to declare their own bank holiday. They had even tried to get the outgoing president to declare a federal bank holiday.

Hoover himself toyed with the idea. He made efforts to get the incoming president to agree to a joint declaration. FDR demurred, leading later critics to argue that Roosevelt was determined that he and he alone—certainly not that arrogant and condescending Hoover—would be the knight in shining armor who would single-handedly save the banks.

This is probably quite true. FDR was certainly capable of devious tricks of that sort, unlike the upright Herbert Hoover. Yet everyone who was working on the idea of a federal bank holiday recognized that there was a serious problem with it. Nothing in the Constitution even hinted that it was within the power of the president to make such a declaration.

As we noted earlier, there were those who were willing for FDR to assume dictatorial powers, enabling him to do whatever he chose to fix the American economy. Mussolini would have had no legal obstacle in assuming such powers. Italian fascism had been founded on the idea that the state could and should intervene in the economy and, indeed, any other aspect of Italian life. Even the recently elected Reich chancellor, Adolf Hitler, did not have such powers, though Article 48 of the still-intact Weimar Constitution provided the German president, Paul von Hindenburg, with powers to meet virtually any emergency the nation might face.

But the Constitution of the United States provided no such procedure. Our system of checks and balances, so carefully contrived, prevented any such usurpation of absolute power by the president.

It was this Constitutional logjam that inclined so many progressives to hope that in FDR they had elected a president who was prepared to cut the Gordian Knot of our fussy, stuffy legal system and frankly declare himself dictator. This, however, was much easier said than done.

How exactly does the president of the United States make himself a dictator? By simply throwing out the Constitution? The very idea was preposterous. Though at its inception the US Constitution had many vociferous critics, such as Patrick Henry, by 1932 it was held to be holy writ, divinely inspired by God— or at least by Thomas Jefferson's curious deity, Nature's God. No one dared touch it. Even Adolf Hitler, after assuming dictatorial power, did not tear up the much less revered, and often criticized, Weimar Constitution. It continued in effect until the final days of the Third Reich.

Yet no written document can ever hope to defend itself against those who are determined to twist its clauses and articles for their own purposes, as Lincoln had done. As we saw earlier, it required much legal fudging and sleight-of-hand to transform the insurrection clause in the Constitution into a pretext for the war Lincoln had launched.

Similarly, those who advocated a federal bank holiday were reduced to finding a legal precedent in the Trading with the Enemy Act passed by Congress in 1917 during the First World War, though what trading with enemies had to do with closing down the banks was never made quite clear. Yet all agreed that something had to be done, and, as is usual in such cases, a pretext was invented, proving again that there is nothing so defenseless as the written word.

Latter day admirers of Calvin Coolidge, with his stern belief in a severely limited federal government, have every right to argue that if Coolidge had only run in 1928, instead of retiring from politics, none of this would have happened. This may very well be true. We might even grant that strict adherence to laissez-faire economics might have avoided the Great Depression altogether. But by the time the banking crisis hit, a return to such an economic policy was no longer possible. Indeed, by that time, Adam Smith's invisible hand had developed a serious case of the shakes.

The fundamental thesis of classic laissez-faire economics is that everyone should pursue his or her own economic self-interests and by doing so, all would be well. The invisible hand of the market would take care of any problems.

Yet in the world of 1933, where you could no longer trust your bank not to lose your money, it became your financial self-interest to withdraw it as quickly as possible, lest it perish with the collapse of the bank. Indeed, you might need to fight to be the first in line.

But in 1933, just getting your dollars out of the bank still did not give you the security you needed. After all, how solid was the dollar? Not only was there the general uncertainty caused by the economic catastrophe, but the sensible investor would also have reason to fear that Roosevelt would be in favor of easy money. As previously noted, economic populism had always been on the side of an inflationary policy, going back to the days of Andrew Jackson and up through William Jennings Bryan's call for bimetallism. The "cross of gold" had traditionally been the target of the inflationists. Therefore, the rational economic actor, having withdrawn their money from the bank, would immediately turn around and ask for its worth in gold.

In the early months of 1933, this was still possible. The United States, like the other leading economic powers, was still on the gold standard. Everyone who had a dollar in his pocket had the legal right to demand that it be exchanged for gold, which was exactly what many people were doing. But where now was the invisible hand?

In the banking crisis of 1933, if everyone followed their rational economic self-interest, they would first withdraw their deposits and immediately claim the gold it represented. Yet if everyone actually did this, the entire banking system would collapse, the gold reserves of the United States would swiftly be drained, and the economy would grind to a complete halt. Total disaster would follow, brought about by a complete collapse of trust in the system.

The paradox here is that the only way to save the economy was by persuading people to act irrationally, to turn their gold back into dollars, and return their dollars to the banks, their rational economic self-interest be damned.

This was the real challenge that no banking wizard had the slightest clue how to meet. They had figured out how to shut down the banks. But they had absolutely no idea how to open them again. How could these lame-duck wizards hope to restore the vanished trust that was utterly indispensable in order to get the system on its feet again?

As events were to swiftly prove, FDR was the political magician who was able to restore that trust. No doubt his unwillingness to agree to a joint proclamation of a federal bank holiday reflected his own Machiavellian instincts. He did want to hog all the credit. But at the same time, his political savvy also came into play. Hoover had lost the trust of the people. This was a simple fact. He had been unable to restore it. Another simple fact. Hence, to bring Hoover in any shape or form into the proclamation of a bank holiday would be to endanger the long game FDR was playing. Hoover and FDR together could shut down the banks, but it would be left entirely to Roosevelt to risk opening them again. You couldn't have a bank holiday that lasted forever.

The banking wizards from the Hoover administration offered their own solution. They arranged to have the federal government print more money—money not backed by gold—and then send this money to the banks so that they would have sufficient funds to deal with further panic withdrawals. In addition, they came up with a list of the soundest banks, which would be reopened first, with the next soundest reopening second, and so on down the line.

Of course, there was another way out of the crisis. In one of his ill-fated presidential campaigns, the populist-progressive hero, William Jennings Bryan had proposed a permanent solution to the perennial danger of bank panics: Let the federal government guarantee the deposits of those who trusted their money to bankers. This idea lay dormant for over four decades. FDR and his advisers were fully aware of it. Many of the progressives who supported FDR also championed Bryan's solution. Those with small savings, like Bryan's own supporters, would no longer face financial ruin from the failure of their banks, as had been the rule in the past, so the policy was intrinsically populist.

Indeed, today, when no one is worried about losing their savings and deposits thanks to the FDIC, it may be a challenge for us to fathom why anyone back then would even think of entrusting their money to so frail a vessel as a bank. Yet this is what virtually everyone did and had been doing for over a century, fully aware of the inevitable risk they were taking if their bank failed, as they frequently did.

In 1933, FDR and his close advisors rejected what seems to us an obvious solution. Their reasoning, however, made sense. If bankers knew that the government would cover their deposits no matter what, this would naturally and inevitably lead them to make riskier investments with their depositors' money than they would have done otherwise. So what if they lost the money, since the federal government was prepared to bail them out.

The risk here was a classic case of a moral hazard. This phrase had first been introduced in the seventeenth century in respect to the insurance companies that were then becoming popular and successful. If a person's home was insured, would they be as diligent in keeping it repaired, or in making sure to snuff out their candles at night? They might even be tempted to burn it down themselves, if they could get away with it, knowing that their insurance company would still pay them what the house was worth.

The Savings and Loan crisis of 1980–1995 was the result of the very moral hazard that FDR and his advisors had feared. The men who ran these once venerable institutions decided to extend speculative and unsound loans to customers who were happy to pay a higher rate of interest, only to lose the money due to their own fecklessness. When the customers were unable to repay the loans, the Savings and Loan banks appealed to the federal government to bail them out, and a vicious cycle was soon underway.

FDR's justifiable concern with moral hazard would continue to make him reluctant to undertake many of the programs for which posterity has given him credit. Yet his reluctance to have the federal government intervene in the economy was not due to his pigheadedness alone. FDR frankly regarded such interference with the economy as un-American. And he was right. One of the chief features of American exceptionalism had always been that individuals who had been given the personal liberty to make their own decisions should alone bear the consequences of their decisions, including their bad ones. Helping those who needed help due to circumstances beyond their control was an act of charity, which Americans had always been willing to provide out of their own pockets. But for the government to help those who had made bad decisions was a radical departure from American tradition. In resisting it, FDR was trying to preserve a core principle of American exceptionalism: that the people of the United

States should and could look after themselves and take responsibility for their own decisions.

Roosevelt has often been derided for his lack of original ideas. Like most practical politicians, he never set out to be a great thinker, and he was distrustful of intellectuals. But it would be wrong to conclude that ideas didn't matter to Roosevelt. They just mattered in a different way from how intellectuals think about ideas. FDR's ideas were not conceptual in form; they were deep-seated, visceral convictions, acquired both from his own experience in the world and by the culture in which he was raised. Intellectuals love to bat around ideas, play with, compare them, evaluate them. But this is not how people treat their deepest convictions. They are permanent, impervious to critique, and compelling. During his term in office, intellectuals both inside his administration and outside, were brimming with ideas. Roosevelt had to listen to them all, but in the end, what made up his mind was whether these ideas were consistent with his own deep conviction.

It was FDR's conviction that often put him at odds with his progressive supporters, including those in his own administration, such as Rexford Tugwell. So Bryan's cure for bank panics was off the table for now. Somehow, FDR had to fix the banking crisis without it. The Emergency Banking Act would have to do.

This new law had been cobbled together with astonishing speed by the banking wizards. It was immediately accepted by Congress. Even before he had had time to read it, the Republican leader of the House told his colleagues to give the new president whatever he wanted. It passed both houses in a single day.

In his inaugural address, FDR had proposed reopening the bank on Friday, just a day after the passage of his banking bill, but he then decided to put off this risky venture to the following Monday. Unconvinced that a new law by itself could quell the panic, Roosevelt devised another and quite novel approach to the crisis.

Since its introduction as a means of public communication in the early 1920s, radio had conquered the world. FDR's keen political instincts made him recognize the critical role of the radio broadcast in influencing mass opinion. He quickly mastered it, and he knew his audience. Unlike Mussolini and Hitler, who had also mastered the medium, FDR used his radio addresses not to rave and threaten, but to calm and reassure. Furthermore, in his first fireside chat, FDR was aware that the whole world would be listening to him, anxiously waiting to hear what the new president would say.

On March 12, 1933, a Sunday evening, Roosevelt took the first and perhaps greatest risk of his whole political career. The idea of a fireside chat was not completely new. The amiable Al Smith, with his folksy ways, had used a similar technique as governor. He used radio not to make a formal address, but simply to talk to people, just as if he had his arms around their shoulders for a friendly chat. FDR had followed his example as governor, but never on a subject as critical as how to save the nation from financial collapse. In the face of such a dire emergency, was this really the time for a cozy little chat by the fireplace?

The chat lasted a mere fifteen minutes, but it was heard by sixty million people, only a bit less than half the population then living in the United States.

Quite possibly, Roosevelt was aided by his own lack of sophistication about how banks really worked. There is no worse explainer than someone who knows too much about what they want to explain. In his chat, Roosevelt did not condescend to his listeners; he just tried to explain to them in terms simple enough for both him and his listeners to understand. As the cowboy humorist, Will Rogers, famously quipped, Roosevelt explained banking so well that everyone understood it, even the bankers.

The next day the world held its breath to see what would happen when the most solid American banks once again opened their doors. If all rushed to the tellers' windows in a feverish panic to make withdrawals, then there could be no saving the banks, or the American economy for that matter. But nothing of the sort happened.

People miraculously came in to put their money back into the banks from which they had rushed to withdraw them only a week or so before. The emergency money printed by the federal government was not needed to restore faith in the banks. Somehow, Roosevelt had saved the banks, and he had done this by merely chatting to Americans on the radio. Here, we should pause and ask the question: Could anyone other than Roosevelt have brought the banking crisis to an end? No one at the time thought so. Somehow, the man whom many besides Hoover dismissed as an intellectual lightweight and a rich momma's boy had managed to deliver the goods. What was his secret?

It was certainly not his superior mind. Even those liberal historians who have admired Roosevelt have never claimed that he was a great intellect. Influential columnist Walter Lippmann had described FDR in 1932 as "a pleasant man who, without any important qualifications for the office, would very much like to be President." All this may be quite true, but that only makes the riddle of his success more perplexing.

The only word for what FDR had is charisma. But what makes a politician charismatic in the first place? It seems impossible to provide in advance a list of the qualities required. It cannot be defined the way we define other words used to describe politicians, such as honest, or educated, or handsome. It is the kind of thing that we can only recognize when we see it. Indeed, charisma is like the It Factor—that intangible mysterious quality that makes us adore certain movie stars, root for certain sport figures, and cheer for certain politicians.

All the American populist leaders we have encountered have had an abundance of charisma: Andrew Jackson, Abraham Lincoln, William Jennings Bryan, FDR, and Trump have all had "it," despite the differences in their personal political styles. This suggests that charisma requires the ability of a leader to connect with his people through their emotions rather than through reasoned arguments or labored displays of oratorical eloquence. There are obviously dangers in this appeal to popular emotions. It can lead to the crudest demagoguery, but in the case of FDR, it saved the banks and the American economy.

Yet there is one indispensable quality that all charismatic leaders must have: the gift of giving confidence to others through their own super abundance of confidence in themselves. Andrew Jackson had this gift in spades. It was blazingly blatant. Lincoln was slyer. He often expressed doubts about himself, but when the chips were down, as they were during the crisis of Fort Sumter, it was his own sturdy sense of self-confidence that won over his far more educated colleagues. Between FDR and Trump, it would be difficult to decide who possesses greater self-confidence. That such different personalities could all have charisma only adds to its mystery.

Yet the fact that we cannot unravel this riddle should not tempt us into the gross error of dismissing charisma as a superficial feature of character, of no significant historical import. The banking crisis that confronted the United States in 1933 was resolved by one thing and one thing only: People trusted FDR. He had "it."

2
DID FDR GO TOO FAR—OR NOT FAR ENOUGH?

With the resolution of the banking crisis, not everyone was singing "Happy Days Are Here Again." On his progressive left, there were many who wanted Roosevelt to seize the banking crisis as a pretext for a federal takeover of the banking system. They wanted to replace the chaos of the current disorder with a national bank that would engage in the centralized planning of policy that had become so alluring to many on the American left in the 1930s, inspired by the Soviet system that seemed to outsiders a shining example of the virtues of a centrally planned economic system.

Indeed, according to many progressives of the 1930s, what the United States needed was a Politburo of its own, in order to achieve the dizzying success that Stalin had achieved by means of his famous Five-Year Plan. As the Great Depression dragged on, without any end in sight, increasing numbers of Americans were prepared to accept radical ideas for fixing their nation.

By 1936, as the second wave of the depression set in in America, Hitler's Germany was up and running. Full employment had been achieved. The Third Reich even had to import workers from other countries to staff its bustling economy. Perhaps America needed a dictator like Hitler, though not quite as rough. Meanwhile, the USSR had been completely unfazed by the Great Depression. With the example of other political systems flourishing, the solution was obvious to many: We must become more like them.

The Great Depression became an epochal crisis for the United States only after the many New Deal experiments failed to turn the economy around. Though FDR might have originally thought that he could cure the dismal economy by a charm offensive, reality had by now sobered him. Just as Lincoln had recognized that there could be no return to the old order after the fall of Fort Sumter, FDR had recognized that the economic ideas he had grown up with no longer worked. Yet he persisted in his efforts to keep America as exceptional as he could, given the challenging historical conditions that he faced.

Roosevelt's savvy political instincts were keenly against such fanciful schemes as those proposed by the Soviet-inspired progressives in his own administration with their Five-Year Plans. European fascism, though it had restored the German economy, had no appeal for him whatsoever. Even if the adoption of such alien models of government might rescue the American economy, FDR did not want an America saved at such a cost to its exceptional traditions. Furthermore, FDR had no use or time for ideology, from whichever side of the political divide it came. As all world-historical figures are, FDR was the consummate pragmatic opportunist. He would do what had to be done, but no more.

Roosevelt only changed his mind when his commanding grasp of his country's political sentiment made him recognize which way the wind was blowing. Leading up to the 1936 election, FDR felt a storm coming out of Louisiana. Its name was Huey Long, also known as the Kingfish, the last major politician who tried to revive the populist-progressive alliance that William Jennings Bryan had achieved at the turn of the nineteenth century.

The Great Depression, as it dragged on, had given new life to the economic populism that many assumed had been rendered obsolete by the booming American economy of the 1920s. This presented a problem for FDR. Agrarian populism was not a foreign import. Its supporters were not ideological radicals but farmers and working men and women whose votes were reliably Democratic. First as governor of Louisiana, and then as its Senator from 1932, Long was winning many of them over to his side with his populist message.

Huey Long was cut from the same populist cloth as William Jennings Bryan, though the cut was rougher and the cloth a good bit more tattered. Yet there was no other politician of his day whom FDR feared as much as Long. The patrician Roosevelt saw a serious threat in the very much self-made Kingfish.

A consummate politician himself, Long was a crowd-pleaser. When campaigning in Louisiana, he had to tread carefully between an electorate made up of fundamentalist Protestants and devout Catholics. On the stump, he loved to tell the story of how on Sunday mornings as a child he had hooked up one buggy for his Baptist grandmother to go to church and another for his Catholic grandmother. The tale always went over well with his audience, though when someone inquired whether it was really true, he replied, "Hell, we didn't even have a horse."

In place of FDR's New Deal, Long offered the American people what he called a fair deal. His slogan was "Every man a king." His program was "Share Our Wealth!" And it was gaining a national following from those who thought the wealth needed to be shared among them. Outside of the small socialist camp, no American politician rejected more vehemently the Social Darwinist dogma that held that the unequal distribution of wealth was the natural result of the unequal distribution of talent, energy, and intelligence. Bluntly stated, the rich deserved to be rich and the poor deserved to be poor. To tamper with this arrangement was to tamper with the natural order itself. But Huey Long disagreed.

He had a point. The Great Depression had revealed the shocking disparity that existed between rich and poor, making a travesty of the egalitarianism that had once made the American

Republic unique among the nations of the world. If some went to bed in Hoovervilles under Hoover mattresses and others slept in feather beds in their gaudy mansions, then by what right could they be called equal? Like many latter-day progressives, Long also attacked concentrations of corporate power, especially going after the railroad interests. He deeply distrusted the Eastern Establishment, which he saw as preying on the poor. In many ways, Long was far more interested in battling economic inequality than many of today's so-called democratic socialists, not a few of whom are themselves multi-millionaires.

Yet Huey Long was not a socialist, at least in the European sense of the word. He did not attack the engine of capitalism that had created so much wealth. He did not propose the takeover of industries or advocate the grandiose Five-Year Plans then in vogue in the Soviet Union. Instead, his plan relied on altering the tax and spending policy of the federal government, a minimalist approach that did not require a radical make-over of government, the establishment of an American Politburo, or the overthrow of the capitalist system.

Long had perfect pitch for what ordinary Americans wanted to hear. Share Our Wealth sounded benign; indeed, it appealed to the core American tradition that ennobled the person who was willing to share with others whatever they had, just as the poor people Long talked to were used to sharing their pittance with passing strangers, even with a bum down on their luck. No people had ever been more generous than America's rural poor, and many of them couldn't understand why those who lived in grand houses could not be as generous with their mighty fortunes as the poor were with their less fortunate mites. After Huey Long delivered a national radio broadcast in February 1934, in which he announced his program, millions of Americans formed and joined Share Our Wealth political clubs across the country.

Though Long today is often derided as a vulgar demagogue, even a fascist thug, his proposals would eventually become the principal policy ideas of sophisticated American progressives. They included free health care for all, a guaranteed minimum income, a cap on personal income, an inheritance tax and a tax on wealth.

But Long was no policy wonk with degrees from Harvard, speaking technical mumbo-jumbo to the masses. He was a man of the people. He spoke their language. He could make his ideas clear to crowds of farmers and sharecroppers. He came from the Southern agrarian brand of populism. Early exponents of this tradition included "Pitchfork" Ben Tillman, a colorful character from the backwoods of South Carolina, who served as the governor of his state from 1890 to 1894. Tillman managed to combine economic populism with the most virulent and unprogressive racism. In contrast, Huey Long, though he recognized that he was appealing to die-hard segregationists, avoided racial demagoguery.

The populist revolt that Long had ignited was naturally feared by those whose wealth he planned to share. But it was even more greatly feared by Roosevelt, who saw in Long and his radical programs the greatest threat to his re-election in 1936. FDR, the builder of coalitions, knew that he could not afford to lose the solid South, so loyal to the Democratic Party that in the election of 1932, many Protestant fundamentalists had voted for the Roman Catholic Yankee, Al Smith, in preference to the Republican Hoover.

The Social Security Act that was signed into law by FDR on August 14, 1935, had been designed, among other reasons, to take the air out of Long's populist sails. It did not provide a national minimum income, as Long had proposed—and an astonishingly high minimum income, for that matter. In today's money, under Long's program, the very least a household would receive from the government was between $50,000 and $70,000 a year. In contrast, even the far more modest proposals of the Social Security Act were at first rejected by FDR. He repeatedly warned that there could and should be no "dole" in America.

The dole was another moral hazard, even worse than the FDIC—another program that FDR first opposed but eventually signed into law. The threat posed by the dole was obvious. If people started accepting even temporary handouts from the government, how long would it be before they came to depend on, and even demand, more handouts? The very idea went against one of the core principles of American exceptionalism, based on the virtue of self-reliance, most perfectly embodied in Cooper's Natty Bumppo who even made his own clothes and hunted his own food. Yet FDR's political convictions had to yield to his political instincts. A Wilson or a Hoover might have resisted the need to appeal to Southern populism, but FDR, always the pragmatic opportunist, realized that he had to offer some kind of compromise policy that would not bankrupt the economy as Long's would have surely done.

3
THE PATRICIAN PATERNALIST

Shortly after FDR signed the Social Security Act, Huey Long's populist revolt was stopped dead in its tracks. On September 10, 1935, just as Long was preparing to challenge FDR for the Democratic nomination in 1936, he was killed by gunshots in the corridor of the Louisiana State Capitol building—yet another example of the role that both bad luck and good luck play in the shaping of human history and in the fate of those who try to make it.

In a speech given in 1935, Long claimed that his many political enemies were plotting to assassinate him, even making the sensational charge that gangsters from Chicago were out to get him. Yet in the aftermath of his death, no conspiracy theorists came forward to accuse his many enemies, including FDR, of plotting to murder Long. There were those who suggested that he had not been killed by Carl Weiss, but by his own bodyguards in the crossfire that ensued after Weiss showed his gun.

Here, we have a striking example of a radical change in the American zeitgeist. Few in the age of FDR thought that the government was out to get them, as is widely believed today. Rather, they turned to it for help in their own lives. Today, the ready fund of trust felt by ordinary Americans in their institutions and leaders has been lost, perhaps forever. Many may regard this as a good thing. Yet such paranoia produces its own moral hazard. Could the American people have faced the challenges of the Great Depression and the Second World War if they had been as cynical about government as we have become today? It was largely due to the immense trust the people had in FDR that the Great Depression did not cause the political upheavals that demanded either an outright dictatorship or the adoption of a Five-Year Plan à la Stalin. This trust allowed FDR to pursue a policy of moderate progressivism, less out of conviction than political expediency. It was this policy that earned FDR the title of "traitor to his class."

There is a good deal of truth in this, yet he was not a traitor to the values of the Old Money aristocracy, the stock from which he himself had come and which he always honored. It was the capitalist class made up of rich and successful businessmen and entrepreneurs that hated him most and regarded him as a traitor to their class. But their class was not FDR's idea of real class. In contrast to the plebeian populist Huey Long, FDR was a purebred patrician. To a man of his lofty station, the sense of *noblesse oblige* was virtually innate. He came from the class that was at the top of the social hierarchy, where only those with Old Money belonged. There were many richer than he, but they were usually those obnoxious and vulgar self-made types called the nouveau riche. They had been required to get down and dirty in their struggle to acquire their tarnished lucre. FDR and other members of the Old Money class inevitably looked down their noses at those who had made their fortunes through their own resources.

This was in accordance with the universal law of snobbery. The class right beneath yours is the one that you must work to distinguish yourself from. Whatever they do, you must avoid doing yourself. They will be expected to ape your ways, but they can never hope to do it with the style and panache that distinguishes yours. In the case of Roosevelt, it led him to regard businessmen with a visceral antipathy. By the same universal law of snobbery, those who fall into classes well below your own are considered objects of sympathy. You may care about them, but of course, this concern will inevitably take the form of a paternalistic interest in their well-being.

FDR felt he had to move to Long's populist left out of political expediency, but there may have been a subtler motive for FDR's renunciation of his previous economic and fiscal conservatism. His earlier economic ideas were merely the ideas he had picked up from others—the same ideas that were held by right-thinking members of the upper class. But in his heart, he remained an elite paternalist.

Old-fashioned nineteenth-century paternalism did not try to disguise its intentions or its motives. It was openly and frankly an act of noblesse oblige. It arose from the charitable interest of an elite class in helping those who were below them on both the economic and social ladder, but with the clear understanding that no amount of help could ever raise them to the same level as those dispensing the charities. There were paternalistic slave-holders, like Jefferson Davis's brother, Joseph, just as there were paternalistic factory owners, like the owners of the Lowell Mills in New England. Roosevelt's family, whose wealth came from the rents paid by their tenants, observed the paternalistic tradition of their class. Though many paternalists looked after the people in their charge due to their Christian or humanitarian ideals, it also made good business sense to treat those making you rich with a modicum of respect and kindness.

Paternalism, however, is not an ideology but a habit of the heart, especially to someone like FDR who had been raised in its traditions. Despite the considerable resistance that his brain put up against what he originally regarded as a dangerous flirtation with moral hazards, his heart gave way before the opportunity to play the role of paternalist-in-chief. But by the 1930s, the new progressivism that arose in opposition to Bryan's populism had itself become increasingly paternalistic. The people could not be trusted to look after their own interests—the basic justification for all paternalist rule—therefore, an elite was required to make decisions for them. A Brain Trust was needed to make the right decisions for the masses.

This would become the foundational principle of the modern meritocratic elite that would arise with the enormous surge of college graduates in the postwar period and their assumption of executive and managerial roles at every level of society. But what the meritocratic elite of our own day fails to understand is that paternalism can only work if the people have trust that their leaders are sincerely looking after their interests and share their values. Once the paternalists are exposed as ideological activists, keen on imposing their own alien values on the people, this trust can quickly evaporate, while the days will always be numbered on a paternalistic regime that is both corrupt and incompetent.

FDR was perfectly aware of this. His political instincts were in harmony with his own desire to keep America as much like itself as possible during the great crisis of capitalism. He knew he must not risk the trust of the American people. He also knew that there were limits to how much paternalism they would tolerate. His gift for appearing fatherly came naturally to him. Many wanted to trust him as they would a father—the way they had trusted Washington and Lincoln.

At its core, the Great Depression was a crisis of trust. Trust had to be restored and, as it turned out, FDR was the only one who could achieve this. It is true that FDR's New Deal did not end the economic crisis, but it prevented the catastrophic collapse of public trust in the national government. We could and did eventually recover from the crisis; but it is highly improbable that we could have survived as a nation without the reaffirmation of public trust that FDR, the political magician, was able to bring about virtually by the force of his charismatic personality, his set of deep personal convictions, and his inveterate optimism. It may have all been smoke and mirrors, but it was smoke and mirrors that did the trick.

It is often said that FDR saved capitalism, but the truth is that he preserved as much of the traditions of American exceptionalism as he could under the circumstances. But in addition to fighting against those who wanted to remodel the United States along the lines of European corporate fascism or Soviet central planning or British cradle-to-grave socialism or Huey Long's Share Our Wealth program, Roosevelt also had to fight against the threat to American exceptionalism posed by the political power that had been amassed by the immensely wealthy capitalists of his era, many of whom had learned how to game the system, just as the land speculators of Lincoln's era gamed the Homestead Act. They bought off politicians by the hundreds and had them virtually in their capacious pockets.

Indeed, the capitalist ruling class was the greatest threat that the principles of American exceptionalism had ever faced. The small businesses that had been the hallmark of an earlier America had been crushed by the rise of giant corporations such as Sears and Standard Oil. Big was driving out small, and by this very process, it was systematically threatening the independence of those who had made their living in small ways, as the vast majority of Americans did. Without this source of independence, their dignity was at risk.

To counter the aggressive ambitions of the new capitalist ruling class, some immense counterforce was necessary. You cannot hope to remove an enormous boulder blocking your path by shoving it away. Sometimes you need dynamite.

Due to his immense popularity, FDR was able to deliver America from a ruling class composed of capitalists, not by liquidating them as Lenin would have done, or sending them to re-education camps, like Mao. FDR simply put them in their place.

This is a feat that could only have been performed by a natural patrician like FDR, whose snobbery, derived from his Old Money, made him feel comfortably superior to the vulgar new money of the capitalist class. Just as Lincoln's rise from lowly origins gave him the gumption and the orneriness to defy the advice of the urbane college-educated William Seward, so FDR's sense of aristocratic entitlement gave him the confidence to defy those whom his cousin, Teddy Roosevelt, had called "the malefactors of great wealth."

The fact that FDR was often unfair in his attacks on the rich might well be held against him, just as Lincoln's dismissal of the Confederacy as an insurrectionary rabble was unfair. But the dynamite that is needed to bring down an arrogant and self-satisfied ruling class will inevitably leave many of the innocent wounded. It is an unfortunate fact of life that no ruling class will ever relinquish its power on its own. There will always be a struggle to bring a ruling class down.

In shifting power back to the people, FDR had himself followed a very crooked road. It was not as violent and bloody as the road Lincoln took. But there were skirmishes all along the way and occasionally a big battle. Eventually, and perhaps even despite himself, Roosevelt also got to the end of his road. In the process, he also became a world-historical leader. Both FDR and Lincoln had salvaged as much of American exceptionalism as they could in the midst of epochal crises that threatened to bring the entire American experiment to an end. By doing so, they kept the United States unique among nations, a feat that made both men world-historical. After FDR, just as after Lincoln, America would continue to be the world's last best hope. By another irony of history, FDR, who had radically underestimated the threat of Soviet Communism, created a nation strong enough to meet this threat virtually alone. Furthermore, it was strong enough to protect dozens of its allies around the world.

Yet FDR eventually overreached himself. Immediately after his stunning landslide in 1936, FDR decided that it was time to do something about the Supreme Court that had frustrated so many of his programs, and in this case, the constitutionality was far from clear. Could the president at his own discretion add new members to the Court? Members, of course, who would reflect his own views? Thomas Jefferson had tried and failed to bring his own Supreme Court in line with his ideas. Now it was Roosevelt's turn.

Contrary to popular myth, howls of protest did not instantly rally to the side of the Court. Everyone who supported FDR had become frustrated as the Court struck down one piece of New Deal legislation after another. Two-thirds of Americans had just given FDR his second term. Most of these voters had no problem with FDR's plan.

After all, it was only by tradition that the Supreme Court had exactly nine justices, no more, no less. The Constitution did not specify this number or any number at all. Before 1867, there had been varying numbers of justices on the Court, but after this date, the tradition of nine justices solidified and had come to seem the only number that the Court could hold.

There was nothing in the Constitution that prohibited FDR's plan to "pack" the Supreme Court. Maybe there was no good reason to have only nine justices. Perhaps seven or eleven might do an even better job.

The problem was once you get rid of the tradition set in 1867, what would replace it? If a president who had the backing of Congress could add new justices to the court every time a Supreme Court decision went against him, where would it stop? If twelve, why not twenty-two, if twenty-two, why not thirty-four, and so on.

There was nothing in the Constitution to keep us from going down that road. Only an unwritten tradition stood in the path of an endless packing and repacking of the Court, until the Court had surrendered its essential function of having the last word, short of the passage of a new amendment to the Constitution. If the Supreme Court did not have the final say, then nobody did. Political life in America would have descended into a game of rock, paper, scissors. You cut my paper, but just wait till I get the scissors.

Fortunately, voices began to speak up in favor of keeping the tradition. They had logic behind them, but for many, it was argument enough that there was something close to sacrilege in scrapping a tradition that had been so long respected and observed.

Perhaps his most audacious display of hubris came in 1940, when FDR decided to violate the all-but-sacred tradition that no president should serve more than two terms. Though both Grant and Wilson had flirted with the idea of a third term, only FDR had the audacity to abandon such a revered convention. Yet there was nothing in the US Constitution to prevent him from running for as many terms he could be elected to. Despite shedding supporters for what many critics saw as a coup, FDR was elected for an unprecedented third term. While the Second World War was raging in Europe, FDR in his campaign would emphatically promise American fathers and mothers that he would never, never, never send their boys to war. In retrospect, it is difficult not to see in FDR's gambit a strain of Machiavellianism that might have shocked even the author of *The Prince*, since at the time of his pledge, Roosevelt was moving heaven and earth to get his reluctant nation to send their sons to fight in yet another European war.

CHAPTER TEN
DR. WIN-THE-WAR: FDR TRICKS AMERICA INTO SAVING THE WORLD

1
ROOSEVELT'S DECEITFUL ROAD TO WAR

In addition to saving our nation, FDR is most widely credited with defeating the threat of both European fascism and Japanese militarism. But once again, Roosevelt's role in shaping these momentous events is not that of a Hero out of Thomas Carlyle. Nowhere else in his career would FDR display his genius for pragmatic opportunism more than in his efforts to put American industrial and military might behind what Roosevelt genuinely believed was a battle to determine the fate of civilization. Nowhere else would Roosevelt be more genuinely world-historical than when he was using all his Machiavellian cunning to try to get his nation to fight this battle that ended one epoch and began another.

Franklin Delano Roosevelt wanted the United States to fight in the European conflict, but he faced a series of obstacles. In the aftermath of the Great War that ended in 1918, Americans in general had decided that their entrance into the European conflict had been ill-advised. The old spirit of American neutrality was revived when Congress passed a number of laws designed to make it virtually impossible for the United States to be dragged into another European conflagration.

Is it any wonder Americans were not enthusiastic about pulling Europe's chestnuts out of another fire they had lit themselves through the Carthaginian peace they had imposed on Germany after their last war? It had only been twenty years between the end of the last war and the beginning of the new one. If the Europeans were going to start a world war every two decades, then many Americans had come to believe that this was their problem, and not America's. "Fool me once, shame on you. Fool me twice, shame on me." This quite sensible attitude to European problems of their own making would come to be dubbed "isolationism." This sentiment would later be expressed in the "America First" movement as fears mounted that FDR was slowly dragging the United States into a new world war.

Modern defenders of FDR's duplicitous conduct during the 1940 campaign argue that the president had to deceive the American people in order to get them to do the right thing. And there can be no question that, in his own mind, FDR believed that the war was not only the right thing, but that it was necessary to save civilization from a return to barbarism. Perhaps the United States should have stayed out of the First World War, but the situation in Europe had changed radically in its aftermath. Three empires fell to pieces: Imperial Germany, the Austro-Hungarian Empire, and Czarist Russia. A whole new set of nations had been created by the Treaty of Versailles—Poland,

Czechoslovakia, Yugoslavia—while the tiny nations of Estonia, Latvia, and Lithuania had been given their independence.

But the war had not made the world safe for democracy. It had brought down empires, but it had also spawned a variety of radical ideologies. First, the Bolsheviks seized power in defeated Russia. Mussolini and his fascists came next in Italy. Finally, the National Socialists, under Adolf Hitler, achieved total control of a Germany that was again a rising power. These were not the autocracies of prewar Europe. They represented an entirely new kind of threat.

FDR, as noted earlier, had always hated militaristic states, as did virtually all other Americans. Even Japan, an ally in the First World War, had become intensely militaristic, and like all such societies, it soon embarked on imperial expansion, in China. Italy had also embarked on its own imperial expansion in Africa, and in neither case could the hapless League of Nations stop them. In Nazi Germany, it was becoming evident that Hitler was determined to make his nation once again into a great military power.

To FDR, the resurgence of militaristic empires was a self-evident danger to the future of civilization. Though they did not threaten America directly in the 1930s, in time this could change. In a world divided up among such brutal empires, how much good would America's vaunted geographical isolation do it? As FDR watched events in both Europe and China, a disturbing pattern was emerging. The Third Reich had absorbed Austria in 1938, making clear that the Treaty of Versailles, which had forbidden such a union, no longer mattered to Hitler.

Meanwhile the Japanese were acquiring ever more territory in China, using the new and terrifying weapons that had first been exhibited by the Germans and Italians during the Spanish Civil War, most notoriously during the aerial bombardment at the town of Guernica, the subject of Pablo Picasso's iconic anti-war canvas of the same name. The three belligerent nations had even formed the Tripartite Pact. The Munich Crisis, followed by the German invasion of Poland, the defeat of France in May 1940, and Great Britain's lonely defiance of the Germans, all convinced FDR that Americans were deceiving themselves if they believed that isolationism could save them. To deal with this epochal crisis, FDR began to systematically deceive Congress and the American people about his own intentions.

While promising Americans that they would stay out of the wars both in Europe and in Asia, FDR set out coolly and deliberately to provoke Hitler into declaring war on the United States. He was hoping that the first shot fired by the Germans would set Americans ablaze as the first shot fired by the Confederates had enflamed the North in 1861. In addition, FDR announced his famous Lend-Lease program to aid Great Britain, an agreement that allowed the United States to provide military supplies not only to the beleaguered British but to other future allies as well. Since Great Britain was virtually bankrupt, FDR agreed that it could "delay" payment for them, which in the eyes of critics meant giving our supplies away for free. To dampen the controversy this engendered among the isolationists, Roosevelt again went on the radio and compared what he was doing with lending your neighbor a hose when his house caught fire—another instance of FDR's uncanny ability to frame his most Machiavellian moves under the guise of homespun wisdom. Finally, in October 1941, FDR even began providing the Soviet Union with materials to assist them within days of the German invasion.

Then came the Japanese surprise attack on Pearl Harbor. Hitler himself was certainly surprised. The Germans had no inkling about what their alleged allies had been long planning to achieve. The Führer would have certainly been happier if the

Japanese had obliged him by attacking the USSR from the east, thereby catching Stalin in a vast pincer movement.

After the attack on Pearl Harbor, the American people demanded war. But unfortunately, it was not the war that FDR had worked so hard to get them to demand. So now, thanks to the combination of American and British arrogance and incompetence, FDR was confronted with a war that he did not intend to start, a Pacific War rather than a war in Europe. His situation was analogous to Lincoln's after the debacle of failing to resupply Fort Sumter. But just as Jefferson Davis had thrown Lincoln a lifeline when he ordered the shelling of the garrison on Fort Sumter, so Adolf Hitler, against the counsel of his closest advisors, handed Roosevelt what he had so long sought in vain. On December 11, 1941, the Third Reich declared war against the United States.

If Hitler counted on the war in the Pacific to distract Americans from Europe, he was underestimating FDR, who instantly announced that the defeat of Nazi Germany would be given priority over the defeat of Japan, stunning both his military advisors and the American public who understandably felt much greater hostility toward the treacherous Japanese than they did toward the Germans. Yet few today would dispute Roosevelt's choice.

From that point on, FDR managed the war as he saw fit. Operation Torch had been an idea of Churchill's that FDR adopted despite the opposition of his military advisors. American troops would land in North Africa first. An all-out assault on the fortress of the European mainland was deemed by both leaders as too dangerous in 1941, and Churchill would still consider it too dangerous up until D-Day. Better to creep up the soft underbelly of Europe—an obsession of Churchill's since the last world war.

On the home front, FDR displayed prodigious energy. He assembled a war cabinet that included Republicans as well as Democrats in order to make the war bipartisan, which it quickly became. Pearl Harbor converted most isolationists, who saw it rightly as an attack on their nation. He selected competent leaders from the great American corporations to manage the variety of responsibilities required to carry out a war on two fronts, though he was careful to see that none of his lapsed supporters were given any such positions. He had a long memory for such things.

But it was also on the home front that FDR left perhaps the greatest permanent blot on his own memory by issuing the order to intern American citizens of Japanese descent for the course of the war. The head of the FBI at the time, J. Edgar Hoover, whose job was to ferret out spies and saboteurs, told Roosevelt that there was nothing to fear from the loyal Japanese Americans.

FDR's decision to imprison Japanese Americans, issued on February 19, 1942, faced immediate challenge in the courts. Did the president—or any president—have the constitutional authority to massively disrupt the lives of over 120,000 American citizens whose only crime was that they were of Japanese descent. Yet when the question was finally presented to the Supreme Court, the verdict was 6–3 in favor of FDR. Today, it is impossible to imagine the Supreme Court issuing such a ruling. We would condemn FDR for being a dictator. He exceeded his authority, just as Jefferson, Jackson, and Lincoln all did; but in this case, unlike in theirs, future generations have not thanked but condemned him. But this is the risk that any world-historical leader must take, and that those they lead must accept, however bitterly. Also keep in mind that it would have required only a single terrorist attack by a single Japanese American to have vindicated his policy.

2

A NEW WORLD RISES FROM THE ASHES
OF THE OLD

As the war continued, Roosevelt's America quietly assumed the charge of the war from Great Britain. Much of FDR's political skill was called upon in soothing the egos of vying generals and rival national leaders involved in keeping the war going. It was in his operational control over the war that FDR came closest to dictatorial power, albeit a power limited by the American tradition of preferring carrots to sticks, and even when a stick was necessary, of using only the sticks least likely to cause irreparable injury.

For many, however, an even blacker mark on FDR's record was what is often called the betrayal at the Yalta Conference, held in early February 1945. It is true that Roosevelt used a charm offensive in dealing with the cunning Soviet dictator, as did Churchill. But their behavior must be viewed in its historical context. By the time of the meeting at Yalta, the Red Army had already engulfed Poland and Eastern Germany. Within three months, it would enter Berlin. Both FDR and Churchill were too realistic to expect that Stalin would simply relinquish the territory his immense army had captured, especially given the staggering cost in terms of the millions of Russian lives, both military and civilian. Both leaders knew that Hitler could not be defeated without the Soviet Union. Both leaders knew that neither of their nations were ready for another world war on the heels of one that had just barely finished. Nothing but brute force could have rolled back the tide of the Red Army, and neither leader was prepared to take this dangerous route. They knew that Stalin did not care how many Russian lives another victory would cost. All they could do at Yalta was to try to charm Stalin. They were out of other options. It is certainly possible to argue that FDR was exceedingly naïve in his expectations that Stalin would play nice if the other side did. But that was the result of wishful thinking rather than any plot to betray the nations that would soon fall under Soviet domination.

Many have argued that neither Roosevelt nor Churchill should have been so quick to offer the Soviet Union aid and supplies after the German Wehrmacht invaded the USSR on June 22, 1941. It is reasonable to argue as well that without this bountiful aid, the USSR could not have survived. But once again, the historical context in which these decisions were made is critical in appraising their conduct. Neither leader expected the USSR to survive more than a few months. In 1940, the German Wehrmacht had crushed the French army, considered at the time the strongest in the world, in a little over six weeks. On the other hand, the USSR had struggled to subdue tiny Finland less than two years before. In 1941, absolutely no one outside the Kremlin thought that the USSR was long for this world. Both FDR and Churchill hoped, ideally, that the Soviet Army would fight a suicidal last stand that might weaken the German forces. Once again, history looks very different once we understand the position of those who were forced to make it.

It was a very crooked road by which FDR got American soldiers to return to fight in Europe. Yet in the end, FDR accomplished his greatest world-historical mission. The war left the United States of America the leading nation of the free world. In retrospect, FDR's success may well seem providential. What the epochal crisis of his time called for was not a profound intellectual nor an inflexible idealist nor an engineer with a blueprint, but an immensely gifted Machiavellian opportunist, like Roosevelt—and perhaps only like Roosevelt, a born politician who knew how to use power. No one else could have done what FDR did.

It is true that the New Deal did not achieve its goal of ending the Great Depression, yet the idea of the New Deal had an immense impact in shaping what the American people expected from their government in the future. After FDR, there could be no return to the hands-off governmental approach of Calvin Coolidge. The spirit of the times had rejected that option and demanded a government that really cared—or at least did a good job of pretending to care.

However reluctantly FDR may have adopted many of the New Deal programs for which he is credited, his most lasting achievement was to transform what the American people would come to expect from their government in the future. An activist government became the new ideal. It was expected now to provide assistance to those Americans who had been left behind to finally get ahead. That this was really possible was demonstrated by the remarkable success of one of FDR's last programs.

The GI Bill of Rights was signed into law by FDR on June 22, 1944, a little more than two weeks after the success of D-Day, when Allied forces finally invaded Nazi-held Europe. Officially known by the bland bureaucratic name of the Servicemen's Readjustment Act, it proved to be the most successful of the various government programs to lend a helping hand to those who needed it. It provided subsidies both for GIs pursuing further education and for those buying homes.

The Homestead Act that Lincoln signed into law had tapped into inspiring myths of our great westward expansion. By giving poor and ordinary Americans access to new lands, where they could establish their little farms, Jefferson's dream of a free society kept free by independent property owners could be realized. Though the Act failed in its ultimate purpose, the ensuing "land rush" became part of American mythology. The GI Bill of Rights operated on the same premise: give the people a genuine stake in their society, a home. Unlike the Homestead Act, the Act that FDR signed proved successful beyond anyone's wildest dreams. It vastly expanded the number of those who wanted to make something of themselves, lifting millions of GI's out of the poverty to which they were born and elevating them to the middle class.

The Act also played a critical role in the great economic and population boom that followed America's victory in the Second World War. This boom had been wholly unexpected. Most believed that the end of conflict would mean the resumption of the Great Depression. Instead, with the help of the federal government, the United States that FDR had created would see a stunning economic recovery that would grow the middle class by leaps and bounds.

The GI program might have been advocated by Huey Long, since it had the stamp of the populist-progressive movement all over it. It was unquestionably progressive to give hitherto marginalized members of society the chance to improve their lot, but it was also populist because it was designed to help the descendants of those ordinary working-class Americans who had risked their lives for their country.

One last point before we move on: Did FDR promise too much? Consider one of his most famous ideas, the doctrine of the Four Freedoms. Americans had long taken for granted the freedoms of religion and speech formally granted to them by the Bill of Rights. But they now expected the federal government to provide them with freedom from fear and from want.

The last two freedoms were certainly devoutly to be wished. Our primitive ancestors would have been thrilled to be provided with the freedom from want and fear, a freedom seldom found in pre-civilized societies. The challenge they and their descendants faced was how this could be achieved on earth.

In earlier times, those who had held out the promise of freedom from fear and want had penned their utopian visions of how such a blessed state might be achieved, though those who tried to implement their agendas on earth and not in heaven failed miserably in their pursuit, even when they were only trying to transform their communes into a tiny piece of heaven on earth.

If even these small utopian communities had failed to fulfill FDR's promise of freedom from fear and want, how could a vast and mighty nation like the United States of America expect to do any better? Many of the welfare programs that would later come into vogue demanded an expansion of administrative bureaucracy without notable success in lifting the left-behinds from their poverty. FDR proved correct. There would always be a serious moral hazard with the dole.

Furthermore, the law of diminishing returns applies to helping people as it does to everything else. Some people are easy to help. Help extended to them, as in the case of the GI loans, pays off. At the opposite end of the spectrum are those whom it is impossible to help, try as one might. Today, in the era of woke liberalism, it is mainly these hopeless cases that receive the most attention from woke liberals: homeless drug addicts, shoplifters, repeat and professional criminals, even convicted illegal immigrants.

That was the world-historical challenge that FDR left us. Eight decades later, it still remains ours. Yet, by one of those ironies that have already cropped up so often in our survey of the American past, the paternalistic welfare state that had been established for the purpose of eliminating want resulted in millions of Americans who, by 2016, were loudly demanding to be granted a Fifth Freedom—freedom from the rule of a bureaucratic elite that regarded itself as a natural governing class on the basis of its superior "merit."

CHAPTER ELEVEN
DONALD TRUMP AND THE CRISIS OF OUR TIME

1
THE REVOLT OF THE ELITES

Hegel believed that world-historical figures could only arise during an epochal crisis, when a dying old order gave way to a new one. We have examined the crises that both Lincoln and FDR had to face, but what is the crisis that Trump faces today? For many of his detractors, Trump himself is the epochal crisis: an American Hitler who, backed by his fascist supporters, poses an existential threat to our democratic traditions and institutions. As Peggy Noonan put it in *The Wall Street Journal*: "This is what it looks like when establishments fail."

All epochal crises are brought about by the failure of an existing establishment to rise to new challenges. However well it might have handled the challenges of the past, it is no longer able to resolve those of the dawning epoch. At exactly what point our current crisis began to unfold is unclear, but in 1995, historian and social critic Christopher Lasch published a prescient book, *The Revolt of the Elites and the Betrayal of Democracy*, in which he exposed the dangerous fault lines that were increasingly dividing ordinary Americans, representing around 80 percent of our population, and an elite of around 20 percent.

According to Lasch, this new elite lived in a different world from the vast majority of the nation. Its members were college-educated and affluent, with considerable social status. So what were they in revolt against? The answer, increasingly clear, is that they were revolting against the power of non-elites, otherwise known as democratic rule by the people, of the people, and for the people.

In 1930, the Spanish philosopher José Ortega y Gasset published *The Revolt of the Masses*, which Lasch intentionally echoed in the title of his book. Ortega wrote at a time of rising fascism in Europe, which he blamed in large part on mass media, particularly the power of radio to carry the dictator's voice into the homes of ordinary citizens. Mass media, in the sociological discourse of his day, produced "mass men"—which is to say, people who don't think for themselves but simply repeat slogans fed to them by master propagandists like Mussolini and Hitler. In short, they were conformists—sheep—worthy of contempt by intellectuals and experts. (Although, let's not forget there were plenty of intellectuals in Europe and the US who embraced fascism as a progressive force.)

Now we have come full circle: Lasch's new elite—consisting of the college-educated children of the postwar baby boom—began its rise by revolting against what they saw as the mass-induced conformity of America in the fifties. Their libertine attack on traditional standards of behavior and decency reached its shrill peak during the sixties, when virtually every American tradition came under merciless assault. The outcome was the rise of a new meritocratic elite, composed of men and women who had achieved positions of power over ordinary Americans, but had nothing but contempt for their conformist ways.

Journalist Chris Bray describes how this attitude today not only pervades elite institutions and media but has led to a kind of derangement, which those institutions project upon the rest of us as received wisdom:

> This derangement, which cannot call a spade a spade, isn't organized by a coherent ideology. It's organized, instead, by a shared contempt. As Christopher Lasch wrote 30 years ago, a set of overlapping status groups have perceived themselves as a "new elite," built around their sense of America as a dark and ugly society. The institutional Left understands itself as high-status, living exclusively in an echelon created by a common opposition: a disgust for an "incorrigibly racist" and backward country. They're self-isolating, withdrawing from a culture they regard as provincial and bigoted. They see themselves as an "expert class" that the country is too dumb to properly obey.
>
> "The new elites," Lasch wrote, "are in revolt against 'Middle America' as they imagine it: a nation technologically backward, politically reactionary, repressive in its sexual morality, middlebrow in its tastes, smug and complacent, dull and dowdy.... It is a question whether they think of themselves as American

at all." [Source: https://tomklingenstein.com/the-end-of-their-authority/]

There have been many societies in which the governing elites had social and economic advantages that set them apart from common folk, yet they shared the same basic values and traditions. The nineteenth-century British upper class was deeply convinced that it should be in charge, but it held a common set of fundamental beliefs with the lower orders. All agreed that Great Britain was the greatest nation in the world, and all looked down on those countries that had the misfortune to be on the wrong side of the English Channel. All were intensely proud of their magnificent history; all prized their ancient rights and liberties as English citizens.

In addition, all shared the Judeo-Christian heritage; all held the Bible to be a sacred and inspired text. They congratulated themselves on their unique ethos of fair play. They all revered the English Constitution, though it was not a written document like ours but a collection of customs, precedents, and traditions passed down from earlier generations. They had no truck with tyrants, despots, or dictators. Like Gilbert and Sullivan's *Pirates of Penzance*, they loved their queen. Naturally, there were a number of intellectuals who wanted to reform the British system from top to bottom, like Jeremy Bentham and John Stuart Mill, but neither the ruling class nor the masses had much use for, or interest in, their radical ideas.

The meritocratic elite that came to dominate the American government and corporate world after the Second World War also shared the values and traditions of ordinary Americans. But by the time Lasch wrote his book, there had been a radical change in the nature of America's elite. For the first time in American history, intellectuals with radical ideas for improving society had virtually seized the power they had always longed to wield.

To put it as mildly as possible, the legacy of intellectuals in power has not been without blemish. Millions of human beings have died as a result of these intellectuals' bright ideas for radically transforming the established social order. In each case, the intellectuals in charge declared all-out war on the customs and traditions of the society that they were hoping to transform into utopias. Perhaps the most egregious example of this phenomenon was the case of Pol Pot. Obligingly educated in revolutionary history by French Marxists at the Sorbonne, his utopian vision of progress required a genocidal civil war in Cambodia. But Pol Pot was only following in the bloody footsteps of Lenin and Mao, intellectuals who saw human beings merely as historical abstractions to be either re-educated or eliminated in pursuit of the socialist dream.

Once confined to campuses, where it was thought they could do little harm, by the beginning of the twenty-first century, intellectuals had taken full control of the American meritocracy. Under the administrations of first George W. Bush and then Barack Obama, intellectuals began to shape American policy to an extent that they had never done before.

Traditionally, each party had adopted the policies that their voters wanted in a bottom-up system of representative government. Each had built coalitions made up of various and distinct interest groups. Both Democrats and Republicans had come to count on their traditional bases, and none risked offending their faithful supporters by advocating policies that had no appeal to them. This sound and prudent approach had worked well for both national parties. The last Democratic president of the twentieth century, Bill Clinton, had been especially adept at listening to voters and building winning coalitions in the old-fashioned way.

Political parties that listen to their voters and cater to their interests can be marked safe from a populist revolt. But the same cannot be said when a party is in the hands of intellectuals who, rather than listening to voters, are convinced that the voters should listen to them. This is what happened to both the Republican and Democratic parties in the twenty-first century.

Disregarding their traditional bases, the two parties turned to intellectuals (a.k.a. Ivy League grads) for advice. The Democrats could reliably depend on liberal academics from the most prestigious universities for their ideas. The short supply of conservative academics, however, led to the emergence of a well-funded network of think tanks, magazines, and alternative media outlets to address their "idea gap" with Democrats. Each of these think tanks had its own ideological brand of conservatism that it wanted to promote and its own pet projects to propose, as did the liberal academics.

The new role given to intellectuals as shapers of government policy dramatically shifted American politics from the traditional tug-of-war among various interest groups to a conflict of ideologies. Since ideology matters a great deal to intellectuals, and very little to the average voter, both parties ran the risk of alienating many of their traditional supporters by pursuing their ideological fixations.

Over time, the meritocratic elite—like all historical elites—began to exhibit the features of a self-perpetuating caste through a combination of credentialism, intermarriage, the accumulation of wealth, and the monopolization of managerial roles across a wide range of institutions, both public and private. While not necessarily a conscious strategy, the pattern ultimately results in the emergence of a ruling class with a well-formed ideology that justifies its power and privileges. Ironically enough, if not for their panicked response to Donald Trump, this incipient ruling class would have remained largely invisible. But Trump forced them to show their hand, and now it cannot be unseen.

2
THE TRIUMPH OF THE EGGHEADS

Intellectuals had long played a role in American politics. Madison was an intellectual, and so too was Thomas Jefferson. The radical Republican Charles Sumner was an intellectual as well. FDR had even assembled a team of intellectuals for his famous Brain Trust. The Cold War also saw the ascendancy of intellectuals, best symbolized in that era by the RAND Corporation. As president, John F. Kennedy launched an era of "New Frontiers" and hired a host of "whiz kids" like the former Ford Motor Company president, Robert McNamara, whose team of quantitative eggheads was given responsibility for strategic planning in Vietnam. The failure of "the best and the brightest" in pursuing victory in this distant war was noted at the time, yet faith in "the best and the brightest" continued unabated. They were put in charge of various top-down social engineering programs of the Great Society and the War on Poverty, neither of which produced the intended results.

Yet there was a major difference between the role played by intellectuals in the 1960s and the one they began to play in the twenty-first century. In the former case, both Kennedy and Johnson called the shots. The causes they promoted were their own and were, at the time, largely popular causes as well. The assignment of the intellectuals under both presidents was to use their technical skills to bring about the success of the programs and policies determined by the president for whom they worked. Hence, the failure of these policies may not have been the fault of the technocrats, but rather due to the overly idealistic goals that had been set for them by their respective presidents.

This changed under George W. Bush. His best and brightest were no longer technocrats following directives. They were now the ones who were designing policy, rather than merely implementing it. The inspiration for the ill-fated invasion of Iraq in 2003 came from the group of neoconservative intellectuals and bureaucrats who had assured the president that the American invaders would be greeted by jubilant crowds, expressing their gratitude to Bush for having liberated them from the tyrant, Saddam Hussein. Furthermore, the same neocons had promised Bush that once Iraq had become an oasis of liberal democracy, the other Arab nations would swiftly follow suit. They were dead wrong, though this didn't keep the neocons from continuing to play a considerable role in American politics, coming together in a united front against Donald Trump in all three of his campaigns for the presidency.

George W. Bush did not consider himself an intellectual. Although a graduate of Yale, the second Bush went to great pains to represent himself as a man of the people. Barack Obama, on the other hand, presented himself as an intellectual. He had once commented that if he could be allowed to talk to ordinary Americans in their own living rooms, he was certain he could persuade them that he was right. It is the role of the intellectuals, after all, that people should listen to them, in contrast to that of the politicians who actually listened to the people.

Unsurprisingly, under the Obama administration, the fatal intellectualization of American politics ramped up. Virtually all of Obama's policies were designed by the liberal intellectuals who had assumed the helm of his administration. As intellectuals and credentialed "experts" replaced seasoned political operators, the tried-and-true wisdom of ward heelers was cast aside in favor of the pet causes espoused by liberal intellectuals and progressive academics.

The response of many Americans to the intellectual takeover of their politics was understandably confused. Labels like fascist, socialist, and communist were resurrected from the past and applied to the current political situation—a sign of the extent to which even ordinary Americans had come to think of politics in ideological terms. The truth was different. It was the old story of an elite that was seeking to become a ruling class and was willing to use any means at its disposal to obtain its goal. The fact that the new elites claimed to be the intellectual superiors of those whom they set out to govern was nothing new. This had been the dream of all utopians from the time of Plato, though in every case in which intellectuals were given actual power to shape events, things went terribly wrong. In his attempts to create philosopher kings out of the tyrants of Syracuse, Plato failed miserably, though without the immense human toll incurred by later philosopher kings, like Lenin, Mao, and Pol Pot.

This blatantly obvious problem, clearly borne out by the historical record, might have persuaded those less eager for power to let ordinary people make their own decisions. But our meritocracy was built on the self-serving myth that, unlike all previous elites, it could be trusted to know what it was doing, since it was a genuine meritocracy based on intelligence and talent, not on fighting ability, inherited titles, or wealth. This meant that its members *had* to be smarter than ordinary people. It was their superior brain power that earned them the right to be elites in the first place. To admit that their decisions were prone to be no better, and often worse, than those made by ordinary people would have denied the liberal elites' very reason for being. And that was unthinkable.

3
THE ANTI-POPULIST POLITICS OF THE NEW MERITOCRACY

Lasch's book would be the first to warn of the dangers of the new meritocracy but although the book received much attention, it failed to put an end to the revolt of the elites. Indeed, rather than recognizing the potential risk of a popular backlash, the meritocracy only grew more emboldened. A handful of thoughtful liberals, like economist Thomas Frank, warned that the Democratic Party was in danger of losing its operating base in the American working class by virtue of its disastrous pursuit of progressive ideological fads. It was as if the Democrats had consulted a hot-shot Madison Avenue advertising agency and asked them to craft programs with the sole purpose of alienating and repulsing the very working men and women upon whom the traditional Democratic coalition had been based. But the Democrats would not listen to the wise and sound counsel of traditional liberals. They chose instead to abandon their working-class base and to become the unofficial party of the meritocratic Establishment.

By the end of the Obama administration, the power of the Establishment rested on a number of formidable pillars. It controlled the immense and Byzantine apparatus of the administrative state, unelected bureaucrats full of bright ideas about how Americans and their business should be ruled and regulated. The liberal elites controlled the major newspapers and media outlets. They decided what we saw on television and cable. They told us what everyone was talking about—and who knew better what everyone should be talking about than those who were doing the talking?

Our liberal elites also held sway over American institutions of higher learning. In public schools, it was they who decided what our children should be taught, which, needless to say, meant teaching them to believe exactly what they wanted them to believe.

They also dominated Hollywood. They made films and TV shows to get their message across to the masses. They had scads of rich and wacky celebrities on board to make sure their message reached even the remotest outposts of the American boondocks. They were also in the process of trying to corner the market on social media. They teetered on the verge of achieving a cultural hegemony over the minds of ordinary Americans, having already won over to their side the affluent college-educated crowd. Their persistent emphasis on "messaging" revealed their underlying contempt for a public who they believed could be swayed like sheep by the scripted blandishments of empty-headed pop stars.

Gradually, it became clear that the hubris of the liberal administrative and cultural elite had brought upon itself the fate that inevitably awaits the arrogant and terminally smug. Nemesis was on the way. It was coming in the form of a populist revolt. Ordinary Americans began to feel that they were being left out of the national debate. They began to feel no one listened to them or even cared what they thought. And they were right. They watched as decisions were being made by the liberal elite as to how they should live, what words they could utter, what opinions they were permitted to have, even in what foolish wars their sons and daughters would be sent off to fight.

If we look at the causes that have dominated the political discourse of twenty-first-century America, we will find an obvious common denominator. None of them began as popular causes, reflecting the views of ordinary Americans. More often, they went against their views. Although Americans wanted revenge for 9/11, few dreamed of using military force to spread liberal democracy throughout the Middle East. This was the idea of the neocons.

The people didn't suddenly demand gay marriage, not even most gay men and women. It went deeply against the grain of the majority of Americans who still believed in what overnight was reduced to the clearly out-of-date "traditional" marriage. But many of the elite, including those who regard themselves as conservatives, went along with the idea. But if someone is prepared to overthrow one of humanity's oldest traditions, it may be asked, what exactly was the point of being a conservative?

Americans did not wake up one day, alarmed by their air-conditioning bills, and demand that something be done about global warming. Unless they had heard it on the news, they would never have suspected it to be "the greatest existential threat" that humanity had ever faced, as President Biden put it. Once more, this was a cause championed by the elite, and not the people, who had to be shown graphs and statistics and lectured by Al Gore and other celebrities to persuade them that they needed to be alarmed. They had to be taught that the science was "settled"; they had to be shown forlorn pictures of stranded polar bears.

The problem was that ordinary people had no personal experience of climate change, unlike their firsthand and daily experience of changes in the weather. Weather is real; climate is an abstraction. We feel the first; we can only speculate on the second. This meant that ordinary people had to take the word of the climate activists who warned of the existential threat ahead. The people would simply have to trust the meritocracy to deal with this unprecedented crisis.

The host of woke causes that unites the modern Democratic party could certainly never claim to be popular in origin. On the contrary, they all seemed explicitly designed to offend traditional sensibilities and values. The attack on white Americans in the name of anti-racism was perhaps the most extreme case of a cause geared to antagonize as many voters as possible, though the woke insistence that men who called themselves women should be able to compete in women's sports was a close runner-up.

In contrast, there was a wide of variety of issues that deeply disturbed ordinary Americans, but which were not being addressed by the liberal media and administrative class. There was the hollowing out of America's industrial base and the export of American factory jobs to Mexico and China, leading to the collapse of regional economies and a range of societal ills including addiction, crime, obesity, depression, and suicide, all of which were ignored by the bicoastal elites and their media organs. These were the "forgotten" men and women whom Trump claimed to represent and on whose behalf he vowed to make America great again.

The movement Trump lead would be characterized by Democrats and their media allies as a reactionary racist attempt to return America to the days of white supremacy. But in hindsight, it is better understood as a counterrevolution against the sweeping attempt by our elites to radically transform the country in their woke liberal image, much as the Jacobins sought to transform the way French people thought, spoke, and dressed, the holidays they observed, and even the months of the year. The elites' inability to see all this is testimony to the seamless, self-justifying ideology that they cooked up in liberal universities, imposed through their control of private and public institutions, and enforced through their monopoly on national discourse. In the end, as with all monopolies, it served them—and the country—very poorly.

CHAPTER TWELVE
TRUMP VERSUS THE POLITICS OF ELITE SNOBBERY

1
THE POPULIST REVOLT BEGINS

The first stirrings of the coming populist revolt began with the Tea Party movement. The movement emerged from the 2008 financial crisis, with its catalyst occurring on February 19, 2009, when CNBC commentator Rick Santelli called for a new "Boston Tea Party" in response to President Barack Obama's mortgage relief plan. Santelli's call for a Chicago Tea Party to protest government intervention quickly gained traction, resonating with those who resented and felt burdened by the bailout, which favored the "one percent" of affluent Americans over the 99 percent of common people.

There was nothing unusual in Americans complaining about taxes. This was how the American revolution began. The right of American patriots to resist British efforts to impose even an insignificant and largely symbolic tax was part of their radical Whig heritage. Yet though the Tea Party movement represented only a rather small sliver of society, the meritocratic elite attacked it as if fighting off the ravaging hordes of Attila the Hun. Decent and quiet citizens, who made a big deal of holding parties where they sipped tea and talked politics, were ferociously villainized by their betters in the media.

Perhaps the most significant result of the Tea Party was that it exposed the true colors of the meritocratic Establishment. Whatever ideological differences its members might have had among themselves, they immediately united in the face of a perceived common enemy: the discontented ordinary Americans who dared to have political opinions of their own.

Pundits from both parties were united in scorn for the movement. They gleefully derided the Tea Partiers' lack of educational credentials, their lack of sophistication, their lack of social status. David Brooks, a pundit whose finger is always on the pulse of the right-thinking elite, quipped that they were "Walmart hippies." Certainly no one Brooks had ever shared cocktails with would be caught dead in a Walmart.

But in what sense could these hard-working and family-oriented Americans be regarded as hippies? They were not dropouts from society. On the contrary, they were politically committed—this was, in fact, what offended their betters. They demanded a government that once again listened to the people.

Like most pundits of the time, Brooks was looking for an unflattering historical analogy to explain (or explain away) the new libertarian-populist movement. This is the normal way educated people have of understanding what is new: by discovering its resemblance to something old. This drawing of historical analogies makes them look clever and learned, but it virtually guarantees that they will miss what is new and significant in the phenomenon they are considering. By calling the Tea Partiers Walmart hippies, Brooks was also perhaps indulging in a bit of wishful thinking. Just as the hippies had been a transient cultural aberration that had come and gone, like the fad it was, this too would be the fate of the equally meretricious Tea Party, which many Democrats pooh-poohed as an "astroturf" phenomenon financed by the nefarious Koch brothers. Hence, Brooks and other critics missed that they were witnessing the first tremors of the political earthquake to come. But behind the smokescreen of their smug rejection of the Tea Party's naïve politics lay the real motive for their contempt. It was simple class prejudice, otherwise known as snobbery: "These people were beneath us."

This was also the approach taken by our meritocratic Establishment when in 2008, John McCain chose Sarah Palin, the popular governor of Alaska to be his running mate. The meritocracy had no issue with McCain. Its members felt he was one of them. But Sarah Palin was certainly not.

Palin instantly became the standard-bearer of the disenfranchised Walmart crowd, thereby becoming the first genuinely populist hero of our time—a fact that became obvious when she spoke at the Republican National Convention. The crowd may have dutifully nominated John McCain, but it was Sarah Palin they loved, Sarah Palin who lifted them from their seats, Sarah Palin they stamped and cheered for.

Naturally, the American meritocratic Establishment turned up its nose at her. It ridiculed her ignorance and gleefully jumped on the many conspicuous gaps in her knowledge of the world, neglecting her sound grasp of the many practical issues that properly concern the governor of a state like Alaska including the management of fisheries, mining, forestry, energy exploration, and the problems of indigenous peoples. The Republican campaign, meanwhile, decided that Sarah Palin badly needed an education, and they inflicted upon her lessons in history, geography, and world affairs as if she were Eliza Doolittle, taken from the gutter for a bet. The charismatic charm that had won over the Republican convention quickly faded under the dreary duty of trying to remember the capital of Kazakhstan and the yearly output of bicycles built in Peru.

Yet if there was to be a genuine populist revolt in our time, it would need a charismatic leader of its own, someone who could directly express the frustration and anger of the millions of working-class Americans who were being disinvited from the dinner table upon which they themselves had set the dishes and for which they themselves had cooked the meal.

No one from either the Democratic or the Republican Party appeared to pick up the populist standard that Palin had been unable to carry. This was itself a sign that both parties had lost touch with the sentiments of ordinary voters, deferring instead to the causes championed by the elite. This meant that if there was to be a convincing leader of the populist revolt, it would have to be a political outsider.

2
ENTER TRUMP

On June 16, 2015, Donald Trump announced that he was running for the presidency of the United States. By any standard, Trump was a political outsider, far more so than either Jackson or Lincoln. Trump had never held a political office.

Born into considerable wealth, Trump, as a boy, had attended the exclusive Kew-Forest School through seventh grade. Considered an unruly student, he was sent by his father to the New York Military Academy, after which he attended Fordham

University for two years, where he toyed with the idea of going into show business. After deciding to pursue a more orthodox business career, he transferred to the prestigious Wharton School and graduated in May 1968 with a BS in economics.

Trump's career in business has long been the subject of controversy. His detractors have pointed out every shady deal he made over the course of many decades, the loans he defaulted on, the bankruptcies he declared. Yet it was impossible to deny that Trump had managed to become a very rich man in the process. But Trump was not content with merely being a billionaire. In 1987, with the help of a ghost writer who later turned conspicuously against him, he published a book entitled *The Art of the Deal*, which quickly became a *New York Times* bestseller. The book's title would become his brand, and Trump would subsequently portray himself as the consummate deal maker, first in business, then later when he entered politics, though the significance of his deal-making style of politics would only become apparent during his presidency.

In 1985, Trump began his rise as a media star. At first, he appeared in cameo roles in TV shows and movies, famously appearing briefly in *Home Alone 2*. He also became involved in the pro-wrestling scene, where he may have picked up his aggressive style of belittling and demeaning his political opponents. But his career in show business really took off in 2004 when he began hosting the reality show *The Apprentice*. By now, Trump had become a household name, as he had long intended it to be. The show was immensely successful, and when Trump finally left it in 2015, it was to run for the presidency.

Despite the fact that Trump had never held office, he had long been a political player. In 1987, Trump paid for a number of full-page ads in leading newspapers to express his ideas on both American foreign policy and the federal deficit. In 1988,

Trump was said to have spoken with Lee Atwater, who was running George H. W. Bush's campaign, to ask if Bush would consider Trump as his running mate. He was turned down. In 2000, Trump had entered the primaries for the Reform Party of the United States but dropped out of the race after a few months. In 2011, he contemplated mounting a campaign against Barack Obama, who was running for his second term, but thought better of the idea.

Trump's decision to run for the presidency in 2015 nevertheless caused a media sensation. He was, if nothing else, the most colorful and media-savvy politician in decades. He had a genius for grabbing attention and cared little whether the press coverage of his campaign was negative or positive. He might have taken his political strategy from Oscar Wilde's famous quip that the only thing worse than being talked about is *not* being talked about. And soon Trump became the candidate that everyone was talking about.

Trump drew howls of mockery from the media establishment when he resurrected the old canard of President Obama's foreign origin and supposed lack of a birth certificate. Trump would later withdraw the allegation, but it had served its intended purpose. It had won him much negative media attention, but it had helped to establish a common cause with his future core supporters, who tended to believe that Obama was not quite a legitimate president. There was, after all, something indefinably "foreign" about Obama. Many wondered how a man with an African father, who had been raised abroad in a Muslim country, could represent traditional American values. Equally alienating was his wild popularity among European elites, his smug self-assurance, and the whiff of Ivy League elitism he gave off. Many voters were deeply offended by his infamous comment that during economic hard times, ordinary Americans instinctively clung to their guns and religion, blaming their problems on immigrants. But as the campaign progressed, Trump made it perfectly clear that his presidency would be just as opposed to the policies of George W. Bush as to those of Barack Obama.

In the early days of the Republican primaries, the smart money was on Jeb Bush to seal the nomination. As a popular governor of Florida, and the son and brother of two former presidents, his position seemed unassailable. But during the Republican debate in December 2015, Trump blasted both George W. Bush and the Iraq War that he had launched and presided over. Liberal pundits did not know what to think. As *Vox* observed, "Trump went further even than most Democratic politicians would, calling the war 'a tremendous disservice to humanity'—adding that it achieved nothing whatsoever, except to leave the Middle East 'a total and complete mess.'" In a later debate, Trump would go even further in his attacks on the war that most Republicans were still trying to defend, calling it "a big fat mistake," adding that the Bush administration had "lied" about Iraq having weapons of mass destruction. By this point, it had become abundantly obvious that Trump was running not only against the Democratic Party of Barack Obama but also against the Republican Party of the Bush dynasty.

Prior to the advent of Trump, presidential candidates tended to be the choice of the party insiders, but in the election of 2016, both parties were confronted with outsiders who showed surprisingly strong support among primary voters: Trump for the Republicans, Bernie Sanders for the Democrats. These two outsider candidates each represented one wing of a broad-based populist revolt against a political establishment that both agreed had become corrupt and was increasingly seen as an elitist bought-and-paid-for "uniparty" with the corporate media as its compliant tool.

The meritocratic Establishment was suddenly under attack by both traditional Democratic and traditional Republican voters. Fortunately for the Establishment, it still controlled the powerful apparatus of the mass media, which allowed it to declare when a candidate was too extreme, as both Trump and Sanders were quickly deemed to be. Furthermore, the establishment media had so perfected the tools of propaganda that it was left up to them to decide even who was conservative and who was liberal. These labels had nothing to do with anything of genuine political substance but served rather as signals to guide voters to support the candidate of the Establishment's choice. The fact that Trump has supported a variety of liberal causes in the past (and also donated to Democratic candidates) did not keep the media from labeling him a conservative, lest naïve liberals actually be tempted to listen to what he was saying instead of what the media said he was saying—which were often two quite different things.

It was around this time that the phrase "the liberal media" gained currency as a partisan term of abuse. Americans were long accustomed to newspapers and magazines that were either liberal or conservative. The late 1990s, however, saw the rise of a conservative reaction to what was seen as the liberal monopoly on public opinion. Talk radio became an alternative for conservatives, with Rush Limbaugh alone gathering millions of dedicated followers. This success was followed up as the internet offered new ways of communicating conservative ideas to the interested public. Cable news also entered the scene. The Fox channel quickly became both the favorite news source for conservatives and a convenient whipping boy for liberals, who, despite their claims of being open-minded, would have died before watching the channel they wittily (in their own minds) dubbed "Faux News." This approach also served to declare information gathered from Fox News beyond the pale of respectability, unsuitable even for entertainment. Yet by refusing to acknowledge any of the legitimate issues raised by Fox during a succession of Democratic regimes, this cynical strategy ended up undermining the liberals' own credibility.

Moderate Americans, on the other hand, who were open to both sides, were increasingly disturbed by liberal media's abandonment of traditional standards of decency and fairness in dealing with the issues and personalities of the day. They became dismayed by the concentrated effort of virtually all the liberal-leaning outlets to attack both Trump and his MAGA movement and to attack them in the exact same way, repeating the exact same thing—for example, "the walls are closing in on Trump"—and rehearsing daily liberal talking points like Aristophanes's chorus of frogs. All of that naturally led many to conclude that they were dealing with a single like-minded entity, henceforth known as *the* liberal media, an octopus with many tentacles.

Thus, despite the fact that Trump had outdone liberal Democrats in condemning the Iraq War, he was dubbed a conservative. By the same perverse logic, political positions that once had bipartisan support, such as securing our borders and obtaining energy independence, were suddenly treated as the manifestations of a narrow and bigoted mind. Indeed, as it became increasingly evident that Trump's string of primary victories would grant him the Republican nomination in 2016, it was no longer enough to scare off liberals by merely calling Trump a conservative. A whole thesaurus of invective was now routinely thrown at Trump. Behind every single one of his policy initiatives, including those previously supported by Democratic presidents, lay a malign and sinister motive. Trump did not want to stem the flow of illegal immigrants crossing our southern border because the vast majority of voters wanted it stemmed, but because he was a racist who hated people of color. From there, it was an easy step to denouncing anyone who approved of Trump's border policy as racists as well. Soon they would also be tagged with the epithets that the establishment media began to manufacture against Trump—he was not only a racist but also a misogynist, a homophobe, a transphobe, a xenophobe. Finally, his portrayal as a populist demagogue reflected the liberal elite's view of populism as a reactionary impulse based in fear and loathing of the Other. It was axiomatic among this elite that ordinary white Americans were full of hate and were determined to keep non-white Americans in their place.

This was the logical consequence of the media's mission to portray Trump as a fiend and a monster. Who with any decency would vote for such a miscreant? The brush that the media used to smear Trump would inevitably smear those who supported him. This alone marked a turning point in America's political history. By vilifying half of the electorate as fascists or hypnotized cult followers, the meritocratic Establishment was escalating the politics of snobbery into its guiding principle.

This unprecedented assault on American voters by the establishment media should have been the big news of the day. There was no surer sign that the United States was in the midst of an epochal crisis than watching elite pundits heap buckets of outlandish abuse upon the ordinary working-class Americans who showed up at Trump's enormous rallies. True to form, the media elite employed the same snobbish put-downs that had been so effective in dealing with the Tea Party movement and Sarah Palin, assuming it would work equally well against Trump and his ebullient fans.

The establishment media could not insult his supporters enough. They were called ignorant rednecks, patriarchal Christian nationalists seeking to create a *Handmaid's Tale*-like dystopia, reactionary racists motivated by a retrograde belief in white supremacy. They were white trash, hillbillies, hicks. The media could not resist trying the same approach with Trump himself. They ridiculed him for preferring a McDonald's cheeseburger to a fancy meal at the posh restaurants where they were accustomed to dining. McDonald's didn't even have a wine list.

Trump's vulgarity also made a fine target, for it was quite genuine. He didn't pretend to like Big Macs for a photo op. He really loved them. The liberal media even claimed that Trump had a golden toilet—a boorish display more suitable to a plumber who had won the lottery than a presidential candidate. (There is no evidence of his ever having owned such a thing.) Then there was Trump's penchant for calling his opponents belittling and insulting names, his braggadocio, his playing to the crowd at his rowdy rallies—antics that seemed more appropriate to a man aspiring to clinch the pro-wrestling championship of the world than a man campaigning for the office of president of the United States.

The Democratic Party insiders, meanwhile, had to deal with the threat of Bernie Sanders. They did not want a self-described socialist at the head of their ticket. Yet his stunning success in the primaries had been a warning that many Democrats wanted a different candidate than the choice of the Establishment, the former Secretary of State under Obama.

Hillary Clinton had considerable experience in politics by the time she ran in 2016. She should certainly have learned the basic do's and don'ts of American electioneering. Yet on September 9, 2016, at a fundraising event in New York, she famously described half of Trump's supporters as "a basket of deplorables," adding for good measure that like Trump, they were "racist, sexist, homophobic, xenophobic, Islamophobic." Her words were greeted with rapturous applause and laughter from her upscale audience. The next day, Charles Blow, writing in *The New York Times*, said that Clinton was wrong. Not half, but all of Trump's supporters were deplorables.

Soon Trump's fans began to wear T-shirts with "Deplorable" written on them. Later, in her memoirs, Clinton would acknowledge the folly of her remark, counting it as one of the factors that led to her defeat. Not since the Republican platform of 1856, which described slavery as "a relic of barbarism," has a party committed itself to writing off a vast swath of the electorate at a single stroke. Even Lincoln tried to soothe and reassure the agitated South in his First Inaugural Address, despite the fact that not a single Southerner had cast a vote for him. True, Hillary had said that only half his supporters were deplorables, but few of Trump's millions of fans spent much time debating which half they belonged to. This unprecedented break from the American political tradition marked just how far the revolt of the elites had betrayed democracy.

Yet Clinton's remark did not come out of the blue. It was not a mere verbal faux pas. It faithfully reflected the attitude toward ordinary working-class Americans that had become increasingly evident among the liberal college-educated elite since the election of Barack Obama in 2008. The liberal elite was not just concerned with defeating Trump. They wanted to defeat the populist revolt against their own increasing domination of our politics and culture. They tried in every way possible to shame the supporters of Trump, who were fond of the meme that showed a defiant Trump with the words "They are not after me. They are after you."

By this time, it had become apparent to Trump's supporters that Trump was not merely taking on Hillary Clinton; he was taking on the entire postwar liberal-meritocratic Establishment that she represented. To them and their prestige, Trump was most definitely an "existential" threat. But he was equally a threat to the Republican "Never Trumpers" in the arena of foreign policy, which they had come to regard as their fiefdom. These were by and large the neocon intellectuals who had convinced George W. Bush that the invasion of Iraq would turn the Middle East virtually overnight into an archipelago of liberal democracies.

Though they called themselves Republicans, these professional political operatives only really represented themselves. During the Reagan-Bush era, they had obtained a near monopoly on the conservative brand. Under the Obama administration, they threw their enthusiastic support behind the regime change in Libya that Hillary Clinton had helped to engineer with the assistance of France and Great Britain. Ironically, despite blaming the neocons for the debacle in Iraq, both Obama and Clinton appeared to be following their playbook in Libya.

Unsurprisingly, regime change in Libya worked no better than it had in Iraq, creating the same fatal power vacuum, leading to two civil wars and a humanitarian crisis that has yet to be resolved. Yet despite their role in creating two international catastrophes, the neocons in 2016 still retained extensive influence through their collection of think tanks and high-brow magazines, and woe to anyone who dared question their bona fides to speak for "principled" American conservatism. But like the liberal members of the meritocratic Establishment, the neocons correctly perceived that the election of Donald Trump would not only be a threat to their authority but to their social standing and livelihood as well. Many—disenfranchised by the collapse of their magazines and purged from their think tanks—quickly became the most vociferous advocates of the "Trump is Hitler" trope, thereby earning lucrative cable contracts and book deals from liberal media and publishing outlets.

At the same time, there were several other crises that concerned ordinary voters far more than the advent of an American Third Reich. Some of these crises were covered by the media, like the epidemic of opioid addiction that was afflicting millions of Americans all over the country as well as the sense of hopelessness in the decaying Rust Belt cities of the North. Yet far less attention was paid by the media to the causes of the economic decline of America's blue-collar working class. As a result of the bipartisan North American Free Trade Agreement passed in 1994, the jobs once done by these workers had been sent (with a "great sucking sound," as predicted in 1992 by third-party presidential candidate Ross Perot) primarily to China and Mexico, where the labor was far cheaper.

This made perfect economic sense to the new managerial class of multinational corporations with a "global" perspective—a detached, almost Olympian point of view that came to be called "globalism." Although these corporations were simply pursuing their own economic self-interest by hiring cheap foreign labor, like all globalists they made a great show of working for the good of all humanity, as opposed to those dangerous nationalists who still held to the old-fashioned idea that their nation's leaders should look after their own citizens. Globalism was thus distinctly in tension with nationalism, which was now viewed as a stage in the onset of fascism. Rather than proud citizens of their homeland, Americans should aspire to be citizens of the world in a new global order managed, of course, by enlightened elites. Add to this the cultural confusion ordinary Americans suffered as tradition after tradition once held sacred was declared

226

to violate the new commandments handed down by the woke meritocratic elite.

The populist revolt was the result of a perfect storm of various grievances on the part of ordinary voters who felt that they had been betrayed and sold out by the establishment in Washington, DC. It was not by accident that the residential ZIP codes around DC are now among the richest in the country. The refusal of the meritocratic elite to take the grievances of ordinary Americans seriously or even listen to them was bad enough. But to deride and mock them was to risk political suicide.

One month before the election and a month after Hillary's "deplorable" remark, *The Washington Post* released a bombshell report that the establishment believed was certain to bring Trump down. There was an Access Hollywood tape in which Trump had made a comment about "grabbing" women's "pussies." This would surely cost Trump the support of both women and the socially conservative Christians who had previously supported him. Yet to the consternation of the media elite, the bombshell fizzled. It had virtually no effect on his poll numbers.

The fact that Trump's supporters continued to cheer him at his now even larger rallies might have been taken as a warning sign to the meritocratic Establishment that it was in serious trouble. It had used its best tricks to make voters turn away from Trump to Hillary, but nothing had worked. Instead of wondering if their own arrogance and snobbery might be to blame for their rejection, they doubled down on their attacks on Trump's supporters, who were now written off as beneath contempt.

To the shock of the meritocratic elite, the voters who went to the polls on November 8, 2016, elected Donald J. Trump the forty-fifth president of the United States. The populist revolt had finally found its leader, though it still remained to be seen what kind of populist he was, or, indeed, if such a maverick could really be subsumed under any of our handy off-the-shelf political labels. Once again, the meritocratic elite had been given the opportunity to abandon its attempt to become an unelected ruling class and return to the voter-oriented politics of an earlier era. It did not take that opportunity. No sooner was Trump declared the winner than a new phase in American politics began, as the meritocratic Establishment now went openly to war against both Trump and the millions who had voted for him.

The various efforts to explain Trump after his victory in 2016 all tried to fit both him and the MAGA movement into the past. Once again, scholars and pundits searched for historical analogies, thereby missing the fact that this was a historical development without precedent. The once proudly anti-populist Republican Party was now the seeming champion of the old American tradition of populism, while self-described liberal and progressive Democrats loathed and feared it. American populism was now the cause of those who self-described as conservatives.

This raised the question: Did the populists stop being progressives? Or did the progressives just stop being liberals?

CHAPTER THIRTEEN
THE ESTABLISHMENT STRIKES BACK

1
THE TRUMP RESISTANCE MOVEMENT

Many sober and sensible Americans were genuinely worried about Trump's victory. What troubled them was the way Trump ran his first campaign. He was wild, flamboyant, erratic, coarse and crude, given to petty tantrums over minor slights, vindictive, mean, and narcissistic. His ego was stupendous. No hyperbole was too far-fetched for his purposes. His rallies were the greatest in the history of humanity. His ideas were perfect. He was the proverbial bull in the china shop. All these factors combined to give reasonable and sober people cause to wonder if he was really presidential material. After all, Trump did not need to become the American Hitler to be a very bad president. Yet many of these skeptical voters were still willing to give him the benefit of the doubt that was part of traditional politics in America.

Not so our meritocratic elite. Immediately after Trump was elected, it set about to destroy both Donald Trump and his administration. The alliance of the Democratic Party, Republican neocons, deep state bureaucrats, and the establishment media essentially said, "You may have been elected, but we will not let you govern."

This was the whole point of the Trump Resistance, as the movement was dubbed by the anti-Trumpers, a name they no doubt chose to evoke memories of the French Resistance to Nazi occupation. The metaphor was apt. The Establishment saw the Trump administration as an illegitimate occupation of the nation. Its virtuous duty was to sabotage this administration by any means available, which was exactly what the Establishment proceeded to do.

Lincoln's election had also split the nation in half. But the opposition of the Southern hotheads to Lincoln's victory was at least open and honorable. In contrast, the Trump Resistance was clandestine and came from inside the government and media-political establishment—what came to be called the deep state. Instead of the media informing the American people that they had decided to wreck the presidency of Donald Trump and would stop at nothing to achieve this end, they pretended to believe that Trump was such an existential menace to the nation that it was their patriotic duty to help in any way they could to remove him.

In resisting Trump, however, the meritocratic elite was in effect also declaring war on his supporters, who were quickly subjected to a mass ostracism at the hands of liberals. Friendships were ended and families torn apart. Facebook became a political battleground. Ideally, many liberals concluded, the United States would be better off not only without Trump but without his sixty-three million supporters as well.

Ironically, considering later charges that Trump was "violating norms" and "shredding the Constitution," the liberal Establishment quickly showed that it would stop at practically nothing to prevent him from executing his duties as president. Even before Trump took office, schemes were floated by Ivy League law professors urging a mass revolt of so-called faithless electors from the states that Trump had won. There was nothing unconstitutional about this procedure. By the letter of the law, an elector designated by a state was at liberty to vote their conscience. Once again, it was only by an unwritten tradition that electors were faithful to the candidate who had won the electoral votes of their state. But this assault on the tradition of faithful electors was just the beginning.

Many more such traditions would be cast to the wind during the first term of Donald Trump. Most of all, it was the tradition of fair play that was jettisoned by his enemies in their attempt to bring him down. The media, the administrative state, and the courts—none treated Trump fairly. No written law can guarantee fair play; no authority can mandate it. It must be what one sociologist has called a habit of the heart, second nature to us. Where the principle of fair play is deeply intertwined in the moral fabric of a society, its members all benefit. We all want others to treat us fairly. We believe that even murderers deserve a fair trial.

The decision to violate the principle of fair play in the case of a sitting president only deepened the epochal crisis. Aside from Lincoln, no American president had ever been treated this way. But while Lincoln's bitterest enemies left the Union, giving him a relatively free hand in the North, Trump's enemies felt that the institutions of government were their personal property, and they were determined to tie his hands as much as possible.

From the moment Trump was sworn into office, the Resistance devoted itself to finding or manufacturing grounds for his speedy impeachment and removal. Many in the media establishment genuinely regarded Trump as such a menace that they felt compelled to set aside the standards of objective reporting to which they had previously at least given lip service. They now saw themselves as warriors in the fight to save American democracy from Trump.

From the first years of George Washington's administration, it is true, the American press had made vile and scurrilous attacks on sitting presidents, and in the case of Andrew Jackson, on his wife. But in the latter half of the twentieth century, journalists had come to see themselves as white collar professionals, with standards of civility and objectivity to uphold. Naturally, the liberal media had always been critical of Republican presidents. That was nothing new. Neither were comparisons to Hitler, from Reagan to George W. Bush. But never before had the media establishment taken as its sacred mission the nullification of a presidency.

As a result, the great epochal crisis of twenty-first-century America went untold by the media, for the simple reason that this was a crisis of their own making and design. The media had no more intention of giving away its own role in the Resistance than any of the other conspirators in history who attempted to seize power. Yet no conspiracy had ever been so public and open.

2
THE RUSSIA HOAX AND ITS ENABLERS

After Donald Trump addressed a rally in Charlottesville, Virginia, on August 11, 2017, the establishment media showed its true colors. Controversy had erupted when it was proposed that an equestrian statue of Robert E. Lee should be removed from its place of honor in a public park. Needless to say, this was an affront to the many who still revered the great Confederate general. Trump had offered the crowd a placatory bromide by saying what any savvy politician would say on such an occasion: that there were "good people on both sides" of the debate over removing the statue.

Yet his conciliatory remarks were immediately taken out of their original context after a riot broke out in Charlottesville in which neo-Nazis and white supremacists participated. Despite the fact that Trump explicitly denounced both groups, deceptive reporting and editing made it appear that he had said there were "good people" marching with the Nazis and white supremacists. Despite fact checks to the contrary even from liberal sources, including *The Washington Post*, the myth has been hard to eradicate. Joseph Biden would later even claim that it was Trump's embrace of neo-Nazis that inspired his own fourth run for the presidency in 2020. As late as 2024, Biden was still using the same red herring to blacken Trump's name.

Yet this assault on journalistic decency paled before the three-year-long saga that came to be known as the "Russia hoax."

In fact, the real conspirators were the opposition research team of the Clinton campaign who generated a fake intelligence report on Trump's corrupt political connections with Russia that they then shopped around to see if any government agency would be interested. Astonishingly, it was taken seriously—or at least seriously enough to launch an investigation into the allegations, despite the fact that it was as bizarre as the many QAnon conspiracy theories in circulation at the time. According to the infamous Steele dossier, Trump had paid prostitutes in a Moscow hotel to urinate on photographs of President Obama in the bed he supposedly slept in. As anyone except Trump should have expected—so the story went—the room was wired and the kinky scene had all been videotaped. When the tape landed on Putin's desk, it was suggested, he instantly realized that if he could contrive to throw the election to Trump, he would be in a position to blackmail the new president, who would supinely submit to become Russia's stooge and lackey.

The lack of a scintilla of evidence to support this fractured fairytale didn't matter. After all, Trump had not only made admiring comments about Vladimir Putin but also said that he wanted to ease tensions between the United States and Russia. Improving relations with the Soviet Union had always been high on the list of liberal objectives in the past. Hillary Clinton had professed the same intention when she became Secretary of State under Obama, with her infamous "reset" button. Nor had Obama done much more than protest and impose "targeted sanctions" when Putin annexed Crimea on his watch. But liberals now regarded any rapprochement with Russia as a deal with the devil incarnate. A few brave liberals, like Russia expert Stephen Cohen of Princeton University, would commend Trump's efforts to ease relations with Putin's government, asking whether we really wanted a new Cold War. But the majority took Trump's efforts to be proof positive that he was Putin's willing stooge.

Yet the Russia hoax had one thing going in its favor. It had the elegance of a beautiful scientific theory in that it explained so much. Previously, the meritocratic Establishment had had to struggle to explain away Trump's political success. It had to be a fluke, they agreed, without any historical import. He would be quickly removed from office and disappear in ignominy from politics. Like the establishment defenders of the geocentric theories of the universe in face of the discoveries of Galileo and Kepler, the meritocratic elites clearly wanted to hold on to their power and positions. Their quick adoption of the Russia hoax was what the philosopher of science, Thomas Kuhn, would have described as a doomed attempt to save a collapsing intellectual paradigm. Why attack Trump for his many vulgar foibles and unseemly peccadillos when you could prove that he was a traitor?

Why had Trump won the election? Because the Russians had stolen it for him. This absolved Hillary Clinton of any blame for her loss due to her arrogant sense of entitlement and her fatally flawed campaign.

Why should every effort be made to remove Trump from office, by any means necessary? Because Trump had become virtually a Russian operative, putty in the hands of his puppet-master in the Kremlin.

How could Trump be removed from office quickly? By appointing a special counsel who would prove beyond the shadow of a doubt that the Russia hoax was true, thereby providing ample and incontestable grounds to impeach Trump and remove him from office.

The mainstream media pushed the story for all it was worth, a stunning testimony to the rise of elitist groupthink within the profession and the erosion of traditional standards of journalism. Rather than investigate the source of this dubious fable, the legacy media was happy to spread it, adding the prestige of their authority to back a conspiracy theory that could only have been taken seriously in the paranoid climate of the American conspiracy mania. The campaign to encourage the public to think that their government was always out to get them had succeeded to the point where half of the American public was prepared to swallow the idea that the new president was a Russian asset.

When Robert Mueller, a respected attorney with considerable claims to integrity, was assigned to be the special counsel to look into these fantastic allegations, it was generally assumed that his report would be released in a timely manner. Those who dismissed the Russia hoax as laughable nonsense believed that it would require only a week or so to dispose of. Those who took it as gospel truth were prepared to wait a little longer, though many noted that his hugely expensive investigation was largely staffed by partisan attorneys. As the investigation dragged on month after month, their hopes never sagged. The Mueller Report became their Holy Grail. Once it had been delivered unto the world, Trump would be toast.

When the Mueller Report was finally released after nearly two years, it was met with shock and disbelief by the true believers. It did not even offer a pretext for the impeachment of Trump, though there were many who insisted that it had not really cleared Trump of the charges—if you read between the lines.

Soon, however, the true believers found a new reason to impeach Trump: a phone call he had made to the president of Ukraine. The Democrats and their media allies declared that this short phone call belonged to the category of "high crimes and misdemeanors" that the Constitution had established as grounds for impeaching a president. The Democrats and their allies knew perfectly well that they could never get enough votes in the Senate to remove Trump, but that was never their intention.

The framers of the Constitution had clearly intended the impeachment clause to be used only as a last resort, when a president had so seriously abused authority that they presented a danger to the liberty of the people, at which point calls for removal would be virtually universal—as in the case of Richard Nixon, or Andrew Johnson before him. Since the framers assumed that Americans would never return to the discredited party system of Great Britain, it did not occur to them that the impeachment clause could be used by one political party for the sole purpose of besmirching its political opponent. But plenty of Ivy League law professors were happy to explain on TV that Trump's phone call was indeed just what the framers of the Constitution had in mind when they spoke of impeachable offenses. More than a few of these legal wizards were also delighted to explain why the partisan impeachment of Trump, which they so vigorously championed, was quite a different affair from the equally partisan impeachment of President Clinton, which they had vigorously opposed.

All this concerted opposition did not entirely prevent Trump from enacting his agenda although it did significantly hinder and distract him. Nor did it cause any of his immense MAGA base to abandon him. Meanwhile, the hits on Trump kept coming. The ultimate aim was not only to make Trump a one-term president but also to quell the populist revolt that had brought him to power, making sure that neither Trump nor anyone else could ever again mount so formidable a challenge to the political establishment, of which the mainstream media was increasingly viewed as a member in good standing.

If it had managed to reduce Trump's role in American life to one inglorious term, then clearly his claim to be a world-historical figure would be laughable. Unfortunately, the political establishment failed to realize that the popular revolt it hoped to stifle had been brought about by its own loss of legitimacy in the eyes of both those who had voted for Trump and those who had voted for Sanders. Our epochal crisis could not be ended by merely removing Trump from the scene, so long as our political establishment refused to mend its own ways. In fact, members of this establishment poured fuel on the culture wars that they themselves had stoked by their adoption of woke causes, including the Black Lives Matter movement and the "Defund the Police" demands made in its name.

When George Floyd died as the result of police misconduct on May 25, 2020, in the liberal city of Minneapolis in the liberal state of Minnesota, it became a cause célèbre virtually overnight. Yet it was a very odd cause célèbre. The Dreyfus Affair that shook France from 1894 to 1906 was one of the most famous causes célèbres in history. It divided the French people into two mutually hostile factions. This, in fact, is the norm of any cause célèbre. It is what makes them celebrated in the first place. People argue about them.

But who was arguing over George Floyd? No one was happy that he died. Derek Chauvin, the policeman who had pinned him to the ground with a knee on his neck, had virtually no defenders, at least in public. There was an overwhelming consensus across the political spectrum that Floyd's death had been tragic and unnecessary, one of the rare instances in which the American public was not divided. Yet his death set off nationwide riots, the most destructive since the Rodney King riots that swept California in 1992. Property damage in Minneapolis was around half a billion dollars, with 60 percent of the buildings burned to the ground being uninsured.

Overnight, George Floyd became a martyr to the great and noble cause of taking down "systemic racism." Cooler heads, who were actually concerned with the welfare of the Black people living in Minnesota, might have urged restraint, or appealed to Black neighborhoods not to burn down the few remaining businesses that catered to them. But nothing of the kind came forth from either the Democratic Party or its media enablers. Instead, the Black Lives Matter movement spread across the nation, while those who naively believed all lives matter were denounced as racists. Many liberals championed the Defund the Police movement, a policy that would obviously hurt those most in need of police protection: the poor and other minorities. The soft-on-crime No Bail movement also began at this time, ultimately wreaking havoc on urban law enforcement in blue states across the country. Much of this was motivated by white liberal guilt; much by race hucksters out to make a buck.

The screenshot of a CNN reporter, with flames rising behind him and debris all around, saying that the protests had been "fiery but mostly peaceful" became iconic, at least to those who still retained the faculty for irony that seemed to have deserted the national media with the wild abandon of lemmings leaping from their proverbial cliffs. No one in the media—now increasingly seen as a virtual extension of the Democratic party—dared to challenge the narrative that the best way to defeat "systemic racism" was to encourage Black rioters to burn down their own neighborhoods.

The very idea that the Democratic Party and its allies in the now-indelibly labeled "liberal media" might have actively encouraged and condoned the George Floyd riots for their own political benefit—as a means of getting at Trump and weakening his chances for a second term—was too cynical for many observers to credit.

Then came Covid. By this time, it was an open secret that the Democratic Party and its media enablers were absolutely obsessed with getting rid of Trump and that they were prepared to avail themselves of any weapon, including the farce of impeachment, which coincided with the first cases of Covid to be reported in the United States in early 2020. But for many, it was still difficult to believe that those in the Establishment would be willing to inflict immense damage on their own country, just to discredit Trump. Yet their behavior in respect of George Floyd set the pattern for their behavior in respect of Covid. The real threat to them was not the disease itself, but the idea that Trump might successfully rise to the challenge of dealing with it. Hence, they did everything in their power to cripple Trump's efforts to cope with the first major epidemic to hit America since the Great Influenza struck in 1918.

Trump swiftly announced his decision to prevent entry into the United States of people coming from the epicenter of the contagion, China. To many, this seemed like a perfectly rational response. It was what all nations had done in the face of such rapidly spreading diseases.

Throughout the wide domain reached by the media establishment, everyone agreed that Trump could not possibly have any other motive for his Chinese travel ban than xenophobia, with which the 2016 Democratic campaign had tarred him, along with the rest of the SAT words that had been employed as a trigger warning to ward off anyone who dared to give Trump the benefit of the doubt. Wasn't it just possible that Trump had issued his travel ban to protect Americans, instead of exploiting Covid to exhibit his hatred and contempt for all things Chinese including egg rolls and shrimp lo mein? No, of course not.

As the pandemic spread, it became increasingly apparent to Democratic operatives and their media friends that here indeed was the golden opportunity to "get" Trump once and for all. Thus, according to the media, Trump told people to go home and inject bleach into their veins—a flat-out smear. Trump didn't care whether he killed our kids and their teachers by supporting states like Florida, where the maniacal Gov. Ron DeSantis insisted that the schools and public beaches stay open. In the advanced-thinking blue states, schools were shut down at the demand of the teachers' union. The teachers naturally still got paid, but their students did not get taught. Even in 2025, the damage done to the education of our children by these completely pointless school closures has yet to be undone. Today, it is generally accepted that the closing of schools was a terrible mistake, saving no lives but jeopardizing many futures.

Meanwhile, a new regime of "anti-disinformation" had been launched during the Covid era. Any departure from the liberal Covid party line could be, and usually was, censored on social media. This was particularly true when those making the posts were politically conservative or questioned the recommendation of the Covid "czar" whom many Democrats referred to as Saint Anthony Fauci. This was frequently accompanied by deplatforming, debanking, and firing.

Perhaps the most egregious example of the Covid establishment's assault on truth came when a group of specialists in epidemiology denounced as a "conspiracy theory" the very idea that the Covid virus might have accidentally come from the Wuhan lab that studied the virus. Such accidents are all too common, even given the strictest safeguards.

By definition, accidents are unplanned and not the result of a conspiracy to bring them about. But smearing a perfectly plausible idea as a "conspiracy theory" had become a standard response of the Establishment to any negative information that might put it in a bad light. This is exactly the playbook that would be used when Hunter Biden's flagrantly incriminating laptop was found in a Delaware computer shop—fifty-one former American intelligence agents signed a memorandum declaring the laptop to have "all the classic earmarks of a Russian information operation." In reality, as the FBI would later admit, the laptop had been in their possession for some time and was exactly what it looked like. But this knowledge was suppressed and when the *New York Post* tried to publicize it, its Twitter account was suspended at the behest of the federal government. It is precisely this kind of partisan political abuse that led supporters of Trump to snicker at charges of fascism.

Ultimately, the open collusion of meritocratic elites in and out of government ensured the election of Joe Biden, who they were fully assured would never think of challenging their bid to achieve cultural hegemony over the American people. The aging Biden was their ideal figurehead, as he quickly demonstrated by shedding his reputation for moderation and becoming the spokesman-in-chief for the Woke Revolution, effectively handing his administration over to the Bernie Sanders left—a purportedly populist movement (mostly funded by activist billionaires) that soon proved infinitely more authoritarian than Trump.

CHAPTER FOURTEEN
THE ESTABLISHMENT GOES WOKE

1
TRUMP'S DEFEAT AND THE RISE OF WOKE POLITICS

Immediately after Biden was declared the winner in November 2020, the cry went up that the election had been stolen. Trump and many others claimed that there had been fraud at the polls. This may well be true, though it is impossible at this date to resolve the question definitively.

Yet, even if you adopt a middle-ground posture that there was likely some fraud, though not enough to swing the election, the Myth of the Stolen Election expresses a much deeper truth. Like the corrupt bargain that made Adams president and Clay secretary of state, the corrupt bargain between the Democratic Party and the liberal media was completely constitutional and broke no law. Yet it was a betrayal of the old American ideal that both candidates in the race for the presidency should be given the same fair and objective treatment. Once again, this new corrupt bargain had successfully gamed the system.

Whether or not the election had been stolen at the ballot box, the question remained: Had it really been fair? Trump had been defeated by a media campaign designed to discredit the populist revolt and the man who led it—a campaign that broke every unwritten tradition that had previously guided how presidential elections would be covered. The liberal media could be expected to slant its news coverage of any Republican candidate, but if Trump had been treated half as well as the liberal media treated Mitt Romney and John McCain, it is likely he would have won handily in 2020.

Many of Trump's supporters quite naturally felt righteous anger at the outcome of the 2020 election. They felt like the victims of a con artist so cunning that they had no clue how they had been swindled. All they knew was that they had been robbed and that they wanted their money back—or in this case, their president.

There was nothing at all novel in claiming that an American election was the result of fraud. In fact, many of them had been. Lyndon Johnson had stolen the 1948 election that made him a Senator from Texas, which jumpstarted him on his path to power. In the presidential election of 1960, no one today disputes that the Democratic machines in Chicago, West Virginia, and Texas had procured votes for Kennedy out of thin air. In 2000, many Democrats claimed that the election had been stolen for George W. Bush from Al Gore by the Supreme Court.

Still, Trump would have been wiser simply to accept the outcome of the election in good grace, then after giving the Democrats four years to make a mess of things—which, in fact, they promptly did—return to the stump and glide to his second term in 2024. Instead, he made the greatest political blunder of his life.

On January 6, 2021, Trump held a rally in Washington, DC, with the provocative slogan Stop the Steal. Trump believed—or at least convinced himself that he believed—a dubious legal theory that had been put forth by another helpful Ivy League professor of law, this time a conservative, who argued that the vice president had the constitutional authority to remand the electors of a state to go back and reconsider the hotly contested election results from the states where fraud was suspected.

The theory was egregious, though no more so than many of the theories of those Ivy League law professors who were on the other side. Vice President Pence, to his credit, did not buy the argument and proceeded to call for the vote of the states, which resulted in the formal election of Joe Biden. It should have ended there, but it didn't. What happened next would become one of the most controversial events in American history, when several thousand riled-up Trump supporters besieged the Capitol building, battling with cops and rampaging through the halls of Congress.

Americans watching these events on television had every right to be appalled. This was the kind of thing that could be expected in nations with a long history of political instability, not in the USA. It was certainly a national embarrassment. But was it really anything more than that?

The meritocratic elite certainly thought it was. The Capitol riot of January 6, 2021, was quickly declared an insurrection, nothing short of an attempt to overthrow the government, and those who participated in it were looked upon as outright traitors deserving the harshest possible punishment. A nationwide law-enforcement sweep resulted in the arrest and imprisonment of some 1400 individuals, many of whom had simply walked through the Capitol taking selfies after being ushered in by smiling guards. By the time of the 2024 election, many of them had been in jail for over three years.

Oddly enough, most of them would spend more time in prison than Jefferson Davis, the president of the Confederacy, who was released after two years, while his vice president, Alexander Stephens, served a mere six months. The victorious Union was more forgiving of the men who had waged an actual war against them for four years, at the cost of 700,000 lives, than the liberal elite of our era were of those who had acted like fools on January 6. But, of course, their real target was Donald Trump, the insurrection's supposed leader and instigator.

Less than a week after January 6, the Democrats in the House of Representatives, with the support of a handful of Republicans, decided to impeach Trump a second time just as he was leaving office. Now at last they felt they had secured victory over their foe. This second vote was truly historic, they thought. Two presidents had been impeached before, but Trump alone had been impeached twice. He was definitely finished.

But this was not the end of it. Hoping not just to drive him out of politics but to hound the ex-president into bankruptcy, jail, or both, district attorneys from bright blue cities like Atlanta and New York found inventive legal theories by which they hoped to entangle him. The emergence of what became known as anti-Trump "lawfare" did not trouble anyone in the liberal elite, nor did the fact that a politically ambitious DA could advance his or her career by going after Trump on the thinnest of pretexts. This was a clear violation of the traditional role assigned to district attorneys, which was to do their job rather than using it as a springboard to greater rewards in the elite hierarchy. Yet the millions spent in the frenetic pursuit of putting Trump behind bars was money tossed out the window. In the end, the unprecedented efforts by Democrats to defeat Trump in the courts rather than the ballot box backfired when each new charge only increased his popularity and encouraged him to run again in 2024.

But once again, the fact that their bright ideas always missed the mark did not lead the liberal elites to look for new ones. Like the foolish gambler down on their luck, they decided to double down. In short, drunk with power and believing themselves in possession of a righteous agenda that no sane or reasonable person could oppose, they went completely woke.

Many Americans had voted for Biden in the belief that his presidency would mark a return to the old-fashioned style of politics in which he had excelled as a senator: Listen to the voters, then try to give them what they want. But Biden didn't listen to the voters. Instead, his administration embarked on a sweeping transformational agenda that no one had asked (or voted) for.

First came the expansion of DEI in the military, including West Point and the service academies. The result was predictable: Recruitment plummeted. Then came out-of-control environmental regulation, including shutting down domestic energy production and pushing mandates against gas stoves. Again, the result was predictable: rising energy costs and interference in consumer choice. In their crusade against the white working class, the Democrats introduced a controversial wave of curricular reforms based on the highly controversial *1619 Project*, which presented America as systemically racist. Another completely predictable result: indoctrination of schoolchildren leading to widespread complaints and a series of videos depicting angry parents being dragged out of school board meetings. President Biden famously declared transgender rights to be *the* burning civil rights issue of our time. When 85 percent of Americans oppose transgender males competing in woman's sports, perhaps this should have sent a warning not to push this particular issue.

While Trump's 2018 nominee to the Supreme Court, Brett Kavanaugh, had been dragged through the mud in a national spectacle that appalled ordinary Americans, Ketanji Brown Jackson sailed to a swift confirmation, her reputation unsullied. But the biggest thumb in the eye was Biden's policies on the economy and immigration, practical issues of broad concern. Nothing expressed the tone-deaf quality of the Biden administration more than the decision to coin the term Bidenomics, as if it were something to brag about. The Inflation Reduction Act turned out to be an Orwellian instance of Newspeak, as billions were spent presumably to fight the sacred cause of climate change, while, in fact, it only made inflation worse.

From the moment they took office, Biden's people took steps to dismantle Trump's border enforcement policies. They openly encouraged caravans of migrants with promises of support and offers of refugee status. They reined in the border patrol and allowed uncounted thousands to cross the border every day, overwhelming local communities with their needs for housing, education, and health care. Many were flown or bussed around the country to liberal sanctuary cities where they were put up in luxury hotels at public expense and given free phones and ration cards. As a result, levels of public disorder and crime shot up. Adding insult to injury, Biden sold off unused construction materials meant for Trump's long-promised border wall.

No policy has ever had such a devastating impact on the very people it was allegedly designed to help than Biden's tacit invitation for migrants to flood across the border unimpeded. White liberals convinced each other that Hispanics could never get tired of seeing ever more Hispanics coming into our country. They would rush to the borders to embrace their racial and ethnic brethren. This was nonsense—people from Latin America identify with the nations into whose culture they were born, just

248

like the citizens of English- and French-speaking countries. The geographical-linguistic term *Hispanic* was never a source of ethnic identity. Its widespread use to cover a multitude of different national cultures only reflected the liberal elite doctrine of identity politics as a means of organizing voter blocs. Woke ideology triumphed over common sense but at the cost of setting back the dream of millions of de facto Americans to become citizens.

Much the same was happening in Europe, where the ruling elites had thrown open their borders to an influx of immigrants from distant and alien cultures, despite the growing resentment of their own citizens who had to bear the burden of trying to assimilate them into their own culture. The result was the rise of populist parties that challenged the dictates of their countries' elites—parties that were quickly dubbed "far right," when not declared outright fascist. In addition, top-down green policies were imposed by fiat. Germany, despite its dependence on energy from foreign sources, shuttered its last nuclear power plant on April 15, 2023. Other equally inept green policies were ended by raising the cost of energy and reducing the individual's freedom of choice. In May 2025, consumers within the European Union could no longer buy appliances that were deemed by bureaucrats in Brussels to use too much energy in standby or off mode.

The meritocratic elites of Europe and America could have changed course in order to avert the political disaster they had brought upon themselves by their arrogance and incompetence. They had certainly been warned multiple times. The backlash against Obamacare, the surprising British vote in favor of Brexit, Trump's 2016 victory, the dramatic rise of European populism in the face of unrestricted mass immigration—all these were signs of danger ahead, but they were ignored. Although they were sailing in uncharted waters under a darkening sky, the elites continued to insist that all was well.

Thus they assured us in 2024 that President Biden was "sharp as a tack," until his debate with Trump revealed him as a doddering and senile old man. Despite the fact that polls after the debate showed that Biden's dismal performance had little effect on his millions of supporters—just a drop of one or two percent—the liberal Establishment of Democratic power players and mega-donors decided that he must drop out of the race. Biden even sounded like a populist when he claimed, with good reason, that he was being pushed out by the party elite—just as Bernie Sanders had done when he was pushed off the ballot by Democrats in 2016.

The coup carried out against Biden clearly showed that the Democratic Party was no longer answerable to its voters. The power of our meritocratic elite in collusion with the press and what conservatives called the deep state had revealed itself in its full majesty. Having lulled Democrats into believing that they were only the loyal servants of the Party, they now revealed themselves to be its exacting masters who could dictate its marching orders. Obeying them, the hastily installed Kamala Harris marched them right over a cliff.

With no accomplishments of her own as vice president, she was left to defend the lackluster record of the Biden Administration and struggled to change the narrative. But her inability to answer direct questions with anything other than a stumbling word salad filled with empty platitudes was embarrassing and unpersuasive. In the last days of her sputtering campaign, she surrounded herself with paid celebrities who spent more money on their gaudy apparel than the average working person could make in a year. But, somehow, even the endorsement of billionaire performer Taylor Swift was not enough to put her over the top, a fact that seemed to genuinely puzzle many liberal commentators.

Only an elite with vastly more power than good sense could have acted with such feckless incompetence. But the same elites had also insisted on hobbling the Democrats with an assortment of woke causes as unpopular as they were perverse. Their slender grasp of political reality was most clearly reflected in their decision to make the election all about Trump and the existential threat he posed to American democracy.

Casting Trump as the reincarnation of Adolf Hitler was a dangerous ploy. There were millions of Americans who already believed this, thanks to years of unrelenting propaganda; but beyond this hardcore base of true believers, it was a tough sell. Why the Democratic Party failed to recognize this fact is puzzling, since many of the largest donors to the Harris campaign had urged their party to drop the "Trump is Hitler" gambit and return to dealing with the issues that the American people were genuinely concerned about, as shown by virtually every poll: immigration and inflation.

Yet the Harris campaign continued to paint Trump as a dangerous fascist up until the very eve of the election. This may only have been the most recent illustration of the old adage, "Whom the gods would destroy, they first make mad." But another factor was in play.

Trump had to be Hitler. For if he wasn't Hitler, then how could the Democratic Party and the liberal media justify their treatment of him? The only way they could defend their wholesale and wanton violation of the traditional rules of fair play was if they had done so for a higher cause. And what cause could be higher than saving democracy from Hitler? This was the slender thread on which the Democrats relied to rally their once-winning coalition.

Yet behind the hysterical scaremongering was the fact that the liberal elites were genuinely terrified of Trump, and their fear had nothing to do with his supposed dictatorial ambitions. The Great Populist Revolt threatened to upset the status quo that had provided them with their wealth and power. It was little different from the fear that aristocrats of the Old World felt when faced with a peasant revolt, which is more or less how the liberal elites looked upon the raucous crowds that Trump held spellbound at his rallies. They were peasants who needed to be put in their place.

Trump's stunning victory in the election of 2024 has been called, with good reason, the greatest comeback in the history of American politics. He was not the first man to be elected for a second term in office after having been defeated after his first. Grover Cleveland held that distinction. Yet Cleveland's return to power in 1892 did not unleash the ecstatic jubilation that greeted the return of Donald Trump among those who had faithfully supported him—nor did Cleveland's victory send his defeated political opponents into a state of total shock and panic, leading many to declare that they were fleeing the country. Trump's victory constituted not just a resounding political defeat but a cognitive challenge to their worldview, not to mention a threat to their safety given Trump's avowed intention—soon to be borne out—to prosecute his enemies as they had prosecuted him.

In the election of 2024, the Deep South was solidly Republican, as it has reliably been, with a few exceptions, ever since the political realignment of the 1960s. Black people now voted in great numbers in the Deep South. Most of its big cities had Black mayors. Hispanic citizens now constituted a larger voting bloc than their Black counterparts.

In the elections of the previous three decades, both groups had strongly supported the Democratic Party, which had become the de facto party of racial minorities. Yet in 2024, for the first time, the majority of Hispanic men voted for the Republican candidate, who also won more Black voters overall than any Republican since 1960. But this was nothing in comparison with the most dramatic political realignment to emerge from the election. The working-class vote, which had once been the bread and butter of the Democratic Party, had largely gone over to the other side.

The most enthusiastic support for the Republican candidate came from working men without college degrees, the very group that FDR had dubbed Forgotten Men and whose fervent loyalty helped elect him to four terms. Somehow or other, the Democratic Party had completely forgotten about the Forgotten Man.

Many voters who had had more than enough of meritocratic overreach would have preferred a candidate other than Trump. Yet history is always stingy with the choices it offers us. There was, in fact, no one else who could play Trump's role. It was either Trump or the sinking ship of the meritocratic elite. There was no third choice.

For better or for worse, that is how history works. Intellectuals often have trouble accepting this. They believe that history provides us with a host of options even after these options are no longer available. The hopeful array of options we could have taken yesterday are cruelly eliminated by the events of today, often leaving us with only those choices that we hoped never to have to make. Still, we have to choose.

2
TRUMP RETURNS TO WASHINGTON

Merely by winning the 2024 election, Trump had delivered a knock-out blow to the meritocratic elite. It was down for the count, but would it stay down forever? Indeed, the relative resignation of the liberal media to Trump's victory in the immediate aftermath of the 2024 election stood in sharp contrast to their hysterical reaction in 2016. No Ivy League law professor was breathlessly interviewed for fanciful theories of how to prevent Trump from taking office. But the meritocratic elite retained formidable strength through its media apparatus that continued to give it the power to influence public opinion by deciding what everyone should talk about. And soon everyone was once again talking about how terrible Trump was. In these attacks, the Trump-is-Hitler line featured prominently.

Meanwhile, across the Atlantic, the European establishment attempted the same fearmongering tactics in dealing with their discontented populations. When ordinary Europeans attempted to resist this new ruling class, they found themselves labelled (ironically) as threats to democracy, far right, or even fascists. The rise of anti-Establishment populism across the globe also belied the favorite trope of the anti-Trumpers, which was to maintain that Trump was a unique threat rather than reflecting a global shift of historic proportions, in which political establishments were under attack in most of the leading nations of the world. As it turned out, the global elite was not a bogeyman invented by Fox News to hoodwink its benighted viewers. The global elite was real, and it was fighting hard to maintain its dominance in a world order in which it was used to being at the helm. Denying its reach and power was as damaging to the credibility of the liberal media as its pretense that there was no crisis at the southern border or in America's big cities or that Biden was cognitively fit to be president until 2028.

On March 31, 2025, the Fifth Republic of France banned Marine Le Pen of the right-wing National Rally party from running for the presidency for a period of several years. She had been formally charged and sentenced for embezzlement. Her many supporters cried foul, accusing the French government of using law-fare to check her rising popularity, just as Trump's supporters accused the Democrats of doing the same to Trump. Those who took both Le Pen and Trump to court naturally claimed they were upholding the rule of law. But the rule of law is a noble abstraction that can be hypocritically invoked by politically ambitious District Attorneys and prosecutors for their own personal ends as well as protecting a moribund Establishment from its populist challengers. Political prosecution under the guise of law has been the policy of all authoritarian forms of government from the absolute monarchies of the seventeenth century to the totalitarian regimes of the twentieth. Arrest those who endanger your own hold on power—that has been an honor maxim of every threatened Establishment. Whatever the legal merits of the charges brought against both Marie Le Pen and Donald Trump, the suspicion is bound to be raised that those who claim to be protecting "democratic norms" have decided that the greatest threat to democracy was posed by the candidate who got the most votes. This was also the policy of Romana, whose elite had crushed that nation's populist candidate, Caălin Georgescu, while the German meritocratic elite has attempted, like the French, to outlaw populism by taking legal measures to hobble its own "far right" party, significantly named the Alternative for Germany.

Nothing better demonstrated the bankruptcy of the European elites than this ham-fisted response to a perceived threat to their hegemony. Having abandoned all attempts to win the people over by their stale and musty ideas, the European elites saw no other recourse than to silence their opponents by outlawing them outright. An elite that can think of no better way of handling a populist revolt than outlawing its candidates and criminalizing dissent is frankly doomed. It may ban the leaders of such revolts, but only at the cost of exposing its own fear and desperation.

The American elites tried repeatedly to do the same with Trump. Our legal system permitted them to concoct charges against Trump that had no legal precedent. But time and again he eluded their traps, which only served to increase his popularity.

In their fury at Trump, they foolishly blamed him for the fiasco for which their arrogance alone was responsible. Hence, it was no surprise that within three months after Trump was inaugurated for his second term, the BBC would claim that "Trump has blown up the world order." Variations on the same theme could be found in other liberal news outlets around the globe. Needless to say, the unspoken assumption behind such articles is always the same: It is not good to "blow up" the world order. But this depends on the health of the order in question. If that order has outlived its original purpose, what reason is there to preserve it? If it is no longer up to new challenges, if it has run out of ideas, if it has lost the faith of the people, if its leaders are corrupt and incompetent, then perhaps it is time for a new one.

3
INTERNATIONALISM AND ITS ILLUSIONS

The world order that the BBC says Trump is blowing up is the "rules-based international order" that came into existence after World War II and was supposedly reaffirmed with the end of the Cold War and the collapse of the Soviet Union. This was undoubtedly a good idea at the time, insofar as it stabilized international relations while guaranteeing American hegemony through a complex system of alliances, international bodies, and economic agreements. But the idea of an international liberal world order had always been based on make-believe, going back to Wilson's League of Nations. It was designed to be a system to assure perpetual world peace—a dream of visionary philosophers as far back as Immanuel Kant.

According to this hopeful theory, strong nations would act in concert to protect the sovereignty of weaker ones. Its premise was that all nations, the strongest as well as the weakest, *should* be treated equally. But how was this possible in a world in which some nations were far "more equal" than others?

It is a simple fact that some nations are vastly more powerful than others. There is no way to alter this arrangement. Stronger nations will invariably create a sphere of influence. They will seek to maximize this soft power to achieve their own objectives. Weaker nations are at an obvious disadvantage in any conflict with stronger ones, meaning that most will tacitly accept their position within the closest sphere of influence. But in any violent conflict in which the stronger nation is judged to be the aggressor, the rule book of liberal internationalism is that its aggression cannot be permitted to stand.

This principle actually worked only once, when Saddam Hussein was forced by a coalition led by the United States to pull his armies out of the much weaker nation of Kuwait, which he had invaded. But this mission was only attempted because Iraq was itself a relatively weak nation. Such international coalitions are far less likely to take on a strong nation, which not only has the will to fight back but the means of doing so catastrophically. This occurred in 1968 when the NATO powers failed to resist the Soviet invasion of Czechoslovakia, and more recently in 2014, with Putin's annexation of Crimea on Obama's watch. Yet liberal internationalism was explicitly designed to keep the strongest nations from aggression, not the weak ones.

The war in Ukraine has shown this fatal contradiction at the heart of liberal internationalism. The strong nations of the West condemned Russia for invading Ukraine and sent money and weapons to its embattled victim; but as in the past, they did not dare to go to war with Russia herself. To do so would risk a thermonuclear response. Whatever else one may think of liberal internationalism, it was designed with the intention of bringing about world peace. But in the Ukraine War, a consistent application of the principle that no territorial aggression should be allowed to stand would risk the most catastrophic war in history. Power, in the form of several thousand nuclear warheads, trumped make-believe, in the form of high-minded globalist ideals about the supposed "community of nations."

Donald Trump did not, in fact, blow up the liberal world order. He simply recognized that it had already imploded, doomed by its own internal contradictions. Contrary to the hopeful expectations of many, the collapse of the USSR in 1989 did not lead to the New World Order envisioned by President George H. W. Bush. Liberal democracy had not conquered the world, despite the many color-coded revolutions across the globe that gave the false promise of a new dawn. Many regimes remain stubbornly authoritarian. Others are mere kleptocracies operating behind the façade of democratic slogans. Donald Trump, the pragmatist, simply recognizes these stubborn facts. America must deal with the world as it is and not as we would like it to be. This reflects his America First policy, but it is ultimately based on Trump's pragmatic recognition that our sclerotic international order is incapable of leadership, setting clear goals, or decisive action. In his bracing address to the United Nations on September 23, 2025, Trump even questioned what purpose the UN now served. Nations might give lip service to the lofty principles of the UN charter, but they will always act in their own self-interest when the chips are down. Trump's realistic grasp of how the world actually works marked a paradigm shift from the internationalist illusions favored by both the Republican party of George W. Bush and the Democratic party of Barack Obama.

Trump here is revealing an aspect of his world-historical role. He has tuned into the emergent zeitgeist expressed by various populist movements around the world that reject the illusions of internationalism in favor of a robust return to nationalism. As might be expected, the globalists decry this return as a harbinger of fascism, conveniently forgetting the role that nationalism played as a progressive force in the past, even the quite recent past. During the decolonization of the various European empires that began after the Second World War, liberals cheered as one nation after another proudly declared its independence from its colonial rulers.

Meanwhile, Trump's domestic critics on both left and right who attack him for making deals with dictators seem to think that he should wait until all the dictators are gone, but that would be a long wait indeed. In the meantime, America has to engage in the real world. This means a rejection of the various make-believe solutions that Trump's critics are so eager to pursue. There will never be a two-state solution to the conflict between Israel and the Palestinians. Ukraine will never again possess the Crimea nor bring Russia to its knees.

Trump understands this, but he also takes it for granted that the leaders of other nations will naturally insist on looking after their own national self-interests. Instead of scolding them for this, as has been the habit of previous administrations, both Democratic and Republican, Trump offers them deals from which all parties, including America, derive some benefits.

Hence, it is no surprise that from his first day in office, Trump made it clear that he would seek to end violent conflicts around the world. Part of this was perhaps a result of his America First mentality, but Trump has repeatedly indicated his sincere ambition to bring an end to pointless bloodshed. The refusal of his enemies even to acknowledge Trump's intention to create a more peaceful world is perhaps the blackest and most shameful mark against them. The same crowd that told Bush (quite correctly) that war was not the answer in Iraq now attack Trump for his desire to bring an end to forever wars everywhere.

Though most attention has been paid to Trump's taxing efforts to end both the war between Russia and Ukraine as well as to bring peace to the conflict between Israel and Hamas, Trump and his Secretary of State, Marco Rubio, have marked up considerable success in brokering peace deals around the globe, though these have received little attention in the liberal press. Rubio was present at the signing of a peace deal between Rwanda and the Democratic Republic of Congo, the first step in ending the decades-long conflict between these two nations.

Considering that some estimates of the human cost of this protracted war make it one of the bloodiest in history, at six million deaths, this by itself should be enough to award both Trump and Rubio a Nobel Peace Prize; but in addition, conflict has also been brought to an end between Armenia and Azerbaijan. To this list of pacific accomplishments must be added a ceasefire brokered between India and Pakistan as well as between Thailand and Cambodia. It is always easier to keep a war from starting than to end it once it has begun, though a war averted will obviously never get the attention of a war that has broken out.

In dealing with the threat of a nuclear Iran, however, Trump showed that he was prepared to offer carrots, but when carrots failed, he had no hesitation in using bunker-busters as a stick. Like Reagan, he believes in peace through strength. Both presidents desired world peace as much as Woodrow Wilson did; but in contrast to Wilson's inflexible idealism, they did not put their hope in a utopian world government, but rather, on pragmatic initiatives aimed at reducing dangerous tensions among nations. Trump has complained, quite rightly, that his enemies in the media refuse to acknowledge these impressive achievements, though they were ecstatic when their hero, Barack Obama, was controversially awarded the Nobel Peace Prize shortly after getting elected, with little in the way of accomplishments at the time. Nor was Obama's award rescinded when he launched the war against Libya in March, 2011.

Yet at the same time, Trump has baffled and offended the international community by his talk of purchasing Greenland from Denmark, making Canada the fifty-first state, and rechristening the Gulf of Mexico the Gulf of America. As often in dealing with the mercurial Trump, even those sympathetic to him are left wondering whether he is joking or actually being serious. Though we now have a Gulf of America, Canada remains an independent nation and Greenland doesn't seem to be for sale.

On the domestic front, the first hundred days of the Trump administration has been compared to the first hundred days of Roosevelt's first term. On his first day back in the Oval Office, Trump signed twenty-six executive orders, breaking all previous records. One of them prohibited the weaponization of the various federal agencies that had become the hallmark of Democratic resistance to Trump from 2016 onward. He banned federal censorship of speech on the internet. He ended the electric vehicle mandate and renewed the call for energy production along traditional lines. He withdrew the United States from both the World Health Organization and the Paris Climate Accords. Controversially, he pardoned over 1,500 of those who had been involved in the mayhem of January 6, though to many, given their treatment, this seemed a matter of simple justice.

One of the greatest scandals of the Biden administration had been its policy of virtually opening the southern border to all comers. Trump had repeatedly pledged to reverse this insane course and began by declaring a national emergency at our border with Mexico. With astonishing suddenness, the border crisis had been thoroughly resolved by Trump's decision. He began once again to "build that wall!" He also proposed ending the birthright citizenship policy, which he believed was helping to incentivize an influx of illegal aliens. In addition, Trump declared English to be the official language of the United States.

Trump's America First agenda was also on display in his economic policies. Though his faith in the value of tariffs was perfectly in line with the thinking of earlier American presidents, it was widely attacked by his critics, including those on the right who, for some time, have been wedded to the cause of free trade. But Trump recognizes that free trade is just another ideology. It has always been supported by those nations that could produce the best goods at the best price, not because it was a sacred economic principle that must always be honored, but because free trade was in their obvious self-interest. Likewise, protectionism is obviously in the interest of those trying to develop their own fledgling industries, and this was the immensely successful policy pursued by America in the nineteenth century.

Here, as elsewhere, Trump is simply being pragmatic. He supports free trade when it is in American interests and opposes it when it is not. This may disturb free-trade ideologues at *The Wall Street Journal*, but Trump is simply trying to work out the best deal for America. The devil is, of course, in the details, but merely trying to get better deals with other nations hardly constitutes a radical break with American traditions. It is, in fact, the duty of the president to seek such deals.

Few of Trump's initiatives raised more of a firestorm among his opponents than his efforts to remove violent criminals who had come to the United States illegally. Though many of his critics behaved as if the deportation of such individuals was the first step in creating a fascist police state, which it certainly was not, there were those, including his supporters, who were disturbed that ICE was also going after illegal immigrants who had come here simply to work. On the other hand, the decision of Democrats to defend the sanctuary policy of cities they controlled was baffling even to those who had no fondness for Trump. Why shelter violent criminals, they asked, and received no good answer. Trump also supported the Laken Riley Act, named after the young woman who had been murdered by an illegal immigrant. Though some Democrats in Congress voted for the bill, the majority opposed it.

Many of Trump's other initiatives in his first hundred days were designed to roll back the wave of woke policies favored by white affluent college-educated liberals, despite the fact that these causes were at odds with the social conservatism of most Latinos and Black people, endangering the Democratic coalition that had served the party so well in the past. First, Trump banned all DEI initiatives within the federal government. A later executive order aimed at banning transgender athletes from competing in women's sports, a policy that had overwhelming support of Americans, but which, once more, the Democrats were determined to oppose. Along the same lines, Trump officially defined males and females as they had always been defined before the advent of the woke revolution—though this, too, was interpreted by his critics as proof of his intransigent transphobia.

Trump also believed that parents, and not activist teachers, should be allowed to make decisions about the education of their own children—another quite sensible position that Democrats felt the need to attack. Indeed, as Trump proceeded into his second term, it began to seem as if he was in charge of Democratic policymaking. He simply had to approve an idea whereupon the Democrats immediately rushed to oppose it, without in the least considering whether the idea was good or bad, or how much support it might have among their own traditional base. It is the nature of Manichaean politics to push its practitioners to extravagant absurdities embraced only by other true believers. From the premise that the "Orange Man" is evil flowed the obvious conclusion that any idea or policy promoted by the Orange Man had to be evil as well.

Naturally, many of Trump's initiatives were challenged, some of which were patently frivolous, others more serious. Though the innovation of nationwide injunctions imposed by federal judges was dangerous to both parties, Trump was clobbered with one injunction after another. A federal judge even told the Trump administration that the jets flying criminal aliens to another nation must be turned around in midair, an instance of the kind of judicial overreach that Thomas Jefferson had so much feared.

As the history of our nation has demonstrated, the Constitution does not exist in the realm of Platonic ideals. Ultimately, the question of what is constitutional can only be answered by the normal process of adjudicating the specific issues in question. Even when the Supreme Court strikes down a law as unconstitutional, as it did in 1895 with the proposal of a personal income tax, the people had a remedy by passing an amendment to the Constitution. In 1913, the Sixteenth Amendment overrode the Supreme Court and, for better or worse, became the law of the land. This fact must be kept in mind, especially when considering the flurry of accusations that Trump is violating the Constitution. Fortunately, the Supreme Court checked the wild abandon of these blatantly partisan injunctions, though the Court was immediately attacked as "partisan" for taking this prudent step.

In reviewing Trump's policies and programs, an impartial judge might regard some of them as ill-conceived, some of them plainly bad, some of them counterproductive. But among the many ideas that Trump has embraced, the same impartial judge will naturally find some of them to be quite on the mark—his securing of the southern border among them. In addition, any sensible judge will recognize that it is simply too soon to tell whether or not several of his other proposals will achieve their objectives. The tariff chaos of Trump's first hundred days may seem in hindsight, a decade or a generation hence, as a desperately foolish scheme or a stroke of economic inspiration. His attempts to bring an end to the war in Ukraine may, in hindsight, be hailed as the commencement of a new era of world peace or as the crooked path by which World War Three was ignited. We simply cannot know how all of this will end. But this is not Trump's fault; it is rather how history works. Unpredictability is unavoidable even in untroubled epochs, but it becomes the general rule during any period in which an old epoch is dying while a new one is struggling to be born.

Yet one feature stands out in the first year of Trump's second administration: his determination to see a return to American exceptionalism.

CHAPTER FIFTEEN
THE RETURN OF AMERICAN EXCEPTIONALISM

The globalist meritocracy both fears and loathes Donald Trump because he is today's champion of American exceptionalism. This is hardly surprising. The mission of the globalists is to get people to think of themselves as citizens of the world, with duties to the global community, rather than citizens of any particular nation. But this mission can only be accomplished if everyone adopts a cosmopolitan ethic that rejects the relics of a more primitive age, such as love of one's country, a steadfast loyalty to its traditions, and the quaint belief that the leaders chosen by the people should look after their people's interests.

Nationalism, from the globalist perspective, is a cardinal sin, virtually synonymous with fascism, while patriotism is a dangerous superstition of the lower orders. In the eyes of the globalists, however, nothing comes close to the obscenity of American exceptionalism. Unless they can rid Americans of this absurd delusion, their project of creating a global utopia is doomed. The United States is simply too powerful to be left to make its own choices. It must be cured of its perverse mania for believing itself to be a providential agent of world history.

The globalists were already well on their way to achieving their mission. Most of the European nations had fallen in line, and the United States seemed ripe to fall into their hands under the administration of Barack Obama. Then came Trump—and with him, the return of the spirit of American exceptionalism.

Trump was not the first president to champion American exceptionalism when it was imperiled by those who wanted to remake the United States to conform to an alien model of government. As we have seen, this was also the challenge taken up in their own eras by Abraham Lincoln and Franklin D. Roosevelt. In the case of all three presidents, living in an age of turmoil and confusion, it was imperative to deal radically with those who wished to remake America. Paradoxically, all three had, at times, to be radicals in order to conserve what was best in the American tradition.

It is all too easy for us to point out the flaws and mistakes of Donald Trump. This is because we are his contemporaries. We share the same historical context. But once Lincoln and FDR have been returned to theirs, it is just as easy to draw up a list of their faults and failures, as well as a long list of the policies they proposed that didn't work and often made things considerably worse. The Emancipation Proclamation did not shorten the war but only made the Southern rebels fight with renewed fury, convinced, not unreasonably, that it had been a cynical call for a servile insurrection. Many of FDR's projects provided jobs only to Democratic loyalists, without doing much of anything to improve the national economy. In his dealings with Stalin, he was at best criminally naïve, as in his decision to include the USSR as a permanent member of the Security Counsel of the

United Nations, convinced of Stalin's pacific intentions once the war was won.

Mistakes, errors, misjudgments—the administrations of both Lincoln and FDR are replete with examples. Even more alarmingly, both Lincoln and FDR were willing to violate the sacred unwritten traditions that had been part of the American political way of life. Lincoln rejected the Dred Scott decision, though it had been duly handed down by the Supreme Court, while FDR—plagued like Trump with judicial resistance to his sweeping agenda—tried to pack the Court to his advantage. Both used the presidency to achieve purposes that were, at best, constitutionally doubtful and, at worst, morally and ethically wrong.

Yet both remain world-historical figures. They are not knights in shining armor out of fairytale history but human beings who, under the most trying and desperate challenges ever faced by the leaders of any nation, fought to preserve what they could of the American tradition of exceptionalism, based on a government of the people, by the people, and for the people. During those historical periods when democracy was in retreat around the world, as in the 1850s and the 1930s, both presidents stayed true to the promise of the American Revolution. Both also embraced the idea that the state could be used to promote the aspirations of ordinary Americans, and not to keep them in check.

As we have seen, throughout our history, the tradition of popular rule has been under continuous fire from those who wanted to establish a ruling elite, a movement that began within a decade after the signing of the Declaration of Independence. The struggle between these two camps has defined American politics since the beginning. Indeed, it seems as if some internal mechanism operated to keep either of the two from having complete success. Too much democratic excess, and an elite arose to tamp it down. Too much power in the hands of an elite, and the people rose up to put it in its place. From this long-term perspective, Trump and his mission will not, in hindsight, seem like aberrations—as his critics claim—but rather part of the indispensable balancing act that has kept America on an even keel.

This balancing act is itself exceptional and can only be partly explained by the genius of the US Constitution. In the twentieth century, the Italian economist and sociologist Vilfredo Pareto argued that no society can escape domination by an elite. These elites come and go. As Pareto remarked, "History is the graveyard of aristocracies." Yet in this "circulation of elites," as Pareto phrased it, the people will always be under the thumb of some ruling class or other. America was an exception to this rule.

It is true that we, too, have had our circulation of elites. The revolutionary gentry elite was replaced by a plutocratic elite in the course of the nineteenth century, and that elite, in turn, was replaced by the meritocratic elite after the Second World War. Yet this process was inevitably punctuated by one or another populist revolt against whatever elite was attempting to achieve political domination over the nation. Whatever havoc and chaos these revolts may have caused at the time, which could be considerable, the alternative would have been worse.

There are two things that explain why America was an exception to Pareto's law. First, we had a sequence of presidents who, like Donald Trump, were prepared to be tribunes of the people, including Jefferson, Jackson, Lincoln, and FDR. Another was the immunity of ordinary Americans to the lure of political ideologies, invariably imports from European thinkers. To see why this matters, we need to consider one of the most striking shifts in the zeitgeist that began in the nineteenth century: the advent of the age of ideology.

The term *ideology* did not enter the English language until 1796 and had to be borrowed from the French. In the nineteenth century, it was used exclusively by European thinkers. The British and American Whigs of the eighteenth century would have been puzzled even by the need for such a concept. For them, politics was not about ideas as such, but was a separate sphere of activity focused entirely on how to safely disperse power and keep it from being monopolized. The nineteenth-century English champion of liberty, Lord Acton, summarized the Whig attitude in his famous maxim: All power corrupts and absolute power corrupts absolutely. For these Whigs, politics was the naked struggle for power among various parties, and history was the record of these struggles.

The emergence of public opinion in the middle of the eighteenth century changed the nature of these struggles, as the various contending parties began to appeal to the general public for support. To win over public opinion, it was necessary to convince the people that your party was *not* seeking power for itself. Unlike your self-serving opponents, your side only wanted power to pursue a noble goal, such as uplifting the masses.

Modern ideologies were invented for this purpose. The old struggles for power continued, but under the guise of being a contest of ideas, a conflict of visions. This kind of politics naturally appealed to intellectuals who love to debate ideas and theories. They were particularly drawn to those ideologies that promised to reform humanity and the world. Power to them was merely the means to achieve these vital reforms. It was not dangerous in itself, as the Whigs had argued; it was only dangerous in the "wrong" hands.

For obvious reasons, those who hold power, and especially those who want more of it, will inevitably be opposed to any doctrine that warns against giving too much power to any individual or institution. The claim of every power seeker is, "Fear not, power will be safe in our hands." But there is another claim as well, though this would not emerge until the twentieth century, when the slogan became, "Trust us. Think of all the good we can do if you just give us the power to do it."

This was the classic argument offered by the totalitarian regimes of the last century, but it is also the party line taken by the meritocratic elite of our own day. With enough power, we can cool the earth; with enough power, we can eliminate bigotry, poverty, racism, sexism, homophobia, xenophobia. With enough power, we can achieve equitable social justice. Just give us this power, and you will see what we can do with it. And, unfortunately, we do.

Trump's Revolution of Common Sense marks both a return of pragmatism as well as a break with the ideological fixations of the past. This can be seen most prominently in his foreign policy, which is purely transactional. Trump is not a crusader for human rights. He has no ideological obsession with spreading our form of government around the globe. He has no interest in regime change. Nor is Trump's version of America First a return to the isolationism of Charles Lindbergh or his successor Pat Buchanan. His various efforts to reduce violent conflicts around the world should make this obvious. He wants to see world peace as devoutly as Woodrow Wilson did, but Trump the pragmatist is too realistic to entrust this noble project to the UN or other visionary schemes of global governance. That is another instance of make-believe thinking that only an academic—or a bureaucrat—could credit. Conflicts will always arise among nations. How could it be otherwise? All nations have interests, and sometimes those interests conflict. But each conflict must be addressed not as a matter of competing moral claims but on a transactional basis, like a business deal, as Trump has sought to do.

If Trump can convince the world to accept his pragmatic approach to global conflict, it will be a singular triumph, definitely putting him among the world-historical leaders who have most benefited humanity. The ideologically driven wars of the past century have destroyed more lives than all the religious wars in history. It is time to bring an end to the reign of ideological fanatics who are willing to waste precious human lives in pursuit of their utopian visions. Indeed, there is something deeply un-American about viewing politics as essentially an ideological struggle.

What perhaps most confuses many Americans about Trump is that he does not think in terms of left or right. He is only concerned with whether or not something works. In an age in which politics has become a venue for ideological virtue-signaling, Trump is attempting to restore the American tradition of politics that sought not confrontation but compromise, not to win at all costs, but to reach a deal that is mutually beneficial. This may prove to be his toughest challenge.

Even within the MAGA movement, there are ideologues who would love to see Trump take up their pet causes. Ironically, many MAGA conservatives are disturbed by Trump's genuine and sincere attempts to be a global peacemaker. Some would like to see him more isolationist; others would love to see a far more bellicose Trump. There is also the old debate about the role of government. Unlike the libertarian ideologues, Trump believes that government is not always the problem.

In fact, sometimes government is the answer. FDR's GI Bill of Rights achieved miracles. It was a program that was at once populist and progressive. And it worked. But in our current political climate, dominated by ideologues on both right and left, Trump will certainly have his work cut out in trying to promote an agenda that pleases both camps.

Trump, by nature, is not an ideologue. But his attitude to ideologies is not simply a matter of temperament. For at the heart of our current epochal crisis is the failure of past political ideologies to have any relevance today. All are bankrupt; they have nothing more to offer than the opportunity for zealots to quarrel and name-call about who is purer and more principled. They offer no fresh solutions, just more of what didn't work in the first place. Contemporary neoliberalism has proven to be a dead end. But so too have been the ideologies of the American neoconservatives and of the doctrinaire libertarians as well. Meanwhile, progressivism has become an elite ideology that has virtually defined itself by opposing any tradition that ordinary Americans have long accepted, while today's socialists are the children of wealth and privilege, with Ivy League diplomas to prove it. But how genuinely progressive can a movement be that disdains to even listen to what ordinary people care about?

The time has come to put the age of ideology behind us. The time has come to return to the politics of the deal. It was the American genius for making deals that in the end has kept us exceptional. It was only when our deals fell through, as in the run up to the Civil War, that we became fatally divided. Yet it was the art of the deal that brought North and South back into a single Union. In the election crisis of 1876, many despaired that another civil war was imminent, but pragmatic dealmakers worked out a compromise. The Democrats wanted to end the military occupation of the South. The Republicans wanted their candidate, Rutherford Hayes, elected president. So they made a deal. Was this another corrupt bargain, as many at the time protested, or a display of the exceptional capacity of Americans to make deals as opposed to tearing their nation apart?

With the election of Trump in 2024, the art of the deal was back. This was not a revival of European fascism, as the liberal media would have us believe, but a revival of the principles of American exceptionalism just at the point when they appeared to be vanishing under the heavy hand of a corrupt and incompetent would-be ruling class invincibly convinced of its own inherent virtue.

Just as it is often said that FDR saved capitalism from itself, the ultimate irony is that Trump may well have saved liberalism from itself. Under his guidance, the Great Populist Revolt did not go off the rails, as it might easily have done without him. It did not descend into a blind rightwing reaction against modernity.

As much as the liberal media tried to paint Trump as a white supremacist and his followers as pitchfork-wielding racists, his own behavior made a joke of their hysterical claims. Trump welcomed people of every race, creed, and ethnicity to his rallies, and many came to look and found what they liked. While those who called themselves liberals were busily engaged in their efforts to take down Trump, by methods that made a mockery of their claims to be liberal-minded protectors of democratic procedural norms, Trump upheld the true spirit of old-fashioned American liberalism. The result has been the rise of a broad-based multi-ethnic coalition that drew from core Democratic constituencies that had been alienated by the party's increasingly strident woke policies and rhetoric.

Donald Trump is a far finer example of the generous old-fashioned tradition of American liberalism than is the woke crowd that routinely denounces him as another Hitler. While these so-called liberals were calling his millions of supporters the vilest of names, Trump treated every potential voter with respect. He was as happy to speak to Black people as to Hispanics and, as noted earlier, he won many over to his side. He attacked only his political opponents, never those who supported them.

The fact that the other party broke this golden rule of American politics is clear proof that in their frenetic quest to bring down Trump, they were willing to abandon every tenet of the American tradition of liberalism. But the liberalism they betrayed can still make a comeback, and Trump may well surprise us by being its new standard bearer. He has surprised us before. There can be little doubt that he will surprise us again.

Finally, if Trump's victory in 2024 did nothing else but keep the essence of American exceptionalism alive for even one more generation, rather than allowing it to be crushed by a corrupt and overbearing elite, he has already achieved enough to make him the only candidate for the position of the world-historical leader of our own time. The fact that the Trump revolution is spreading across Europe and potentially the rest of the globe is evidence that America leads best when it leads by example.

This, too, is part of the Make America Great Again movement. By reviving the original spirit of exceptionalism in our own land, the United States will have far more influence for the good than if it squandered its resources and the lives of its men and women in the vain attempt to impose a new world order. The world will always be disorderly. It is a fantasy to think otherwise. The wisest policy only tries to keep disorders from getting out of hand.

America did not become great by imitating the rest of the world, but by being unique. And it is by staying unique that it offers the best hope for the future of the world. Ours became the freest nation in the world, a fact of which Americans were quite proud, but this was not because we sought to achieve some abstract and hitherto unrealized concepts of liberty, such as those championed by the political theorists and which the French revolutionaries had tried but failed to bring down to earth. Rather, Americans have traditionally fought to preserve the exceptional degree of liberty that they saw as their unique heritage. Their idea of liberty was not based on a set of philosophical abstractions but arose from the visceral sentiment that people should mind their own business and let others mind theirs. This had long been the way of life for most Americans, who had little interest in imposing their own way of life on others, or in pursuing impossible dreams of world government or eternal peace or any other of the pet projects favored by the ideologically driven intellectual elites of our day.

In the aftermath of the assassination attempt at his rally in Butler, Pennsylvania, Trump stated that he believed God had "spared" him to save America, and so did many of his devoted followers. Throughout American history, this same faith in providence became part of the fabric of American exceptionalism, a fact that may dismay those of a secular mindset, yet one that has been indispensable in the creation of the world's oldest and most successful democracy. The belief that we were special *made* us special—an idea that William James would have endorsed, based on his famous essay "The Will to Believe," which argued that religious beliefs should not be judged by whether they correspond to the facts, but rather on how effective they are in shaping for the good the individuals or communities that hold these beliefs. The American belief in providence has clearly shaped our nation for the better, unlike those beliefs begotten of an ideology that have invariably doomed to historical oblivion those who held them, as happened to the European fascist regimes as well as the USSR.

Whether our peculiar heritage, so favorable to democratic values, was due to Divine Providence or to a long series of serendipitous accidents remains an open question. Fatalism requires its own peculiar leap of faith. But it is not difficult to see why so many ordinary Americans still believe that we were blessed by God.

Is this a superstition to be suppressed or is it a faith that has proven its "cash value" by helping to keep so much of the world free? If America had not been convinced that God looked after us, would it have dared to defy the British Empire, end slavery, fight European fascism and Japanese militarism, or take on international communism?

Trump wants to restore to America its providential role in world history. The globalists are disturbed by this, as well they should be. The restoration of the spirit of American exceptionalism would be a challenge to their hegemony, which is why they rightly see Trump as an existential threat. The struggle between the meritocratic elite and a people they have pushed too far is the defining issue of our age. Its outcome is still uncertain. Trump may fail due to any number of intractable obstacles, not least of which may be his own besetting flaws. Yet if Trump were to drop dead tomorrow, he will have already achieved something that may turn out to be of lasting importance. Like the little boy in Hans Christian Andersen's fable, Trump has dared to point out that the emperor has no clothes. The global meritocracy has been exposed as a racket, so deeply discredited by its own ham-fisted efforts to crush the populist revolt that it is difficult to see how it can ever win back the legitimacy it squandered in pursuit of its ideological fantasies.

Given the unraveling of the meritocratic world order, the only way now is forward. But who can say what comes next?

POSTSCRIPT
WHAT IF TRUMP FAILS?

At this point in Donald Trump's presidency—the end of 2025—
the MAGA movement appears to be unraveling as isolationist
elements demand disengagement from foreign adventures and
antisemitism rears its ugly and divisive head. Meanwhile the
Democrats (who have coalition problems of their own) are heart-
ened by off-year victories in Virginia, New Jersey, Florida, and
New York City where a socialist has been elected mayor. It now
seems possible, even likely, that the GOP will lose its majority
in Congress, a correction that often occurs in midterm elections.
If so, Trump becomes a lame-duck president and his energetic
debut may turn out to be a proverbial flash in the pan.

Even without that electoral outcome, Trump has aroused so
much anger and resistance from elites and the political left that
we cannot rule anything out. This book began with the MAGA
rally in Butler, Pennsylvania, where Trump narrowly missed a
bullet intended for him. Three months later, there was a less
spectacular attempt on his life while he was golfing on one of
his own courses in Palm Beach. It is certainly conceivable that
there will be other attempts in the remaining three years of his
term. It is also possible that there might be other ways to remove

him from office or render him politically impotent. Given any of these possible future scenarios, what becomes of the thesis that Trump qualifies as a world-historical figure?

If we look back over the world-historical leaders of the past, it is striking that most of them failed to carry their grand mission to completion. Julius Caesar and Abraham Lincoln were both assassinated by men who were deeply convinced that they were slaying a tyrant. Napoleon ended his spectacular career on the bleak island of St. Helena in the middle of the Atlantic Ocean. The English who kept him prisoner wanted to remove him as far from land as possible, lest he stage another miraculous comeback, as he had done in 1815 after his escape from Elba, an island within easy reach of France.

Yet in none of these cases did their death or defeat result in a return to the old order. The senators who assassinated Caesar thought they were restoring the Republic, but after one last bloody civil war, the Roman Empire would be governed by men who took the title of Caesar. The murder of Lincoln did not restore the Old South that had been vanquished in the war. The slaves were eventually freed, although Lincoln did not live to see it, and the Union was preserved, surviving as Lincoln intended to keep the torch of liberty alive and pass it on to future generations. Napoleon died in exile, his empire disbanded; yet he created the modern French state, established a meritocratic system that rewarded talent over birth, spread liberal ideals across the world, and left behind an enlightened legal code that remains the foundation of French society today.

The fact is that if Trump dies tomorrow, or is turned into a lame duck by a Democratic victory in the midterms, he would still be consequential enough to be considered world historical. Consider his accomplishments to date: He has solved the immigration crisis by closing the border, which previous presidents pretended was impossible; exposed the corruption and self-dealing of the meritocratic elite, including its propaganda organ, the mendacious establishment press; taken steps to undo the globalist economic revolution, using tariffs to re-shore American industry; reinvigorated the domestic energy sector; defunded the activist left and its network of taxpayer-supported NGOs; disestablished DEI in the military and federal government; brought order to crime-ridden cities ruled by feckless and incompetent Democrats; cracked down on universities for promoting antisemitism; revived the Monroe Doctrine by reclaiming the Panama Canal, seeking the overthrow of the Venezuelan communist regime, challenging the drug cartels with military force, and basically kicking China and Russia out of the Western hemisphere; he has ended numerous conflicts around the world through his strategy of economic dealmaking and reshaped the Middle East by defanging Iran's strategy of regional domination through the pursuit of nuclear weapons and a network of terrorist proxies; he has restructured the global economy, shored up the dollar, tamed inflation, and laid the groundwork for a new system of economic alliances. And this is just a partial list.

Not all of his initiatives succeed, nor are they handled with the tact and aplomb that many of us might prefer. His critics have a point in this regard. But these are matters of execution, not policy, and his supporters are prepared to overlook them, just as we are prepared to overlook the flaws and failings of both Lincoln and FDR in light of their world-historical achievements.

Finally, if Trump's victory in 2024 did nothing else but keep the essence of American exceptionalism alive for one more generation, rather than allowing it to be crushed by a corrupt and overbearing globalist elite, he has already achieved enough to make him the only candidate for the position of the world-historical leader of our time. The fact that the Trumpian national-populist revolution is spreading across Europe and potentially the rest of the globe is evidence that America leads best when it leads by example.

This too is part of the Make America Great Again movement. By reviving the original spirit of exceptionalism in our own land, the United States will have far more influence for good than if it squandered its resources and the lives of its men and women in a vain attempt to impose a new world order.

America did not become great by imitating the rest of the world, but by being unique. And it is by staying unique that it offers the best hope for the future. Ours became the freest nation in the world, a fact of which Americans were naturally proud. But this was not because we sought to achieve some abstract or hitherto unrealized ideals of liberty and equality such as those which the French and Communist revolutionaries tried—with catastrophic results—to bring down to earth. Rather, Americans have traditionally fought to preserve the exceptional degree of liberty that they saw as their unique heritage. Their idea of liberty was not based on a set of philosophical abstractions but arose from the visceral sentiment that people should basically mind their own business and let others mind theirs. This had long been the way of life for most Americans, who had little interest in imposing it on others, let alone pursuing impossible dreams of world government or eternal peace or any of the other pet projects favored by the ideologically driven elites of our day.

Looking back on the first hundred days of Donald Trump's second administration, the sober Peggy Noonan—herself no fan of Trump—summed up our current epochal crisis with admirable simplicity: "Donald Trump is what he wanted to be, a world-historical figure, and we have entered a new time. It sounds dangerous. This is what it looks like when establishments fail."

It sounds dangerous because it is dangerous. Indeed, it is always dangerous to replace an established order with a new one. The Bourbon monarchy was no doubt doomed to pass away, but the Revolution's Reign of Terror quickly demonstrated the dangers inherent in the overthrow of even the weakest and most corrupt established order. The Southern aristocracy of slaveholders was equally doomed, but it required a bloody Civil War and a decade-long military occupation to convince Southerners of that fact; while the collapse of the moribund USSR led to vast corruption, gigantic theft, the impoverishment of the people, and political chaos.

Even the worst established order, despite its abundance of vices, will always have one great virtue. Life under it is predictable. There is a routine for everything. We do today what we did yesterday and will do tomorrow. Traditions tell everyone how to behave under virtually every circumstance. But during an epochal crisis, everything is suddenly up in the air. It is during this transitional period that the gravest danger arises.

An epochal crisis has the tendency to bring out both the worst and the best qualities found in human nature. So Noonan is right: We do live in dangerous times. But Americans have survived many such times in the past and may well survive this one as well—which may explain why simple trust in Divine Providence has gotten America so far. The sagacious Otto von Bismarck, a keen observer of world affairs, is said to have remarked: "There is a Providence that protects idiots, drunkards, children, and the United States of America."

At the very least, it is permissible to hope that this is true.

ACKNOWLEDGMENTS

I must first of all thank my editor, Adam Bellow. In writing a book that tries to put Donald Trump into historical perspective, I was always aware of what a questionable mission I had undertaken. Having no crystal ball at my disposal, I could not see how the second administration of Donald Trump would end. After all, there have been few leaders in history whose conduct was as hard to predict as Trump. In truth, there were many moments in the composition of this book when I was ready to throw in the towel on my absurdly ambitious project. Fortunately, Adam Bellow was always there to hold my hand (metaphorically) during these fits of panic. In addition, throughout the entire process of rewriting the book, Adam never failed to indicate ways in which I could make it both stronger and more relevant. His help has been invaluable.

I also want to thank Lauren Campbell, my managing editor, for her assistance in guiding me to the finished product. And, of course, I need once again to thank my agent, Andrew Stuart.

Now to all the friends whose conversations have provided me with new insights. Ellen Vivet, Michael Lynch, Mary Grabar, Stevan Apter are high on this list, but I must particularly thank Adam Linnell for his patient reading of my manuscript throughout its various stages, and for the encouragement he has given me to prod on.

Finally, I must, as always, express my profound gratitude for Andy Fuson. He has stood by me for thirty-nine years now. He has always made sure that I had the time and leisure that I needed to take on such long and involved projects such as this book. I also want to thank his partner, Mau Quezada, for his kindness and wonderful meals.

ABOUT THE AUTHOR

Lee Harris is the author of *Civilization and Its Enemies, The Suicide of Reason, The Next American Civil War,* and *What's Wrong with The Right Side of History.* His many articles on a wide range of subjects are available at Harris.Pundicity.com. He lives in Roswell, Georgia.